THE
DEVOURING
DRAGON

THE
DEVOURING
DRAGON

How China's Rise Threatens Our Natural World

CRAIG SIMONS

St. Martin's Press
New York

THE DEVOURING DRAGON. Copyright © 2013 by Craig Simons. All rights reserved. Printed in the United States of America. For information, address St. Martin's Press, 175 Fifth Avenue, New York, N.Y. 10010.

www.stmartins.com

Library of Congress Cataloging-in-Publication Data

Simons, Craig.
    The devouring dragon : how China's rise threatens our natural world / Craig Simons.—1st ed.
        p. cm.
    ISBN 978-0-312-58176-3 (hardcover)
    ISBN 978-1-250-02318-6 (e-book)
    1. Environmental policy—China.   2. Environmental responsibility—China.
3. Nature—Effect of human beings on—China.   4. Environmental degradation—China.
5. Environmental protection—International cooperation.   I. Title.
GE190.C6 S55 2013
363.70951
                                                                                    2012037791

St. Martin's Press books may be purchased for educational, business, or promotional use. For information on bulk purchases, please contact Macmillan Corporate and Premium Sales Department at 1-800-221-7945, extension 5442, or write specialmarkets@macmillan.com.

First Edition: March 2013

To Jen and my parents,
and to Sierra, who—like all children—
will inherit our decisions

CONTENTS

Author's Note   ix

Map of Asia   x

Map of China   xi

Prologue   1

PART I: CHINA'S BASELINE

1	The Yangtze	25
2	Baselines	41
3	The Three Gorges Dam	49

PART II: LIFE ON THE BRINK

4	Tiger, Tiger, Burning Bright	67
5	The Sixth Great Extinction	83
6	Corbett National Park	103

PART III: OUR SHRINKING FORESTS

7   A Forest Laid Flat   121

8   New Guinea   137

9   Our Future Forests   155

PART IV: OUR WARMING SKIES

10   Time Travel   175

11   Hopenhagen   203

Epilogue   219

Notes   231

Acknowledgments   271

Index   275

AUTHOR'S NOTE

Anyone who writes about China faces the challenge of how quicu19 it changes: China's economy is growing by almost 10 percent each year and, with that growth, everything gets bigger. This book includes various numbers that describe China's rise and will soon be overtaken. But that will not make them less meaningful: they will remain signposts of trends that anyone who visits the country can feel in his bones, shifts so profound that they are changing the physical planet. They also help us grasp China's scale: one-fifth of humanity, one-quarter of global greenhouse gas emissions, almost half of all the coal burned on earth. We should not be distracted by the constant search for new numbers. Without a major change in China's—and the world's—direction, they won't provide new answers. They will only get bigger.

Speaking of numbers: the language of science is metric, but American readers are used to dealing in feet, miles, gallons, and degrees Fahrenheit. I have tried to make the units I use clear to readers in the United States and abroad. If not otherwise specified, they are given in metric amounts.

I took the major reporting trips for this book between January 2009 and March 2012. But I have lived and worked in Asia for over a decade and make occasional reference to earlier reporting.

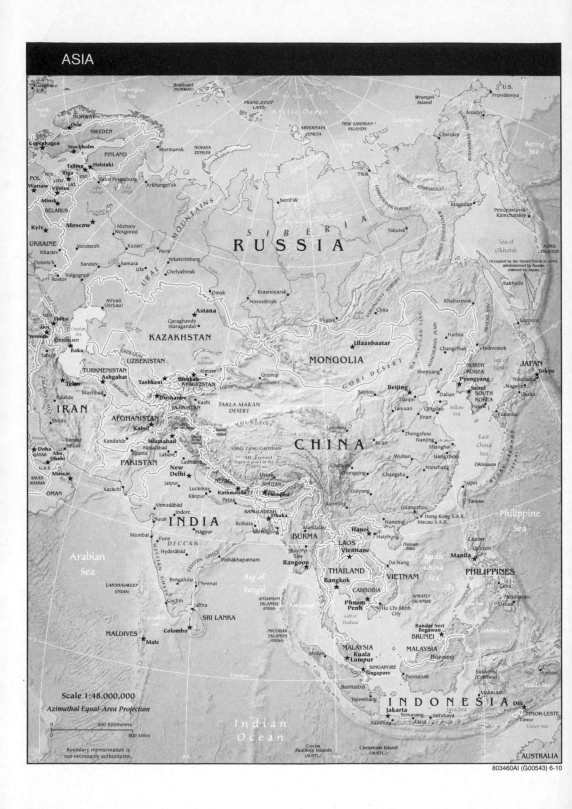

Scale 1:48,000,000
Azimuthal Equal-Area Projection

0   800 Kilometers
0   800 Miles

Boundary representation is
not necessarily authoritative.

803460AI (G00543) 6-10

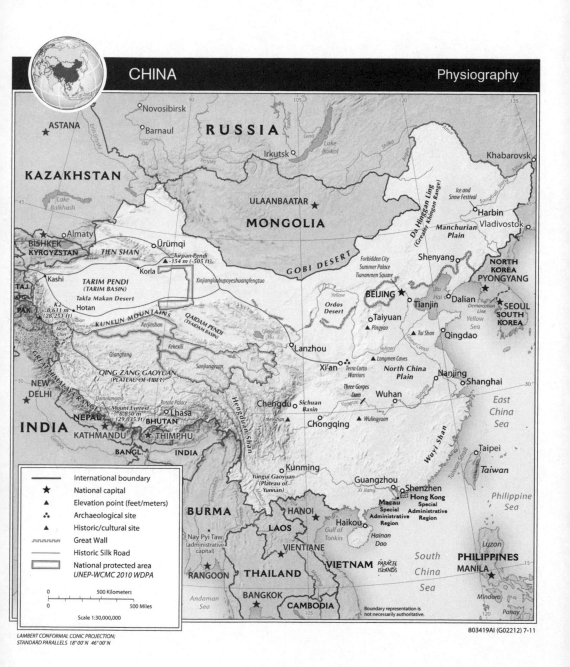

ASTANA

KAZAKHSTAN

RUSSIA

Novosibirsk

Barnaul

Irkutsk

Lake
Baikal

Khabarovsk

ULAANBAATAR

MONGOLIA

GOBI DESERT

Ice and
Snow Festival

Harbin

Vladivostok

Manchurian
Plain

Da Hinggan Ling
(Greater Khingan Range)

Shenyang

NORTH
KOREA
PYONGYANG

BISHKEK
KYRGYZSTAN

Almaty

Ürümqi

TIEN SHAN

Turpan Pendi
▲ -154 m (-505 ft)

Korla

Xinjianglubupoyeshuangfengtuo

Forbidden City
Summer Palace
Tiananmen Square

BEIJING ★

Tianjin

Dalian

Bo
Hai

Demarcation
Line

SEOUL
SOUTH
KOREA

Kashi

TARIM PENDI
(TARIM BASIN)

Takla Makan Desert

Hotan

Yellow

QAIDAM PENDI
(TSAIDAM BASIN)

Ordos
Desert

Taiyuan

▲ Pingyao

▲ Tai Shan

Yellow
Sea

Qingdao

TAJ.

AFG.

PAK

K2
8,611 m
(28,251 ft)

Aksai
Chin

KUNLUN MOUNTAINS

Aerjinshan

Kekexili

Qinghai
Hu

Lanzhou

▲ Longmen Caves

Nanjing

Shanghai

1972 Line of
Actual Control

GREAT HIMALAYA RANGE

Qiangtang

QING ZANG GAOYUAN
(PLATEAU OF TIBET)

Sanjiangyuan

Xi'an

Terra Cotta
Warriors

North China
Plain

Yellow

Grand Canal

NEW
DELHI

INDIA

Domlongma

Mount Everest
8,850 m
(29,035 ft)

Botala Palace

Lhasa

Three Gorges
Dam

Wuhan

Chengdu

Sichuan
Basin

Yangtze

East
China
Sea

NEPAL

BHUTAN

Emeishan

Chongqing

▲ Wulingyuan

KATHMANDU

THIMPHU

Hengduan Shan

BANGL.

INDIA

Kunming

Yungui Gaoyuan
(Plateau of
Yunnan)

Guangzhou

Shenzhen

Wuyi Shan

Taipei

Taiwan

Taiwan Strait

BURMA

HANOI

LAOS

Haikou

Gulf of
Tonkin

Macau
Special
Administrative
Region

Hong Kong
Special
Administrative
Region

Philippine
Sea

Xi Jiang

Nay Pyi Taw
(administrative
capital)

VIENTIANE

VIETNAM

Hainan
Dao

South
China
Sea

Luzon

PHILIPPINES

MANILA

RANGOON

THAILAND

BANGKOK

CAMBODIA

PARACEL
ISLANDS

Andaman
Sea

Boundary representation is
not necessarily authoritative.

Mindoro

Panay

Legend:
— International boundary
★ National capital
▲ Elevation point (feet/meters)
⁘ Archaeological site
▲ Historic/cultural site
⌁⌁⌁⌁ Great Wall
— Historic Silk Road
▭ National protected area
UNEP-WCMC 2010 WDPA

0   500 Kilometers
0   500 Miles
Scale 1:30,000,000

LAMBERT CONFORMAL CONIC PROJECTION;
STANDARD PARALLELS 18°00'N 46°00'N

803419AI (G02212) 7-11

THE
DEVOURING
DRAGON

PROLOGUE

Modern humanity was born, so to speak, about ten thousand years ago with the invention of agriculture and the villages and political hierarchies that soon followed. Up to that point our species had perfected hunter technology enough to wipe out a large part of Earth's largest mammals and birds—the megafauna—but it left most of the vegetated land surface and all of the oceans intact. The economic history that followed can be summarized very succinctly as follows: people used every means they could devise to convert the resources of Earth into wealth.

—EDWARD O. WILSON, FOREWORD TO COMMON WEALTH: ECONOMICS FOR A CROWDED PLANET, BY JEFFREY SACHS

On a warm spring afternoon I left the Trail's End Motel in Trinidad, Colorado, to search for signs of something I had come to think of as "China speed"—the countless ways that China's rapid growth has raised our global metabolism, the ways its enormous appetite is reshaping the physical world. At first glance, Trinidad seemed like an odd place to look for ties to China. Sitting twenty miles north of New Mexico on a dry plain just east of the Rocky Mountains, it appeared insulated from global trends. Each morning locals gathered at the Savoy Café, a small restaurant that seemed frozen in the 1950s: Marilyn Monroe posters and pressed-metal Coca-Cola signs hung on the walls, Elvis crooned from a small radio, discussions tended toward cattle prices, weather, and high school sports. In the afternoon the students of Trinidad High School—home of the Mighty Miners—pulled their pickup trucks and rigged-out sports cars into the parking lots of fast-food restaurants. Older residents sometimes bragged that the town's courthouse was floored with marble cut from a quarry that supplied the Lincoln Memorial.

But I knew what I was looking for. Several months earlier, halfway around the world in Beijing, I had come across a short newspaper story about a coal mine that had quietly reopened more than a decade after being mothballed. The mine was called New Elk and its owners planned to send much of its coal south to Texas and then by ship to Asia. According to a local paper, at least some of it was bound for China.

I suspected that China was more than a peripheral part of the story. In 2009, China had burned 3.5 billion tons of coal, almost half the world's total. But it was China's *potential* demand that was creating a global mining renaissance. In 1976, when Mao Zedong, the first leader of Communist China, died, the country had used only 550 million tons of coal each year, one-sixth of today's total. By 1997, its demand had exceeded that of the United States, but it still used what now looks like a quaint number: 1.4 billion tons. Then—in the thirteen years from 1997 to 2009—China added over 2 billion tons of annual coal demand, the equivalent of two new nations as voracious as the United States, which—until China surpassed it—had been the world's biggest coal consumer.[1] And experts predicted that China's growing energy appetite wouldn't peak for many years.

The mine seemed like a perfect example of how China's rapid growth—growth that since 1992 had multiplied the size of its economy sixfold—has raised the world's metabolism in unexpected ways.[2] But five weeks of emails to the company's headquarters had gone unanswered. When I finally reached its CEO by tracking down his number and cold-calling, he said the mine was too busy for even a brief visit.

I suspected the reason was more complicated. China's rising fortunes—almost all of it powered by fossil fuels—had pushed it past the United States as the world's top emitter of greenhouse gases in 2006. A group of environmental organizations had recently protested new coal ports planned along the West Coast partly because they viewed exporting U.S. coal to China as undermining decades of work to slow global warming. Together with other groups, the Sierra Club had petitioned Colorado's Bureau of Land Management to delay reopening the New Elk mine. Among their chief arguments was that coal from the mine could add millions of tons of carbon dioxide—the chief gas responsible for global warming—to the atmosphere over its life.

So, even without permission, I had decided to go.

I drove west from the Trail's End Motel—a reference to Trinidad's place at the end of the Santa Fe Trail—down Main Street, itself a reminder of the fickle hand of fortune. Trinidad is one of America's early success stories. Early settlers found thick coal seams in nearby hills and wealthy East Coast families invested in iron and steel mills. The city grew rich enough to build Colorado's first public schools and hospitals.

But slumping U.S. demand over the second half of the twentieth century—in Trinidad a product of new iron smelting technologies, stricter environment laws, and the end of the great American era of road, dam, and bridge building—bankrupted its mines, and as Trinidad's fortunes withered, people drifted away. Halfway up Main Street, I passed the Trinidad Historical Society, where a pamphlet explained that the people of Trinidad "lived and worked among the tarnished splendor built by former wealth." Just beyond the history museum was the old Opera House, built in 1883 but recently chained shut after its most recent renter—the owner of a clothing shop—had given up. Just down the road, the Buffalo Smokehouse Barbecue was for sale. The Mary Ann Apartments were boarded up. The most prosperous looking businesses were the Corral Pawn Trading Post and Shirley's Thrift, where a handwritten window sign read, "$5 to fill a bag with any clothing or shoes."

———

Beyond the Savoy Café and Trinidad High School, the city fell away into prairieland speckled with distant homes, pickup trucks, and cattle herds, and thirty minutes later I pulled off the road in front of the mine. It consisted largely of two huge concrete storage silos and a boxy building where machines washed newly extracted coal. The hills behind the structures were still dusted with the last remnants of the winter's snow.

I walked to a tiny wooden guardhouse and talked with Lance Ross, a friendly man who said he couldn't let me in but was happy to share what he knew. He pointed to a large pile of coal gleaming dully in the distance and said that, as far as he knew, it was the first coal mined in Trinidad since 1991. He echoed something other locals had already told me: the return of mining was Trinidad's best news in years. "This is some of the best coal in the world," Ross said. "We should be selling it. We know we need the jobs."

When I asked how quickly the mine would expand, he said managers expected it would happen fast. The company, called Cline Mining, expected to dig up to 6 million tons of coal each year and ship it south by rail to Corpus Christi, Texas, where it would be packed into boats.[3] When I asked where it would end its journey—where it would be burned—he pushed his chin sharply toward the snow-capped Rockies and said, "China's where the money is, so they say that's where it's going."

———

A week earlier I had seen another unanticipated impact of China's rising demand. I was standing near the top of Mount Bachelor, a nine-thousand-foot peak in Oregon's Cascade range, with Dan Jaffe, an atmospheric chemist from the University of Washington. Jaffe is one of the world's top experts on long-range air pollution and he'd just pulled a metal tube from a pipe mounted atop a ski lift. He unscrewed the tube's cover and we peered down at five perfectly round gray dots—dust and black carbon that had been carried on the jet stream from Asia, mostly from China, and dropped on a place that until only a decade or two earlier had recorded some of America's cleanest air.

In a corner of a building used by the lift operators, an expensive stack of equipment measured various pollutants. One machine pulled in a puff of air every few minutes and then tested it for tiny particles of dust—in the language of science called particulate matter—that have been linked with heart disease and lung cancer. Another machine sniffed for traces of ozone—the chief component of smog, a gas formed when sunlight reacts with nitrous oxide. Still others looked for carbon monoxide and mercury, a potent neurotoxin.

All four pollutants are considered urban blights, the products of cars and power plants, and before Jaffe's research few people thought that they could be carried across the Pacific Ocean in dangerous amounts. But the instruments were picking up both a steady flow and, occasionally, hazardous spikes of each. Less than a week before I visited, the machines had shown a higher concentration of ozone atop Mount Bachelor than in downtown Los Angeles. Measurements of airborne mercury suggested that Asia is responsible for nearly half of the global total, some of which is finding its way into American lakes and rivers, contributing to toxicity that has forced almost every U.S. state to issue warnings to fishermen.[4] A decade earlier, equipment at the mountaintop laboratory had recorded one of the most significant "dust events" in American history: an Asian storm had dumped 110,000 tons of dust on the United States, an amount equivalent to everything picked up by the winds across the country on an average day. Atlanta issued a health alert as the particles settled earthward.

For Jaffe, the pollution was equally important as a metaphor. It was hard evidence of how interconnected the world has become: coal mined in Trinidad and countless other small communities is shipped to Chinese power plants. When it's burned, it contributes to clouds of pollution that drift back into the United States. "People don't really understand that we're living in a world full of airborne pollutants," he said. "If the world doesn't make any progress on these pollutants and our economies keep growing, things could get very bad."

———————

After I visited Mount Bachelor, I traveled to Boulder, Colorado—two hundred miles north of Trinidad—to learn about a more lethal gas spewing into the atmosphere as China burns through billions of tons of coal. I had arranged to meet with Jim Butler, the director of an office at the National Oceanic and Atmospheric Administration (NOAA) tasked with monitoring everything that might impact the world's climate. (The full name of the group is the Earth System Research Laboratory, Global Monitoring Division.) According to NOAA's website, Butler's job was to oversee "the nation's continuing measurements of atmospheric constituents that affect the world's climate, including greenhouse and ozone-depleting gases, aerosols, and surface radiation."

On a sunny afternoon, I met Butler and his colleague, Pieter Tans, in Butler's office, a room filled with plants and books and thick binders bearing titles like "Carbon Cycle Initiative 2008." Huge windows looked out toward beautiful, jagged peaks that Coloradans call the Rockies' Front Range. A bottle sitting on a shelf was labeled with a pretty picture of a hummingbird and the words "Humboldt Hemp Ale."

The two men, obviously friends, made an interesting pair. Butler looked like a scientist who could just as easily address a room of senators as he could a conference of physicists. He wore a tan button-down shirt and silver-rimmed glasses. His tightly cropped beard was flecked with gray. When he spoke, he chose his words carefully. Tans, a Dutchman who moved to the United States in 1978 as a postdoctoral physicist, struck me as more of a prophet: he spoke fast and passionately and emphasized key points by swinging his hands through the air like a conductor.

I started our conversation with my biggest, broadest questions—What should Americans know about China's rise and global warming? How does China's growth change the picture?—and Butler replied with a brief history of climate change: "As you watch carbon dioxide's increase since about 1800"—the beginning of the Industrial Revolution—"its growth rate has doubled about three times per century," he said, leaning forward in his chair. "When you think about that, it's pretty incredible. It's a factor of eight by the end of the first century and a factor of sixty-four by the end of the second century. That can't continue to happen, but we haven't seen it stopping yet. The emissions from the United States have not increased at all over the last ten years. In Europe it's the same. They may even have decreased.

"So when you think about it, it really points toward the China-and-India theater as what's driving the growth. In the early eighteen hundreds it was land use—cutting down forests and putting in farms and burning fields and all that stuff. In the 1900s it began to be driven by oil and the U.S. and Europe. But now it's sliding over to China and India and coal."

Tans put things more simply: China's carbon dioxide emissions had more than doubled between 2000 and 2008 and, given China's growing demands, if the world doesn't wake up to the science of global warming and find the political willpower to do something about it, "we'll all be in deep shit.[5] Climate change is upon us," Tans said, staring at me with steely blue eyes. "The observations show that it's happening. The temperature is rising, but a lot of other things are happening too."

"Glaciers are melting like crazy," Butler said.

"That's a big feedback," Tans said, "because there's a reduced albedo," the amount of energy reflected from Earth, which is high for things that are light-colored or white, like snow, and low for everything dark, like open water.

Butler and Tans had recently calculated that since 1990, roughly when Americans began to pay attention to China's economic growth, the world's rising greenhouse gas emissions had locked in almost another degree Fahrenheit in temperature increase.[6] "It looked like the growth of fossil fuel emissions was leveling off until, say, the twenty-first century, when China really started to take off," Tans said. "Now they're already dominating the total emissions and their emissions are increasing at a clip of maybe 7 percent a year. For the Chinese to use as much as we do per capita, we're going to hit a wall."

Like Jaffe, the University of Washington chemist, Tans was also concerned about all the other ways China's growth is rearranging the atmosphere. "Mankind is starting to dominate the global metabolism and the Earth is trying to cope with all of it," he said.

Butler laughed quietly, as if Tans had just told a good, dark joke. "In 1960, the human population was three billion," Butler said. "Now we're almost at seven billion. It's like we've played a game of low-stakes poker but somebody's been raising the stakes as we go along.

"Now, every hand will take a huge slice out of everything that you've worked so hard to earn. It could just go in one hand. The stakes are going up, absolutely."

This is a book about how China's rise is changing the physical planet. For many readers the facts about how quickly China has grown since the late 1970s and what that means for the global economy and geopolitics will be familiar, even if we don't always keep all the facts straight. Many will have heard that China is not only the world's fastest-growing large economy but that it is the *only* large economy that has ever sustained such a high growth rate—roughly 10 percent each year for three decades, enough that it has moved from being the world's tenth-largest economy (in 1979 wedged between the Netherlands and Spain) to its second-largest today.[7] Only the United States earns more each year, and much of that is derived from investments and outsourcing, not from actually making anything. Most economists predict that the Middle Kingdom—the direct translation of the Chinese *zhongguo*—will surpass the United States as the world's top economy sometime during the next two decades.

We know that with 1.3 billion people (in mid-2011), China is the world's most populous nation. Before it peaks, its population is expected to reach somewhere between 1.4 and 1.5 billion.

And it takes only a glance at our closets to see China's manufacturing prowess: the made-in-China label has become history's most successful. Largely because of China, we have 99-cent T-shirts and $2.99 action figures and electronics cheap enough that when they break we can simply throw them away and buy new ones. In 2004, *Businessweek* reported that Chinese manufacturers could generally produce goods for 30 to 50 percent less than American factories, "a big factor in the loss of 2.7 million manufacturing jobs since 2000."[8]

It is a testament to China's rising power that we keep reminding ourselves of these facts.

* * *

What we are only beginning to grasp, however, are the great environmental costs of China's manufacturing success. The problems that are obvious across China—millions of pollution-related deaths, plunging water tables, the eradication of wildlife—are beginning to stretch far beyond its borders to reshape the physical planet: the air we breathe, the health of the oceans and last remaining tracts of untouched forests, the diversity of plants and animals, the climates that shape where and how we live—the very metabolism of our rapidly crowding world.

Consider, for example, China's growing demand for timber. Until the late 1990s China was largely self-sufficient in lumber. Then, in the summer of 1998, heavy rains flooded the Yangtze River, killing more than three thousand people and causing billions of dollars in damages. China's leaders realized that widespread logging had caused massive erosion and increased runoff, damaging the natural buffers to heavy storms. With the power wielded only by single-party states, Beijing banned logging across most of the nation.

Like squeezing a balloon, that decision forced demand outward and forests began to fall across Asia. Today, most of the natural forests of Southeast Asia are gone. Russia's—the world's largest remaining tract of temperate forest—are falling at record speed. China takes growing quantities of African hardwoods: 90 percent of Mozambique's log exports; 70 percent of exports from Gabon and Cameroon.[9] In total, *nearly half* of all the tropical logs and pulp made from tropical logs, which is traded for use in paper, passes through a Chinese port.[10]

For most of the last decade, much of that wood—particularly the expensive tropical hardwoods—was churned into furniture and floorboards and exported to richer nations. But now China is beginning to hit its own consumer stride: one recent report found that nine-tenths of wood entering China now ends up in Chinese living rooms or bedrooms or in any of the other places that citizens would rather see wood than concrete or tile.[11]

Or look at China's impact on the species that share our planet. With its millennia-old beliefs in natural cures ranging from grasses and leaves to bones and horns, its growing legions of millionaires seeking reminders of the now-distant wilderness, and a widespread desire to eat wild animals—itself an outgrowth of traditional beliefs—China has become the world's biggest and fastest-growing market for illegally traded wildlife.

As with the smuggling of drugs or people, the global wildlife trade is shadowy, but it has pushed many species to the brink of extinction. China, for example, is now the world's largest market for illegal ivory, rhino horn, and tiger parts.[12] Because of demand for an expensive soup, millions of sharks are hunted each year—fishermen cut off their fins and then drop the sharks into the sea to drown. China is also the major consumer of scores of lower-profile species, animals like the pangolin, a loping anteater whose scales some Chinese believe can—after being fried with sand, soaked in water, and ground into paste—be eaten to reduce pain and improve circulation.

How China's rise has accelerated climate change is more widely known, but amid the steady drumbeat of warnings and political jockeying, we seldom step back to look at the big picture. When experts do, they generally agree that without a stronger Chinese commitment, limiting warming to 2 degrees Celsius (3.6 degrees Fahrenheit)—the goal of recent international climate accords—will be impossible.

And, of course, China is hitting its stride at a time when the world is already reeling from environmental problems. The Chinese often argue that they are only doing what Western nations have done and, in many cases, continue to do. And behind China, scores of other nations are also growing rich as their people seek the material comforts taken for granted in the West.

———

Those overlapping layers of history and trade complicate the story and my own journey to realization was slow. When I first moved to China as a Peace Corps volunteer in 1996, I knew little about the country. I remembered a few history lessons mentioning Mao Zedong and the televised coverage of the 1989 Tiananmen Square protests. But, largely, China had been a hole in my education. Only its scale impressed me: I sensed that China might play an important role in the twenty-first century and wanted to learn more.

For two years I lived in Pengzhou, a small city in southwestern China's Sichuan Province that felt isolated from the world. I taught English at a college that trained future high school instructors and, because the classrooms had no heat, my students showed up for winter classes in hats, gloves, and heavy coats. Like almost everyone in the city, I walked and bicycled everywhere. If I needed to go farther, I flagged down a three-wheeled pedicab that charged a flat rate of 35 cents.[13] Internet cafes had yet to open, and I kept in touch with friends by writing letters that took weeks to cross the Pacific. The tallest building in town was a slightly leaning Buddhist pagoda.

Then, in 2003, I moved to Beijing and settled into magazine writing. As I traveled I was often astonished by the changes I saw. China began its era of road building—between 1998 and 2009 more than tripling the length of its highway system—and cars followed. Pengzhou installed its first stoplight just before I left in 1998. When I returned in 2004, its downtown was clogged with traffic.

In Beijing, the changes were more profound. The quiet alleys around the Forbidden City, the old imperial palace at the city's center, were torn down at a dizzying pace. Construction workers ripped up bicycle lanes to make room for parking. Changes came so fast that I sometimes got lost. Returning to my apartment from reporting trips, I found whole buildings gone, roads closed, businesses that had ceased to exist or changed owners in a span of days: I would go to a favorite restaurant after a week's absence and in its place find a hair salon or grocery or toy store.

After a while I grew to expect such transformations. It became more jarring to return to my parents' home in Massachusetts, where I grew up. On each trip it looked like *nothing* had changed. The same four-story plastic cactus still advertised the Hilltop Steakhouse; the sign for the Fern Motel still flickered forlornly along Route 1. It looked as if the United States was standing still while China rushed forward.

* * *

As in any monumental change, however, there were costs to China's rise. Chinese inequality grew to record levels, by some accounts surpassing that of the United States. Conditions in China's factories and mines might have shocked even Charles Dickens: according to official government statistics, a quarter of a million Chinese have died in coal mines since 1949, a number experts believe greatly underreports the real toll.[14] Chinese moving to cities from rural areas were happy to find jobs, but many were also underpaid, overworked, and generally exploited, and I reported on dozens of private tragedies: urban residents forced off their property by corrupt officials, farmers infected with HIV when they sold their blood, activists jailed for demanding greater political freedom.

Among the problems, China's domestic pollution crisis quickly became the clearest example of the heavy toll the nation is paying for its breakneck growth. Even in the late 1990s, the environmental costs of China's rise were obvious. As a Peace Corps volunteer I often read on the balcony of my fifth-floor apartment. When the wind blew toward me, it carried so much soot from a nearby factory that particles rolled down each page, leaving thin gray trails. A stream near my apartment was choked with trash and smelled like sewage. After my Chinese improved, I translated the sign on a factory where thick red liquid poured into the channel and learned that it produced thermometers using mercury, a potent neurotoxin that interferes with the brain and nervous system.

Newspapers and reports were also full of dismal facts: only 1 percent of China's 560 million urban residents breathed air considered safe by the European Union; a World Bank study found that sixteen of the world's twenty most polluted cities were Chinese; half of China's rivers were so polluted that their water could not be used without prohibitively expensive treatment; rain falling in southeastern China had the same acidity as vinegar; China's groundwater supplies were quickly drying up; every year, deserts were spreading over an area the size of Connecticut.[15]

The details often were more frightening. Scientists looking at the Songhua River, a waterway that stretches across an industrial section of northeastern China, found mercury levels five times higher than the 1960s concentrations in Japan's Minamata Bay, where thousands of people were poisoned by mercury pollution.[16] During a reporting trip to a small village in central China I talked with farmers who blamed toxic runoff for a surge in cancer deaths—twenty-five people had died over a year and a half, the youngest of them seventeen. The director of the United Nations Development Program's China office told Chinese officials that the "negative health effects of China's air pollution and water contamination annually cost China over four hundred thousand lives" and 9 percent of the country's gross domestic product.[17]

The statistics were sobering but—as it did with my Chinese friends—the degraded environment became my new normal. The problems were more a curiosity than a concern to the American audience I wrote for, and I learned to live with the pollution. I stayed off my bike when the sky was the color of wet concrete. I gave up eating fish and swam only in indoor pools.

———

Then, in 2005, I took a job covering Asia for a chain of newspapers and began to travel across the continent. In country after country I heard how China's environmental crisis had reached beyond its borders. A college friend in Seoul told me how South Koreans had been forced indoors by a days-long sandstorm that blew in from China. An environmentalist in Phnom Penh worried that Chinese dams were killing Cambodia's fishing industry. The director of an orangutan orphanage in Indonesian Borneo worried that Chinese demand for lumber could drive wild orangutans to extinction. The United Nations had warned that most of Indonesia's original forests could be gone by 2022, with lowland jungles falling sooner. Many, possibly most, of those logs were shipped to China.[18]

I sought out reports about how Chinese demand was driving the poaching and wild collection of everything from elephants and rhinoceros to seahorses and mushrooms, and when a friend forwarded a letter written by

Robert Pitman, an ecologist at the National Oceanic and Atmospheric Administration, it resonated. Pitman argued that the extinction of a dolphin unique to the Yangtze River was the first large animal ever killed off "merely as an indirect consequence of human activity: a victim of market forces and our collective lifestyle."[19]

The loss, Pitman wrote, "is perhaps a view of the future for much of the rest of the world and an indication that the predicted mass extinction is arriving on schedule." I printed the letter and pinned it to my bookshelf.

As the stories accumulated, I began to see the individual shocks as preludes to larger changes and decided to explore how China's rise has reconfigured environments around the world. Besides specific impacts, I wanted to find places that provided a glimpse of a future where not only China but also India, Brazil, Russia, and scores of other nations strive for the rich material lives of the West. China—the world's most populous and fastest-growing nation—seemed like the front edge of a much larger wave of environmental change, and I wanted to understand what its reach says about how we will live on an increasingly crowded, busy planet.

———

As I began to report, I realized that to answer the central question of journalism—"So what?"—I had to look at how humanity had already rearranged the environment. If China is changing the planet, how healthy was that world to begin with? What was the baseline?

I began to study the history of global environmental change and was reminded that scientists have warned for centuries that we—the now 7-plus billion people of Earth—are approaching physical limits to our exuberant demands. One of the first warnings came from Thomas Robert Malthus, a British scholar who argued in 1798 that the "power of population is so superior to the power of the earth to produce subsistence for man, that premature death must in some shape or other visit the human race."[20]

Over the last century, warnings have come more frequently. In 1968, Garrett Hardin, a biologist at the University of California, took Malthus's argument a step further by popularizing a dilemma he called the "tragedy of the commons." Hardin's achievement was to recognize that because many of the world's resources—our atmosphere and oceans are good examples—are shared "commons," economic logic dictates that people, companies, and nations will relentlessly plunder their wealth. "Therein is the tragedy," Hardin wrote. "Each man is locked into a system that compels him to increase . . . without limits—in a world that is limited. Ruin is the destination toward which all men rush, each pursuing his own best interests in a society that believes in the freedom of the commons. Freedom in a commons brings ruin to all."[21]

A few months after Hardin's paper was published, the Club of Rome, a group of academics, business leaders, and civil servants, met in the Italian capital to kick-start an undertaking they called the Project on the Predicament of Mankind. Among other things, the group commissioned scientists at the Massachusetts Institute of Technology to model "five basic factors that determine, and therefore, ultimately limit, growth on this planet—population, agricultural production, natural resources, industrial production, and pollution."

The result was a slim book called *The Limits to Growth*, which argued that because population was growing exponentially—in 1970 doubling every thirty-three years—and people lived increasingly rich material lives, humanity was due for a rapid reckoning: "If the present growth trends in world population, industrialization, pollution, food production, and resource depletion continue unchanged, the limits to growth will be reached sometime within the next one hundred years," the book warned. "The most probable result will be a rather sudden and uncontrollable decline in both population and industrial capacity."

———

Environmental optimists point out that such prophesies have not come true. But it is also clear that the speed of change has accelerated, and mainstream environmental institutions have issued increasingly urgent warnings. In

2000, the United Nations convened a four-year effort to take stock of the planet. To "check the accounts," in their words, they spent $24 million bringing together more than thirteen hundred scientists. Their final report—the "Millennium Ecosystem Assessment"—identified twenty-five critical "ecosystem services" that ranged from recreational and aesthetic benefits provided by the natural world to the basic health of the land, air, and rivers we rely on to grow and forage for food, collect natural resources, regulate the climate, and replenish drinking water. The experts studied tens of thousands of scientific papers and concluded that sixteen of the twenty-five services were being used at an unsustainable rate.[22]

The board of directors for the assessment summarized their findings with what they called a "stark warning": "Human activity is putting such strain on the natural functions of Earth that the ability of the planet's ecosystems to sustain future generations can no longer be taken for granted. . . . In effect, the benefits reaped from our engineering of the planet have been achieved by running down natural capital assets."

The World Wide Fund for Nature (in the United States called the World Wildlife Fund or just WWF) issued a similar warning in its 2010 "Living Planet Report." To measure "changes in the health of the planet's ecosystems," they tracked changes in twenty-five hundred animal species. Compared with the 1960s, they recorded a 30 percent drop in the "health of species that are the foundation of the ecosystem services."[23]

Another nonprofit, the California-based Global Footprint Network, estimated that human demands on the planet's resources are 50 percent greater than the "regenerative capacity" of those resources. If present growth continues until 2030, "humanity will need the capacity of two Earths to absorb carbon dioxide waste and keep up with natural resource consumption," the group stated.[24]

Underpinning the reports is a growing body of research that shows that humanity is using natural resources unsustainably—in ways that deplete them faster than they can be replenished or their wastes safely dealt with. Since the beginning of the Industrial Revolution, for example, we have cleared more than one quarter of the world's original forests and an even larger fraction of its wetlands and plains; set off the world's sixth great era of extinctions—with losses occurring at a rate scientists consider between one hundred and one thousand times greater than before humans dominated Earth; pumped enough carbon dioxide and other greenhouse gases into the atmosphere to heat the planet by more than 1 degree Fahrenheit; depleted the oceans to the point that the UN Food and Agriculture Organization classifies more than one-quarter of fish species as "overexploited" or "depleted"; and released billions of tons of toxic and hazardous materials into the air and water.[25]

According to Edward O. Wilson, the Harvard University biologist famous for his impassioned pleas to protect the natural world, half of the "great tropical forests" have been cleared and as much as half of the world's plant and animal species may be gone by the end of this century.[26] "An Armageddon is approaching at the beginning of the third millennium," Wilson wrote in *The Future of Life*. "But it is not the cosmic war and fiery collapse of mankind foretold in sacred scripture. It is the wreckage of the planet by an exuberantly plentiful and ingenious humanity. . . . The living world is dying; the natural economy is crumbling beneath our busy feet. We have been too self-absorbed to foresee the long-term consequences of our actions, and we will suffer a terrible loss unless we shake off our delusions and move quickly to a solution."[27]

———

The more I read, the more I realized that China is hitting its stride just as the planet is reaching environmental tipping points. And the more I looked at estimates of China's future growth, the more I came to believe that when historians look back at the twenty-first century, they will see China's greatest impact not as economic or political but as environmental. They are likely to judge China's history by how it has changed the physical world.

To get a sense of how much China's demands will grow, it is important to remember that despite the nation's rising riches, most of its people remain poor. In 2011, China's average per capita earnings were less than $4,000, one-eleventh of the U.S. average.[28] And, as in the United States, those earnings are unequally distributed: hundreds of millions of Chinese still lack the basic material goods taken for granted in the West—single-family apartments or homes, vehicles, televisions, washing machines, dishwashers, and all the other things that comfortable consumers enjoy.

To get a sense of how far China still has to go, it helps to compare an average Chinese citizen with a typical American. The average American is responsible for 13,647 kilowatt-hours of electricity each year—enough to run 136,470 one-hundred-watt lightbulbs simultaneously for one hour. He (or she) uses 933 gallons of crude oil and 2,156 cubic meters of natural gas. He is responsible for roughly 18 metric tons of carbon dioxide emissions and eats 238 pounds of meat. He almost certainly owns a car. Every day, he throws away four and a half pounds of trash.[29]

The average Chinese citizen, by comparison, looks as green as a Vermont wind farm. She (or he) uses just 18 percent of the American's electricity demand, one-tenth of his oil demand, and less than 5 percent of his natural gas demand. She is responsible for less than one-third of the American's carbon dioxide emissions and—even though Chinese demand has more than doubled in recent years—eats half as much meat as her American counterpart. China surpassed the United States as the world's largest auto market in 2010, but odds are high that she does not own a car. (In 2008, only one in twenty-eight Chinese owned a motor vehicle.)[30]

The relatively eco-friendly lifestyle of Chinese citizens, however, is more a product of China's economic stage than of green-minded choices and—for better and (mostly) worse—their lives will increasingly look like ours.

This, then, is not just a book about China. It is also about what it means that billions of people—the Chinese and, close behind them, Indians, Russians, Brazilians, and the rest of the people of the developing world—are beginning to achieve the rich material lifestyles enjoyed in Western nations.

To write it I have had to grapple with several intellectual complexities. The first problem was how to fit China into a history of environmental change driven largely by the United States, Europe, Japan, Australia, and the rest of today's wealthy countries. To deal with that issue, I chose to include history about how biodiversity, the world's forests, and the climate fared over the twentieth century, background that provides context for China's rise and reminds us that the environmental changes we are seeing now were created over generations.

A more difficult problem was that in this globalized age, it is impossible to entirely disentangle China's environmental reach. The Chinese, for example, buy most of the tiger pelts and bones funneled by poachers from India. But tigers are also at risk because of increasing conflict with encroaching society: Indian farmers who clear forests don't like wild cats stalking their livestock; hunters kill off many of the species that tigers feed on.

Likewise, China is the world's top emitter of greenhouse gases, but roughly a third of those emissions are created for the production of export goods.[31] Since almost all of the money made in exporting the products goes to foreign companies that own the factories and stores and to middlemen who shuttle the goods around the globe, and since the products end up in the hands of foreigners, who benefit from their low prices, can we really say that China is responsible? Shouldn't Western consumers share the blame?

Instead, I began to think of China as a combustive agent. Thrown into the already churning global stew, China has brought our combined productivity to a rapid boil and touched off countless unexpected reactions. I wanted to trace those distant, global combustions back to their internal sparks and began to think of the project as a planet-sized chemistry experiment: How will a growing Chinese economy force ever larger changes? Where will they happen? What will our world look like if and when they burn themselves out?

To make those connections, I traveled to places where China's consumptive reach is clear and found that in our globalized world, it is possible to trace the impact of supply and demand, cause and effect. Along the way I began to ask questions that are harder to answer: Why would it matter if the last wild tiger is killed? Beyond storing carbon and protecting against floods, what is the value of an untouched forest? Since the world's poor will suffer the worst impacts of climate change, what will make the rich care, given a history of neglect? Can we convince Chinese, Indians, Russians, and the people of other developing nations that they can't take from the natural world the way Americans and Europeans have? Can we convince the world's wealthy to scale back their demands because, in a finite world with finite resources, we are running out of margin? What is a fair balance?

In the end I was simply amazed at how much China has raised our global metabolism. Everywhere I went people said the same thing. There was the port worker on the north coast of Papua New Guinea who threw his arm toward the Pacific, as if casting a stone at China, to show where a huge pile of blood-red logs was headed. In Colorado, a shop owner smiled when I asked if she thought the community might have a second renaissance: "China's going to need a lot more coal," she said. In Copenhagen, an environmental activist was downbeat: "China is showing no leadership on climate change," he said, "so we're doomed."

At the end of my journey I saw China's domestic environmental crisis as a warning of what a world brimming with productive people might look like. We have managed to develop our global economy to great riches. People in rich nations live in ways people never dreamed about even a generation ago. We did those things, arguably, without tripping too many ecological barriers.

But China is the crest of a second, greater wave of demand that will play out—faster and faster—over the coming decades, and the fears expressed by generations of scientists may well be realized. Perhaps a few decades from now we will be struggling to survive on a hot, denuded, degraded planet. Or maybe we will address the problems before they grow too large. Beijing's leaders are capable of swift political acts and, at least for climate change, it seems possible that they will bring us together to save what's left.

Either way, it is time to confront arguably the century's most important questions: Can we save our last old-growth forests? Can we protect the greater community of species? Is there a way to live in a crowded, busier world without pushing the thermostat past critical thresholds? What, even, is at stake?

To answer those questions we must first confront the elephant in the room—China. And to do that, we must start at the beginning.

PART I

CHINA'S BASELINE

Down the Yangtze the awful prediction has been fulfilled. You expect this river trip to be an experience of the past—and it is. But it is also a glimpse of the future. In a hundred years or so, under the cold uncolonized moon, what we call the civilized world will all look like China, muddy and senile and old-fangled: no trees, no birds, and shortages of fuel and metal and meat; but plenty of pushcarts, cobblestones, ditch-diggers, and wooden inventions. Nine hundred million farmers splashing through puddles and the rest of the population growing weak and blind working the crashing looms in black factories. . . . Our grandchildren will probably live in a version of China. On the dark brown banks of the Yangtze the future had already arrived.

—Paul Theroux, *Sailing Through China*

1

THE YANGTZE

On a warm, gray afternoon I found myself standing on a cracked mud bank of the world's third-longest river thinking about what it is and was and could become. The scene looked nothing like the Yangtze popularized in scroll paintings and travel guidebook photographs. There were no mist-shrouded mountains or wooden fishing boats, no swooping sparrows or spindle-legged herons, no blue-water waves or Buddhist pagodas.

Instead, I looked across a quarter mile of turbid, rust-colored water flecked with trash. A dirty rubber ball, a few soda bottles, and a crumpled potato chip bag floated next to a hunk of Styrofoam. Two medicine vials and a rotting cabbage had washed ashore near the disintegrating hull of an abandoned ferry. A half-dozen barges carrying small mountains of goods—coal, steel, motorcycles, giant metal containers—pushed upstream against foot-high waves, each pouring a chimney of smoke into the smoggy sky.

The Yangtze cuts a line through the heart of China, traveling thirty-nine hundred miles from a glacier high on the Tibetan plateau to where it empties into the East China Sea just north of Shanghai, and I was standing roughly at its midpoint, in the center of Chongqing, a city most famous to Westerners as the launching point for trips through the Three Gorges, the narrow, steep canyons through which the Yangtze funnels on its journey east. Until 2006, when the Chinese Communist Party celebrated the completion of the Three Gorges Dam, tens of thousands of foreigners traveled to Chongqing each year to board cruise ships that took them through the gorges, and the river became as well known outside of China as the Great Wall or Beijing's Forbidden City. Early visitors included people like Archibald Little, a merchant who boated through the gorges in 1887 and was careful to write down each day's date because, as he put it, the "river varies so wonderfully at different seasons that any description must be carefully understood only to apply to the day upon which it is written."

But the dam had changed everything. Standing by the river, watching the barges grind their way past a landscape of construction cranes and half-finished apartment buildings, listening to the din of traffic, I couldn't imagine any seasonal variation. Soon, the only way the river would mark the movement from summer to fall and fall to winter was by where its waters fell against black and white numbers painted on concrete banks. On the day I stood on its shore, the Yangtze had reached 163. Translated, that meant the top of the Three Gorges Dam reservoir was 163 meters—534 feet—above the base of the dam, still too low to reach Chongqing but close.

———

For China, the Yangtze River and its Three Gorges hold an almost mythical prominence. The Chinese call the Yangtze the *Chang Jiang*—the Long River— and it has played a central role in history as far back as one cares to look. Many of China's earliest-known Neolithic societies lived along its banks: two and a half millennia ago, the people of a kingdom known as the Ba buried their dead in caves high in the cliffs of the gorges, a practice that showed an early sophistication of both communities and technology. More recently, the river became the locus of revolutionary history: the Heavenly Kingdom of the Taiping, a band of rebels that almost toppled the Qing dynasty in 1860, built their capital in Nanjing, the first major city upstream from Shanghai; the Republican Revolution of 1911, which finally ended two millennia of imperial rule, began in Wuhan, a sprawling city on the Yangtze's middle stretches; during World War II, Chiang Kai-shek, the leader of the Nationalist government, the Kuomintang, retreated up the river with a flotilla of junks carrying everything from dismantled power plants to the nation's treasury.

After the Three Gorges Dam split the Yangtze in half in 2003, it had taken on grander meanings, becoming a symbol of both China's ambitious rise and how that growth has damaged the natural world. When the dam was completed, Beijing released a list of world records set by the project, among them that the dam and power plant were the world's biggest, eventually capable of supplying 85 billion kilowatt-hours of electricity—enough to run a city of 17 million people; required the largest-ever forced-resettlement for a single structure—necessitating the movement of some 1.4 million people; and used more dirt, stone, concrete, and steel than any other project ever built anywhere.[1] It also created the world's longest man-made lake, a reservoir stretching 360 miles—nearly half the length of California—that has turned what was once a beautiful and challenging river journey into a pancake-flat lake with a dirty bathtub ring. Today, fewer foreigners make the trip. But just as Americans flocked to the Hoover Dam in the 1950s, Chinese tourists have made up the difference as they rush to gaze proudly on a cradle of their nation's early history and, sometimes more ardently, on their own wonder of the modern world.

I, on the other hand, had flown to Chongqing in search of a fish. A few months earlier I had come across a brief article about Chinese sturgeon, a fish I knew little about, and clicked open the link to find a photograph of a scientist holding a man-size animal with giant, armor-like scales. The story explained that the species had lived in the Yangtze for 130 million years but now teetered on the brink of extinction. Its size was also impressive: Chinese sturgeon, *Acipenser sinensis*, can live for forty years and grow to sixteen feet, making it one of the world's largest freshwater fish. (I would later learn that the Chinese paddlefish, another Yangtze species, can reach twenty-three feet, giving it the title, but none had been seen in the wild since 2003 and it is probably extinct.)

The approaching extinction of a species that had seen the arrival and disappearance of the dinosaur age seemed more important than the daily drumbeat of Chinese economic and political news, and over the next months I became obsessed with the fish. I read books and journal articles and learned that, like salmon, Chinese sturgeon spend much of their lives in the Pacific Ocean, sometimes traveling as far as Japan before finding their way home. Before the Three Gorges Dam and an earlier, smaller dam, they swam more than a thousand miles upriver to spawn in what must have been one of nature's most spectacular wildlife moments: thousands of minivan-sized animals flopping around in shallow streams and marshes.

I visited a hatchery where a Chinese scientist explained that sturgeon are among the oldest surviving members of Actinopterygii, the class of fish that dominate today's rivers, lakes, and oceans—accounting for 96 percent of all fish species—and represent a delicate thread to the biological history of mammals, including humans. The earliest sturgeon fossils so far found are 300 million years old, squarely in the Paleozoic Era, and some scientists believe they evolved 100 million years before that.[2] If they're right, sturgeon would have been alive when the first fish crawled out of a river, establishing the long tradition of land animals. (The first vertebrate to leave water— *Tiktaalik roseae*—is believed to have emerged from an equatorial river roughly 375 million years ago.) One source put their seniority into perspective by collapsing the last 600 million years into a single year: January 1 represented the day the first multicellular animals appeared; the first vertebrates arrived on the morning of February 27; assuming that sturgeon evolved 400 million years ago, they punched in on May 2; the first primate emerged on November 9; modern humans—*Homo sapiens*—evolved at three hours before midnight on December 31.

I was also struck by how badly sturgeon fared over the twentieth century and, in the bigger picture, what their plight says about the future of the world's rivers. One book noted that "as recently as 1890 the biomass of Atlantic and short-nosed sturgeons in Delaware Bay was in the neighborhood of 48 million pounds."[3] Native American tribes built weirs from tree branches and trapped Atlantic sturgeon as they migrated to breed. In Europe, members of the Viennese royal court amused themselves along the Danube River by firing cannons at "fleet-sized squadrons of migrating beluga sturgeons."[4]

Today, there are no sturgeon in the Delaware Bay or anywhere between there and North Carolina's Cape Fear River, and a person would be extremely unlikely to kill a beluga in the Danube with a cannon or any other weapon, since they're almost all gone. In 2009, all twenty-seven of the world's sturgeon species were listed on the Red List of the International Union for the Conservation of Nature (IUCN), the most important tally of endangered species. A recent notice by the U.S. Fish and Wildlife Service stated that "the Caspian Sea population is believed to be so depleted that natural reproduction in the wild may be insufficient to sustain the species." In Russia's Volga River, "the number of female sturgeons . . . was considered insufficient to even support artificial propagation efforts."

I decided to learn about sturgeon—and particularly Chinese sturgeon, perhaps the most endangered of the group—while a few still survived, and, a few phone calls later, was talking with Wei Qiwei, a professor at the Yangtze River Fisheries Research Institute and one of China's top sturgeon experts. Wei was happy to help. In fact, a student named Wang Chengyou was planning to spend a few weeks looking at sturgeon just west of the Three Gorges Dam. Would I like to tag along?

Wang Chengyou was tall and whip thin, like a tree that has spent all its energy growing upward and had nothing left to add heft. At twenty-five, he had the distracted look typical of graduate students—disheveled, with his hair unkempt and his glasses smudged. When I met him, he was wearing blue jeans, battered knockoff Nike sneakers, and a white and yellow T-shirt that he had put on, intentionally or not, inside out. His enthusiasm was even more striking: he had the energy of someone who needed to collect thousands of data points to make more than the 700 yuan—just over $100—monthly salary his position offered. He was on the river, where he could collect copious amounts of information, and so he was hopeful.

When I'd called Wang a few weeks earlier, he had sketched out our plan. The Chinese Academy of Fisheries Sciences, a national agency tasked with managing China's fish populations, had learned to raise sturgeon in captivity and each year dumped several thousand fish into the river just east of the Three Gorges Dam. Then its scientists crossed their fingers and hoped some would make it to Shanghai without getting hit by boats or caught in fishing nets or killed by passing pipefuls of industrial pollution. If they swam that gauntlet, the sturgeon would eventually reach the Pacific, and from there they might return years later to spawn.

But the Yangtze River Fisheries Research Institute had started releasing fish more than a decade earlier and the program had been a failure: in 2008, only six sturgeon had made their way up the Yangtze to spawn in their last remaining breeding ground and most of their eggs were defective, possibly because water flowing from the dam comes from the bottom of a five-hundred-foot-deep lake and is colder than what sturgeons have been used to for millions of years.

The institute was desperate to find another way to keep wild sturgeon alive and had tasked Wang with releasing five adult fish upstream from the dam to see if they survived. Since sturgeon have evolved to spend much of their lives at sea—sometimes traveling for ten years—it seemed unlikely that they would adapt to a giant, dirty reservoir, but Wang looked at the problem scientifically: until he had enough data to say that it couldn't be done, hopefully in the form of a doctoral dissertation, anything was possible.

And so we stood together on a bank of the Yangtze River in the middle of Chongqing waiting for a truck carrying five *Acipenser sinensis*. As we kicked at bits of trash that had washed ashore, I asked Wang how he had ended up studying the fish.

Western scientists generally have stories about how they fell in love with their subjects, but Chinese are almost always more practical: for Wang, the journey to the Yangtze had started in a poor farming village where his parents had invested their savings to help him escape. He had studied hard and tested into a teachers training college, and when he was about to graduate, a professor had asked if he wanted to study sturgeon.

Wang knew nothing about the fish, but the job sounded better than teaching at a rural high school and, without thinking much, he accepted.

When he arrived at the research institute he walked to a tank holding Chinese sturgeon and looked at the animal he would spend years of his life trying to understand. He found them beautiful.

"I remember thinking they were very large and had a good color," Wang said. He was even more impressed by their pedigree: "When I learned that Chinese sturgeon are one of the world's oldest-living species, I realized it would be a shame if they went extinct."

As I got to know Wang, I learned that he was also concerned because the Chinese sturgeon is akin to a canary in a coal mine. That night we met for dinner at a restaurant where diners cooked a wide variety of vegetables and indistinguishable animal parts in huge vats of boiling oil and water. As we picked through the meal, Wang explained the plight of sturgeon as one of greater ecological collapse.

To get a sense of how badly the Yangtze has been misused, one needs to imagine it thousands of years ago, before people began to dominate its ecology. From its headwaters in China's northwestern Qinghai Province, it flowed through one of the world's most diverse landscapes. In China's far west, it wound through accordion-like valleys on the Tibetan plateau that even today protect dwindling populations of snow leopards, cranes, wild goats, and takin—a relative of the ox that looks like a cross between a moose, a cow, and a bear. From the thin, clear air of Tibet the river rushed down remote canyons to the Sichuan basin, where it widened and slowed through forests teeming with wildlife. Historical and archaeological records show that the wilderness along the Yangtze's eastern half sheltered rhinoceros, tigers, deer, several species of monkeys, pandas, and a forest-dwelling cousin of the African elephant. Few people have studied the river's ichthyological history, but because Yangtze exploitation became severe only in the 1970s, it preserves a remnant of that earlier diversity. More than 350 species of fish have been recorded in its basin, one-third of them found nowhere else. Among the unique endemic species are, or in some cases were, the Chinese sturgeon, a rare finless porpoise, a dolphin, giant soft-shelled turtles, and the only alligators found outside of North America.

Chinese have lived along the Yangtze for millennia, but the beginning of the river's rapid deterioration can be traced to a push for industrialization in the beginning of the late 1970s. Today the Yangtze River basin accounts for 40 percent of China's economic output and almost one-third of its people. It supplies more than 70 percent of China's rice and fish—most raised in ponds laced with antibiotics—and absorbs more than 40 percent of its sewage, four-fifths of it untreated.[5]

Because the river annually carries 900 billion tons of water, enough to fill Lake Erie twice, experts once assumed that it would flush out any toxins people threw into it. But the combination of slow-moving reservoirs and factory-dumped chemicals has led to serious health problems. A 1998 study of irrigation water used in the Yangtze basin found cadmium levels 160 times above the allowable standard.[6] Tests found that people living in the area had consumed levels of the heavy metal nearly high enough to cause *itai-itai,* a disease that weakens bones and causes kidney failure. In 2008, a group of Chinese and Swiss scientists measured pollution in the river and found cadmium, mercury, and chromium, a sometimes carcinogenic heavy metal, exceeding European safety standards by as much as 500 percent. "The enormous loads . . . may assume a disastrous effect in the Yangtze estuary where it flows into the East China Sea," the scientists wrote.[7]

Wang also knew that the Three Gorges Dam is making the situation worse. The reservoir has submerged more than one hundred cities and towns and tens of thousands of acres of farmland, most of which had not been cleaned before they were flooded.[8] A 2006 report by Chinese hydrologists called the Yangtze "cancerous" and warned that more than two-thirds of its length could be effectively dead—unable to support most of the plants at the bottom of the food chain—within five years.[9] Landslides also became a problem as the reservoir rose, and scientists warned that its weight might hasten or intensify earthquakes.[10]

To me, the four decades of abuse looked like an enormous experiment in how quickly people can destroy large, seemingly impervious ecosystems, with the species that lived in the river acting as bellwethers. Between 1980 and 2005, the catch of wild Yangtze fish had fallen by 75 percent, leaving many species threatened or extinct.[11] Most had slipped away with little notice, though the *baiji*, a blind white river dolphin that inhabited the river for 20 million years, had attracted a brief upswell of concern. A team of international scientists spent six weeks looking for *baiji*, pronounced bye-gee, in 2006. After failing to find any, they declared the dolphin extinct, earning it the distinction of being the first large mammal killed off since the Caribbean monk seal was hunted out of existence in the 1950s.[12]

Wang drew his own lessons. For him, the Yangtze's collapse was a worrying marker of modern China's greater environmental crisis. "We need to do a much better job at protecting the environment," he said. "We're only beginning to realize how bad things are and what the consequences could be."

Our sturgeons arrived late in the afternoon on the back of a blue East Wind truck, the ubiquitous workhorse of China's economic growth, and we followed it through Chongqing's urban sprawl, past a China Telecom office and a branch of the Bank of Chongqing and a shop advertising "European-style furniture." It was a warm June day and hundreds of stores had set their merchandise on the sidewalks: air conditioners, plastic mahjong tables, racks of clothing, bins of toys, and all of the other thousands of things that people buy.

Like most Chinese cities, Chongqing is better measured by its population density than by its population: 7 million people live in an area roughly half as large as New York, which—with 8 million people—is the most densely settled part of the United States. The result is that people are everywhere, all the time, and while China's crush is often invigorating, that afternoon it reminded me of Francisco Goya's Black Paintings, which I had seen years earlier in Madrid's art museum. Goya had painted the works when he was in his seventies, embittered by recent wars and depressed by his approaching death, and they show a mass of humanity tumbling over itself in competitive despair.

We passed street after street of busy shopping malls and rundown hotels and characterless apartment buildings. Chongqing is built on steep hills that rise from the Yangtze and is famous for its *bangbangjun*, a phrase that literally translates as "stick-stick army": because many of its traditional lanes are too narrow for cars, thousands of people find work lugging goods around the city on bamboo poles, and we passed dozens of men bent double under small mountains of plates or car parts, washing machines or baskets stuffed with chickens and rabbits headed to their imminent deaths. Outside the Chongqing train station, a hulking building that could compete as the world's ugliest structure, an image of Goya's darkest work—a painting called *Saturn Devouring His Son*—emerged from my foggy memory: built by the Communist Party at the height of its utilitarian drabness, the building had a blank tile façade punctuated by bare lightbulbs. Hundreds of people wandered through an enormous parking lot ringed by dirty billboards and asphalt gray roads that rose in elevated loops. A huge crowd had gathered around two middle-aged women who stood screaming at each other.

Ten minutes later we turned past a pair of steamrollers and pulled to a stop beside a front-end loader digging sand from a Yangtze riverbank. At the edge of the river, a thirty-foot boat stenciled with the Chinese characters for "Sturgeon Seeker 2" bobbed beside a decommissioned ferry. Wang introduced a thin man wearing worn-out tan slacks and a blue oxford shirt as Yang Xiaohua, our driver.

———

Over the past decade I had been on the Yangtze a half-dozen times. As a Peace Corps volunteer I rode crowded river ferries to visit friends in cities east of Chongqing. As a journalist I cruised through the Three Gorges in a self-proclaimed five-star ship where I shared my room with a mouse. But this was my first time on the Yangtze in a small boat, and as I rushed to put on my life jacket, I could feel the Yangtze's power in a way I hadn't before: the reservoir had yet to reach the city, and the river coursed under our boat in a pulling wave that felt strong enough to send us hurtling eastward. As Wang untied our ropes and Yang throttled the engine, I took a seat in a small, enclosed cockpit and plotted my escape route, should the river prove too strong.

As we slid away from the shore, our engine buzzing over the din of distant car horns, it became clear that *Sturgeon Seeker 2* could overpower the
Yangtze's flow and I relaxed enough to focus on where the East Wind truck
had pulled to a stop. Two men in rubber hip waders had climbed its side and
were struggling to lift a large sturgeon onto a canvas stretcher: the sun had
broken through the haze and its gun-metal shine reflected dully through the
damp air.

The plan for the rest of the day, and for the coming weeks, was simple: we
would release the sturgeons and follow them. Each of the five large fish had
been fitted with a small tracking device and Wang had submerged a dozen
fixed receivers in the river at various points to the east. He dropped a four-
foot-long metal tube—a Vemco VR100 ultrasonic tracking receiver—off the
side of the boat and hooked a cable into his laptop. Its screen flickered and
then displayed the rough contours of the river bottom. A speaker emitted a
static buzz that Wang explained was noise from a coal barge grinding its way
up the middle of the channel.

Onshore, the scene was akin to a Federico Fellini movie. A group of
men in tight Speedo suits had been swimming at the river's edge—pushing
themselves ten or twenty feet away from the bank and then being swept
downstream—and they crowded around as the scientists carried the first
sturgeon toward the river. Watching from the boat, thinking about how
sturgeon had inhabited the Yangtze for millions of years, the moment seemed
a potent metaphor for man's impact on the natural world: without help, few
Yangtze species will survive the coming decades. And then the men waded
into the river and released the fish. As it slipped beneath the waves, sharp,
metallic beeps cut through the computer's static.

Wang had given each of the fish a number, and the second release—
number 8268, a fish that was five years old and three feet long—seemed un-
prepared for the Yangtze. Dropped into the river, it moved a few feet from
the men and then floated with its head out of the water, its ebony eyes just
visible above the dark brown surface. Scientists have written that sturgeons
sometimes behave in playful ways—the editors of one academic text admitted

surprise at how young sturgeons "demonstrate an uncanny similarity to puppies, swimming in somersaults, wagging their tails and watching with beady, reflective eyes," behavior that "often allows an attachment between researcher and subject that is unknown with other fish species"—and, to me, the fish seemed sane.[13] After being raised in concrete pools, 8268 was finally in the river nature had intended, but it was skeptical of the dirt and noise.

After several minutes, one of the swimmers—a middle-aged man carrying a red buoy as large as a beach ball—swam to the sturgeon and pushed its head underwater. But the fish quickly resurfaced and the surreal dance—the man pushing the fish underwater; the fish returning to look at him—continued for several minutes before the fish finally accepted its fate and, with a slap of its metallic tail, disappeared. Wang's computer tracked its movements as it dove from eighteen feet to twenty-one feet, heading east, for a few moments one of only two sturgeon alive west of the Three Gorges Dam.

———

The scientists released the other adult sturgeons and then pulled open a hatch at the back of the truck to dump two hundred sturgeon fry—month-old fish smaller than my hand—into the river in what seemed certain to be a death sentence. Then Yang swung the boat around and we followed the larger fish. Sonar can travel hundreds of feet in rivers, but the noise from boat traffic interfered with the signals and within ten minutes we had lost them. The speaker emitted a static hum that sounded like a soundtrack for a light rain that began to fall.

We cut the engine and drifted east, moving at between ten and twenty miles an hour as the river widened and narrowed, deepened and became shallow. We slipped under two massive suspension bridges and by remnants of the past and tributes to the future: a crumbling stone pagoda sat near a fat power plant cooling tower; packed-earth farmhouses abutted a port where cranes stacked tractor trailer–sized containers into colorful cubes; Chinese characters painted on a large sign read, "Energy comes from nature; save energy to protect nature." At steady intervals, red 175-meter markers—the height, in meters, that the Three Gorges Dam reservoir would reach when full—were painted on the riverbanks.

We drifted for several hours, the drone of the sonar resonating with the rain, and I tried to imagine the Yangtze as it once was, a majestic river supporting a wide variety of life. But the longer we searched, the more the effort to reintroduce sturgeon seemed a fool's errand. Instead, I was reminded of the history of global sturgeon exploitation, a slaughter neatly summed up by a group of academics as a story "of human gluttony and greed" and "one of the most telling ways in which humanity has failed in our stewardship of the planet."[14]

Even for a fish tale, the details of that extermination are lurid. The first European colonists to North America, for example, initially disdained sturgeon—along with salmon and lobster—at least partly because Native Americans ate it and the colonists wanted to maintain clear culinary boundaries. Until a few colonies faced starvation, they stuck to cod and shad. But after they were forced to eat the fish, they realized sturgeon was easy to catch and tasted fine.

From there, economics began to dictate desire. As European immigrants poured into North America, the prices of more favored fish rose. By the 1850s poorer citizens had developed a taste for smoked sturgeon, which peddlers marketed door-to-door as "Albany beef." To maximize profits, fishermen found uses for previously discarded parts of the fish: heads were boiled to make oil; swim bladders were used in gelatin.

In 1870, a German immigrant named Bendix Blohm began packaging sturgeon eggs—caviar—along the Hudson River and selling them to Europe, a simple idea that marked the beginning of the end for most of North America's sturgeon. As Blohm became rich, fishermen began targeting the species, and by 1880, Caviar, New Jersey, had become the world's top producer of the delicacy, sending fifteen train cars of wild-caught sturgeon eggs to New York City each day. In New York, the best-quality eggs were repackaged and shipped to Europe, but lower-grade eggs were plentiful enough that bars offered them like today's offer peanuts. The Denver and Rio Grande

Western Railroad sold American caviar in its dining cars at the same price as olives and celery.

The rising trade drove sturgeon fishing across the country. By 1885, almost 9 million pounds of sturgeon meat were being fished from the Great Lakes each year. By the end of the century, Sandusky, Ohio, a small city on the edge of Lake Erie, had replaced Caviar as the world's top sturgeon market. And as that fishery began to give out, people began hunting sturgeon in the cold, fast rivers of the American northwest, slower southern rivers emptying into the Gulf of Mexico, and the Mississippi River watershed.

The resulting collapse has been repeated countless times. Sturgeon can live for over one hundred years and need between seven and twelve years to reach sexual maturity. Mature females spawn only once every few years. By 1900, the thirtieth anniversary of the American caviar industry, most of the sturgeon that would have been swimming up the Delaware River had been killed. "The fish that should have been spawning for the first time in 1900 had never been born," Inga Saffron writes in *Caviar: The Strange History and Uncertain Future of the World's Most Coveted Delicacy*. "Their eggs had long ago been eaten."

The collapse spread west. In 1885, fishermen caught 5 million pounds of sturgeon in Lake Erie. Ten years later their total catch was 200,000 pounds. In 1914, the U.S. Fish Commission reported: "Even in the present generation we have seen the shores of the Potomac River in the vicinity of Mount Vernon lined with the decomposing carcasses of these magnificent fishes, witnesses to the cruelty, stupidity, and profligacy of man, and the same thing has been observed everywhere in our country."

––––––––

Two hours after we left the dock, the *Sturgeon Seeker 2* drifted into countryside. Rows of corn were planted like dress-brigade soldiers and the land's fertility was obvious: everything was green—the fields and, between them, narrow pockets of bamboo and palm trees. Sparrows, noticeably absent in the city, skimmed the water hunting insects. But the sonar continued to emit a low static hum and, as dusk fell, Yang started the engine.

An hour later we docked under the neon glow of Chongqing's night skyline. As we unloaded, I could hear the muffled noise of the city above us—car horns and the dull, thudding bass of a discotheque. We climbed a long concrete staircase toward a looping highway and near the top I turned to look again at the Yangtze. Under the light of a smog-dimmed moon, a tiny wooden fishing boat puttered into the current and passed behind a barge carrying a mountain of coal.

In the gloom I could just make out its name. It was called *Giant Ship 99*.

2

BASELINES

In 1995, Daniel Pauly, an ecologist at the University of British Colombia, published an article in *Trends in Ecology and Evolution* that introduced what he called the "shifting baseline syndrome." Pauly worked as a research ecologist and fisheries adviser, and he had become concerned that the world's fish stocks were slowly failing.

In the article—which in typically bland academic style is titled "Anecdotes and the Shifting Baseline Syndrome of Fisheries"—he spent just three sentences summarizing the bleak state of the world's oceans: fishing fleets, many heavily subsidized by governments, had exceeded "by a factor of 2 or 3" the size needed to harvest the 90 million tonnes of fish reportedly caught each year, raising concerns that many boats weren't reporting their full catch; levels of bycatch—fish killed by nets and lines that have little commercial value and are dumped back into the ocean—had reached "staggering levels . . . that perhaps raises the true global catch to about 150 million tonnes per year, well past most previous estimates of global potential"; and the "overwhelming majority" of over 260 fish stocks monitored by the United Nations' Food and Agricultural Organization faced "collapse, depletion or recovery from previous depletion."[1]

The findings weren't new, but the main thrust of Pauly's article—the concept of shifting baselines—was. "Essentially," he wrote, "this syndrome has arisen because each generation of fisheries scientists accepts as a baseline the stock size and species composition that occurred at the beginning of their careers, and uses this to evaluate changes. When the next generation starts its career, the stocks have further declined, but it is the stocks at that time that serve as a new baseline. The result obviously is a gradual shift of the baseline, a gradual accommodation of the creeping disappearance of resource species, and inappropriate reference points for evaluating economic losses resulting from overfishing, or for identifying targets for rehabilitation measures."

In plainer words, Pauly was pointing out that fisheries experts trying to figure out how many tuna or salmon or sturgeon fishermen can sustainably take from a lake or river attempt to keep the populations similar to what they saw when they started their careers. Over time, because of overfishing, uncounted bycatch, and natural cycles, some of the species decline in number and new fisheries experts use those smaller numbers as their starting points, creating a downward shifting baseline. (Some scientists have also used the term "sliding baseline.")

For nonspecialists, the concept could be used to describe any downshift in expectations, but it is particularly helpful for thinking about ecological change. People who began scuba diving in the 1960s and 1970s, for example, know most coral reefs have been heavily degraded by fishing, overzealous tourists, and bleaching caused by warming water. But when their children dive for the first time, they have no reference point and find the reefs beautiful, which, of course, they still are. Scientists have also used the shifting baselines concept to explain why people aren't upset by falling numbers of birds and mammals: most people have simply set new baselines; their ideas about what is normal have shifted.

The idea of baselines—that somewhere, sometime, there was a pristine natural environment we can reach back to—is central to understanding what we have lost, and to find China's baseline we have to reach further back than with any other nation.

Largely, this is a testament to China's early development. In 1800, China was arguably the world's most advanced society. With a population of 330 million people—then more than one-third of the world's total—it was the largest unified realm on Earth.[2] Its scientists and craftsmen had made many of the world's most important early inventions, among them the compass, gunpowder, and methods to make paper and print books, and its economy accounted for as much as one-third of the global total. Its cities were filled with grand architecture that made Europe's castles look puny, and its arts—stylized paintings, delicate silks, beautifully glazed porcelain—were treasured globally. Its bureaucracy was also well established: an imperial system had been in place for over two millennia, ever since the emperor Qin Shihuang—literally "first emperor of the Qin dynasty"—unified the realm in 221 BC.

That long period of political and economic strength, however, heavily damaged China's physical environment. Mark Elvin, an environmental historian at the Australian National University, argues that China's environmental exploitation "had few parallels in the pre-modern world."[3]

"Through more than three thousand years, the Chinese refashioned China," Elvin writes in *The Retreat of the Elephants*, an environmental history of imperial China. "They cleared the forests and the original vegetation cover, terraced its hillslopes, and partitioned its valley floors into fields. They diked, dammed, and diverted its rivers and lakes. They hunted or domesticated its animals and birds; or else destroyed their habitats as a by-product of the pursuit of economic improvements."[4]

By 1800, little remained that could be called natural. China had once been home to a wide variety of megafauna. Elephants roamed as far north as Beijing. Tigers stalked the Yangtze valley. Mencius, the fourth-century BC Chinese philosopher, taught about a Zhou dynasty king who "drove the tigers, leopards, rhinoceroses, and elephants far away," to the delight of his people.[5]

But as China grew richer, its large population and productive state steadily ate away at its natural heritage. While wars and disease kept European communities small, China's advanced economy and relative stability allowed its cities to flourish. An eighteenth-century memoir written by a Jesuit priest noted that a "hundred and twenty years of peace have so increased the population that the pressing need for survival has caused the plow to enter all those lands where there has been the slightest hope of a harvest. Hard work has outdone itself and gone so far as to create amphitheaters of harvests on the slopes of the mountains, to convert sunken marshes into rice-paddies, and to gather harvests even from the midst of waters by means of inventions of which Europe has as yet not an inkling."[6]

———

Two centuries after the priest wrote, Harvard ecologist Edward O. Wilson coined the acronym HIPPO to describe the greatest threats to natural environments and the creatures that live in them: habitat destruction, invasive species, pollution, population increase, and overharvesting. Ancient China provided case studies for each.

As the Chinese pushed outward, they cleared forests for farmland, an act generally viewed as a sign of strong leadership and one that allowed the exploitation of wildlife for food and medicine, setting a precedent for today's global plunder by an increasingly wealthy Chinese state.[7] Elephants were hunted for their ivory and for their trunks, which were considered a delicacy. One Tang dynasty (618–907 AD) writer noted that there were "numerous wild elephants" in southern China and that people "competed to eat their trunks, the taste of which is said to be fatty and crisp, and to be particularly well suited to being roasted."[8] Rhinoceros were targeted for their skins—used to make armor—and horns, which, ground into powder, were considered a cure for fever, rheumatism, gout, and other disorders. Peacocks were killed "not only through habitat destruction, but also because they are tasty to eat, particularly when fried in oil," Elvin wrote.

For people who have studied Daoism or Chinese Buddhism or who know Chinese history primarily through the landscape paintings popular among its imperial-era elite, such destruction is often surprising, but it is because China destroyed so much of its natural heritage that it produced some of the world's first environmentalists, thinkers whose philosophies resonate millennia later in the modern green movement.

Foremost is Zhuangzi, a philosopher who lived in the fourth century BC and who is credited as having a profound influence on Daoism, a religion that advocates living simply and in harmony with the natural world. A typical teaching ascribed to Zhuangzi celebrates a time when "people lived in sameness with birds and beasts, side by side as fellow clansmen with the myriad creatures," and so were "Not parted from their Inner Power."[9]

One story, as recounted by Jonathan Watts in *When a Billion Chinese Jump*, has Zhuangzi resting under a bent and gnarled tree when he is confronted by a passerby.

"Your teachings are as useless as this tree," the man sneered. "None of its branches will produce a single straight plank. Nothing can be carved from its knotted grain."

"Useless?" Zhuangzi replied. "Oh yes. I certainly hope so. You could plant this tree in a wasteland and still rest in its shadow, still eat its fruit. No axe will ever be sharpened to chop its trunk, no saw will ever trim its branches. If your teachings are more useful, you are the one who should worry."[10]

Such thinking helped create the Chinese concept of *ziran*, a word used in China today to mean "natural" and that can be translated, in the Daoist philosophical tradition, as "being so of itself," existing without interference from humans. *Daziran*, literally "big natural" but used to refer to nature, can be thought of as Mother Earth, a linguistic history that reveals a strain of popular Daoist ideology that meshes well with Western environmental concepts like the Gaia hypothesis, an argument, popularized by the British scientist James Lovelock, that the earth functions as a single living organism.

Chinese Buddhism, an Indian transplant, also espouses eco-friendly messages. Its adherents believe in reincarnation and—partly because a person might return as an animal—respect for all living things, buttressing the philosophy that man exists as part of a greater natural whole.

———

Just as modern environmental movements have failed to convince the majority of Westerners to live simple material lives, however, Daoism and Buddhism have largely existed on China's fringe. The dominant philosophy has been Confucianism, which stresses order both among people and between society and the natural world.

Confucius lived a century before Zhuangzi and taught that social harmony could be achieved only through strict adherence to hierarchy. This top-down order applied to the natural world as well, and Confucians actively sought to manage, use, and control nature.[11] As Elvin makes clear in *The Retreat of the Elephants*, the clearing of forests, damming of rivers, and extermination of wildlife reached an early low point in China: "More than any premodern northwestern Europeans, the Chinese were driven by a desire for *the rational mastery of the world*," he writes.[12]

Confucius tempered his utilitarian messages with the creed of *tian ren heyi*, "harmony between nature and humankind." But after the Communist Party claimed China, driving the Nationalist government to Taiwan in 1949, Mao Zedong—a revolutionary leader who spent much of his early life battling the Nationalists—largely abandoned any pretense of maintaining harmony. Even in his youth, his passion for conflict was clear: "To struggle against the heavens is endless joy, to struggle against the earth is endless joy, to struggle against people is endless joy," he wrote in one poem.[13] By 1940, his philosophies had hardened: at the inaugural meeting of the Natural Science Research Society, he told an audience, "For the purpose of attaining freedom in the world of nature, man must use natural science to understand, conquer, and change nature and thus attain freedom from nature."[14]

As Judith Shapiro describes in *Mao's War Against Nature*, the disastrous environmental policies of Mao's twenty-eight-year rule defied both science and common sense. In the late 1950s, Mao responded to warnings that China's population was growing unsustainably by calling on citizens to have more children, a step toward what he saw as increased productivity and strength. He attacked Thomas Malthus's argument that populations could outstrip Earth's ability to provide for them by saying that "realities in the Soviet Union and the liberated areas of China after their revolutions [showed that] . . . revolution plus production can solve the problem of feeding the population."[15]

During the Great Leap Forward, a terribly misnamed three years that ended with between 35 million and 50 million starvation deaths—the greatest famine in history—Mao took more direct aim at the natural world. In 1958, he called on the nation to double its steel production within six months. Communities met the target by building millions of backyard smelters, clearing forests, and then burning the wood to melt tools and utensils into worthless lumps of metal. During the same year, citizens were mobilized to kill sparrows, which Mao blamed for eating grain. Across China, people knocked down bird's nests and banged pots together to keep birds flying until they died of exhaustion. The government called the campaign off only when officials realized that the insects the sparrows ate were more damaging than the birds themselves.

Mao's longest-lasting impact on the land, however, grew from a traditional Chinese fable called *The Foolish Old Man Who Moved the Mountains*. In the tale, an elderly man can't bear the sight of two mountains outside his house and begins to move them, a stone at a time. A passerby sees the man laboring and chastises him for wasting time, but the old man replies that there is no reason the mountains can't be moved: when he dies, his sons will carry on and when they die, their sons will continue the work. Eventually, the mountains will be gone. The emperor of the gods hears the explanation and is so struck by the man's determination that he flattens the mountains.

Mao cared little for gods, but the fable was a convenient metaphor for his effort to reshape China: equating the Communist Party with the old man and the mountains with imperialism and feudalism, he made the story required reading across the country. In many local communities, however, people took the parable as a literal call to reclaim land. Across the nation, communes competed to "destroy the forests, [and] open the wastelands."[16] Forests were cleared without consideration for erosion. Grasslands were planted with crops, only to have the fields quickly degrade into deserts. Lakes were drained, with disastrous impacts on fish populations. Three-quarters of the lakes in Hubei Province, once known as China's "land of a thousand lakes," disappeared.[17]

To understand China's modern environmental crisis, one needs to grasp those historical roots: Confucian ideology both bolstered the belief that the natural world should be controlled to serve man and created a top-down political system with weak support for civil society—the checks on power provided by democratic elections, a free press, an active nongovernment sector, and the rule of law. Mao Zedong sharpened those historical forces by nurturing a revolutionary zeal that often ignored and silenced science and common sense. And China's post-Mao era has greatly increased the speed of environmental damage and pushed it far beyond the nation's borders.[18]

In China one can see how those roots have created a perfect storm of environmental damage. For me, its epicenter became the Yangtze River. And at the center of the Yangtze River is the Three Gorges Dam.

3

THE THREE GORGES DAM

The first time I saw the Three Gorges Dam, the Yangtze River still ran freely through China's mountainous center. It was early in the winter of 1997 and over the Chinese New Year three friends and I boarded a series of battered ferries and spent several days churning slowly downstream from Chongqing, stopping in millennia-old towns, chatting with passengers heading home for the holiday, and visiting ancient temples where visitors burned fake money to ensure that their ancestors were well provided for in heaven. In the Three Gorges, we snapped photographs of trails where trackers had pulled junks upriver and gaped at tall, slotlike canyons rising into fine mist, the kind of mystical Chinese vision that inspired countless poets and travelers.

In its own way, the dam was just as impressive. Workers had begun construction five years earlier and the site looked like a denuded anthill: thousands of laborers dotted low dirt ridges; giant red-and-white signs showed the almost unfathomable height of the future reservoir; armies of cranes and bulldozers pawed ponderously at the earth. The construction zone seemed improbably long, and as we chugged through it, the ferry's passengers crowded on deck. Propaganda blared through tinny speakers: the dam would alleviate devastating floods that had plagued China for centuries; it would provide electricity that Sun Yat-sen—the doctor who led the overthrow of China's imperial order in 1911—dreamed would produce "one hundred million horsepower"; it was the patriotic child of the Chinese state—Sun had created its initial plan, Chiang Kai-shek had invited American engineers to survey its location, Mao had recruited Russian experts to draw up blueprints, Li Peng, the Chinese premier under Deng Xiaoping, had finessed its approval through the nation's central government.

A scar on the landscape, it seemed both monstrous and necessary, and I was more impressed than worried. For the energy-starved nation in a world beginning to worry about climate change, it seemed better than dozens of coal-fired power plants, and I hoped its engineers would succeed.

———

Thirteen years later, my views were more nuanced as I walked up the gang-plank of the *MV Dragon*, a tourist ship docked in Chongqing. (MV stood for "modern vessel.") I had spent another day tracking sturgeon with Wang Chengyou and had realized it would take the *Sturgeon Seeker 2* weeks to reach the dam. The tourist boat would take three days and was better deco-rated: its front end was fitted with a forty-foot-tall metal structure shaped like a dragon's head; a second-floor shop sold paintings of pandas and pine trees; its staff wore yellow and blue silk gowns, the women's slit high up their hips in dresses called *qipao*.

I had booked a private room with a bathroom and a balcony—a step up from the tiny, windowless space Wang had arranged in downtown Chongqing—and began the trip by falling asleep. When I woke, we had reached the reser-voir: the Yangtze had widened to a half mile of slack chocolate-colored water punctuated by tiny, bald islands.

I picked up an English-language introduction to the boat's services. Opening to the first page I read, "When traveling through the Yangtze River by ship and standing on deck glancing at both banks, you will have a deep impression because the best scenery as well as the magnificent waters and mountains." My half-awake mind struggled with both the sloppy English and the false advertising: outside my window a rusting fishing boat listed at the end of a cracked mudflat. A barge loaded with thousands of logs—possibly the remains of a patch of once-pristine Southeast Asian forest—

pushed west. Behind it, a factory smokestack spewed a plume of gray pollution into the morning haze. I rolled over and went back to sleep.

As on trains, the best part of boat travel is the chance to meet other passengers, and as we cruised east, I spent much of my time talking with an engineer named Wu Bo. I met Wu at dinner on our first day out of Chongqing. We were seated together at a large round table where *qipao*-clad women served a series of tasteless dishes—vegetables stir-fried in a thick cornstarch sauce, underseasoned meatballs, white rice—all erroneously aimed at keeping the boat's single foreign customer happy. Next to Wu was a twenty-nine-year-old businessman surnamed Luo. Across the table, two tour guides named Allan and Lucy, names they had chosen because they were easy for foreigners to remember, looked bored by their umpteenth trip on the river.

Initially, our discussion was as bland as the food. Over my decade-plus in China, I have gotten used to a series of questions people often ask, and Luo quickly ran through several: "Do you like our China?" (The question is generally phrased like that—not 'Do you like China?' but 'Do you like *our* China?') Then, even though I was using a pair to balance a meatball, "Can you use chopsticks?" And, in rapid succession, How much money did I earn as a journalist? Did I find Chinese women beautiful? If so, did I know that the women of Hunan Province are the most beautiful of all?

I mumbled replies and tried to redirect the conversation by asking the group if the reservoir had changed the scenery of the Three Gorges. Allan, who worked for the cruise line, had prepared an answer: "The lake is different from the river, but it's just as beautiful," he chirped. "Some foreigners think it's even more beautiful now."

Lucy, a thirty-five-year-old with a bob haircut and too much makeup, admitted the higher waterline had covered many of the Yangtze's most important historical sites, including tracker trails and several temples, but offset the problems by noting that the higher waterline allowed people to see things they couldn't before.

"Like what?" I asked.

"Well," she said, pushing food around her plate, "there are all the new cities the government has built. There are many beautiful buildings."

Earlier in the day we had stopped at a city called Fengdu, and I had seen a new development. As the government resettled almost one and a half million people, it was housing most of them in what might be called instant cities, places with row after row of six-story concrete buildings set along newly paved traffic-free roads. I had skipped a tour of a Daoist temple to see the new urban landscape and ended up with a taxi driver surnamed Ran.

Over two hours, Ran drove me through the city, pointing out its first building with an elevator, its first Kentucky Fried Chicken franchise, and its first luxury hotel, a structure built with money embezzled from a fund meant to resettle displaced families. The official who stole the money had been executed, Ran said matter-of-factly.

Ran was particularly proud of a section of Fengdu that locals called "Four Big Bank Intersection." China's largest banks—the Bank of China, the Industrial and Commercial Bank of China, the China Construction Bank, and the Agricultural Bank of China—sat at each corner of two newly paved four-lane roads. "Before the new city we had two banks and neither was any good," Ran said.

On our way back to the boat, we picked up one of his friends, a middle-aged man wearing a worn leather jacket, and I asked what he thought of the changes. The man dragged on a cigarette, smiled, and said that everyone still young enough to work was happy. "We are developing," he said. "The new city is better than the old city. Only old people worry about lost memories."

———

Sitting at the dinner table aboard the *MV Dragon*, heading east on the reservoir, I told that story. I understood why locals preferred the newer buildings: they were more comfortable than where they'd lived and represented China's new era, growth that had largely missed the Three Gorges region before the dam. But, to me, they were poor compensation for the majestic landscapes and smaller, history-rich towns I remembered from earlier trips, places that recorded thousands of years of organic, human evolution. I recalled a reporting trip with Chinese archaeologists unearthing Han dynasty tombs in a village east of Fengdu. The group found relics dating to 5000 BC along a stretch of riverbank that would be flooded by the end of the year. Millions of similar sites had never been examined and, as the waters rose, a wide swath of history was being erased.

Allan and Lucy looked up sadly from their meatballs, but Wu, who had been silent, nodded. "In any change, something is always lost," he said. "But you have to balance those losses against the benefits. People can now live in cleaner, more efficient towns. We've been able to minimize flooding. We're providing clean energy.

"The dam is China's greatest engineering feat," he added. "You could say it's one of the greatest engineering feats in the world."

An engineer by appearance as well as trade, Wu wore giant glasses that seemed to be rimmed with stainless steel. He arrived at our table each day dressed in the same white button-down shirt and black slacks, both perfectly pressed despite the humidity. He talked quickly and punctuated his sentences with numbers: he had grown up in Yichang, the Yangtze city just east of the Three Gorges, in the 1970s, when one-third of the city worked on the Gezhouba Dam, a training run for its larger upstream cousin; the China Gezhouba Dam Group, where he worked in sales, had developed its international business by more than 60 percent each year since 2005.

I kept prodding him to tell stories. I wanted to understand what growing up beside China's biggest dam had been like, particularly as the Communist Party proclaimed taming the Yangtze its greatest project. How had people thought about the interplay of costs and benefits he had pointed to at our first dinner?

As the gorges slid past our windows, Wu slowly spun out his story, and the more he talked, the more it struck me as a parable of China's growth—the ambition that has driven China's economic rise and pushed it into the world; the faith, central also to American and European history, that a richer material life will bring greater happiness.

Wu's story started in 1972. He was born in Yichang only blocks from where an army of laborers was working to divert the Yangtze to begin construction of the Gezhouba Dam. His first memories are of thousands of laborers shoveling mud and carrying it up the riverbanks in baskets and wheelbarrows. "Everything was done by hand," he said. "There were hardly any machines back then because our relationship with Russia wasn't good and we still hadn't established relations with the United States."

His most vivid early memory was of the Yangtze flowing away from its riverbed. In the late 1970s, laborers completed a cofferdam to divert the river so work could begin on the main dam. As the Yangtze drained away, the city's residents gathered each evening to scoop fish from thousands of small ponds. "There were so many that people could simply reach into the water and grab them," Wu explained.

He also remembered the infusion of political zeal the dam provided. Workers staged rallies glorifying the Communist Party and hung thousands of banners. Teachers told children to help the laborers "in order to make China strong." Sometimes he and his friends played at building their own miniature dams. "Everyone had the idea that we were doing something great for our country," he said as we passed through the first of the Three Gorges.

That zeal helped China transition from a nation with little technical knowledge to the most experienced dam-building country on earth. On its first try, however, the effort to dam the Yangtze failed. During the chaos of Mao's Cultural Revolution, many of the country's best-trained engineers were accused of harboring bourgeois sympathies and sent to work in remote villages. By 1972, the whole project was in such poor shape that construction was suspended. "The irrationality of revelatory zeal and huge-crowd strategy defied laws of science and technology," a doctoral dissertation about the dam states.[1]

The experience engineers gained, however, was invaluable. Work began again in 1974 and the Gezhouba Dam was finally finished in 1989, setting the stage for two decades of rapid dam construction. Today, China is home to more than half of the world's large dams and its state-owned hydraulic engineering companies have become the world's most competitive, driving down costs and pushing the environmental impacts of damming rivers around the world.[2]

Wu's passion epitomized that recent rapid development. When he finished high school, he earned a spot studying civil engineering in a Beijing university. In 1996 he took a job monitoring construction of a section of the Three Gorges Dam and moved into a small, shared room beside the Yangtze. He spent his days poring over plans and triple-checking the work of laborers. Often, he made them tear sections down and start over. "None of them liked me very much, but we needed to make sure the dam was absolutely safe," he explained.

As in the heady days of growth in the American West, everyone was expected to put in long hours. The company required laborers to work six 10-hour days and one 4-hour day each week and supervisors were expected to do more. Wu regularly spent fourteen hours at the work site. During one five-month stretch, he worked every day. In compensation he received room and board and the equivalent of about $60 each month.

Occasionally he took time at the end of a long day to climb a hill that looked over the Yangtze. "I would sit there looking at the river and thinking about China's place in history," he told me. "I felt strongly that building the Three Gorges Dam was historic. I felt it would remake China."

We passed through the long, steplike lock of the Three Gorges Dam overnight and by daybreak had moored just west of it. After breakfast, we filed onto a blue-and-white tour bus. A guide introduced herself as Little Yu and quickly launched into a lecture on why the dam was good for both China and the world.

Little Yu made the usual references to clean energy, flood control, and the economic logic of creating a river highway that can move seven-thousand-ton ships between Shanghai and Chongqing. There was the story of how Sun

Yat-sen had dreamed of using the dam to modernize China and a proclamation that the Communist Party had realized his dream.

As we drove past power-line towers and the construction site for a ship elevator, Little Yu mentioned the ten world records set by the dam and its benefits to the local community. She mentioned the dam's dimensions and the number of turbines it fed and the names of foreign dignitaries who had toured it. She even dabbled in geology, pointing out that the rolling hills surrounding us were the best possible site for the dam because they rested on a bed of granite.

Little Yu was employed by the state-owned China Three Gorges Project Development Corporation and what she didn't mention were the environmental and social costs of the dam's construction. The only reference she made to the 1.4 million people relocated to make room for the reservoir was that the Communist Party had built "new, better" cities. She never talked about sturgeons or dolphins or porpoises and didn't address the possible health concerns for people living along the river or the risk the reservoir posed to people living below the dam: some experts had warned that a terrorist attack, a military strike, or an earthquake could cause the dam to breach.[3] If the dam suddenly failed, millions would die.

The same one-sidedness was on display at the official Three Gorges Dam Museum a few miles downstream. A movie called the dam "a symbol of China's remarkable reinvigoration" and announced that "for thousands of years, the Chinese people have yearned for the day that the Yangtze River is tamed." Display after display touted the dam's benefits. There were photographs of villages inundated in 1998, when Yangtze flooding had killed more than one thousand people. A map showed the South-North Water Diversion Project, another mega-scheme that—using the Three Gorges reservoir to feed its central arm—will move Yangtze water more than six hundred miles north to China's arid, rapidly drying plains, a distinctly Confucian solution to a man-made problem.

More interesting than the propaganda was the history the museum ignored. It made no mention of the dam's foremost critics: Li Rui, the director of the General Bureau for Hydroelectric Construction under Mao, and Dai Qing, a journalist and environmental activist who published two collections of critical essays. Li had argued that the government could achieve better results with smaller dams on Yangtze tributaries.[4] Dai's books had raised concerns about pollution, sediment buildup, archaeological and biodiversity losses, and the dam's design.

Both had been silenced. After Li opposed the Great Leap Forward—the failed three-year government drive to industrialize—he was banished to a rural farm. During the Cultural Revolution he was imprisoned as an enemy of the state. In 1989, Dai Qing met the same fate. Shortly after her books were published, the government crushed the protests centered around Tiananmen Square. The works were banned and she was imprisoned in the same jail where Li had been held two decades earlier.[5]

The Communist Party's unwillingness—perhaps even inability—to accept serious criticism is central to China's environmental meltdown. Like China's emperors, some of the party's elite think of those outside its ranks as too uneducated to participate in government, an attitude famously evoked by Karl Marx in 1852, when he compared peasant society to "a sack of potatoes" because he believed it lacked cohesion and class consciousness.

China's central management, of course, has benefits. There are none of the endless public debates about policy that foil economic growth in many countries. Unlike Russia, which spent years grappling with its Soviet legacy, or India, where political squabbles make it difficult to build anything, China has focused its energy on moving forward. In the process it has lifted hundreds of millions of people out of poverty.

But, far from Beijing, China's top-down approach has failed to prevent abuses. Without nosy journalists and nongovernment organizations, hard-pitching politicians, and independent courts, China's elite and powerful largely do as they please, a condition captured by an age-old Chinese aphorism: "The mountains are high; the emperor is far away."

The failure of the party's top-down directives to solve environmental problems was highlighted most dramatically in 2001, when heavy rains flooded billions of gallons of polluted water into the Huai River, a large Yangtze tributary. Only a few months earlier, the head of China's State Environmental Protection Agency, its top environmental bureau (now called the Ministry of Environmental Protection), had declared a seven-year cleanup effort successful, returning the Huai from one of China's most lethal waterways—one in which factories dumped untreated pollutants with impunity, water turned black, and fish died—to one suitable for drinking and fishing.

As the river again deteriorated in 2001, it became obvious that it had never truly regained its health. The central government had tightened restrictions on industrial firms and ordered the closure of hundreds of polluting factories. But "the imperative of economic development continued to overwhelm environmental concerns," Elizabeth Economy, a China expert at the New York–based Council on Foreign Relations, wrote.[6] Chinese researchers found that factories stopped polluting only when investigators were watching. The U.S. Embassy reported that within two years of their closure, 40 percent of the shuttered factories had reopened.[7] "Sadly, the saga of the Huai River is typical of today's China," Economy wrote in *The River Runs Black*, an analysis of the country's environmental crisis.

As with the deteriorating Yangtze, such failures are routinely swept out of sight by the Communist Party, and over my years in China, I often wondered how often government elites discuss the costs of central rule. Undoubtedly, some officials, jaded and corpulent, recognize the problems but fear losing the perks of power. Others may simply believe that their leadership is infallible: they recognize China's problems but cling to the notion that the nation's masses need to be tightly controlled. When environmental problems arise, they believe the party is best able to handle them.

———

The night before we docked at the Three Gorges Dam, I received a lesson in how that second type of cadre thinks. I was reading in my room when a steward knocked on my door. A man named Deng Weiming wanted to buy me a drink, he said.

I had met Deng the day before, and when I arrived at the bar, he was sitting at a table looking out at the flickering lights of distant houses. A bottle of expensive *baijiu*, strong Chinese grain alcohol, rested on the table in front of him. I pulled up a chair, grabbed the glass he pushed at me, and downed my first fiery shot.

As we sailed east on the dark river, Deng explained that he had invited me because he liked the United States. He had recently retired as the head of the food and consumer product safety bureau in Nanjing, a city near the Yangtze's eastern end, and, in 1997, he had traveled to the United States on a study tour. In Los Angeles, he had been shocked to see drivers at a four-way stop yield to each other. "In China, that could never happen," he said. "Everyone would just rush through trying to get out first."

He was also impressed by the quality of American-made products. He was wearing a light blue T-shirt he had bought on the trip. "Every year it just looks better than it did the year before," he said. "Chinese-made shirts fall apart in a year or two."

When the topic shifted to the Three Gorges Dam, however, we found less to agree on. Deng scowled when I suggested that China would have been wise to dam only smaller rivers. He had traveled through the gorges several times before the dam was built and found the reservoir beautiful. He liked the dark brown rings on the gorge walls. To him, they were a reminder of China's growing power.

As we pushed farther east, we drifted further apart. I argued that while the Communist Party has racked up incredible achievements, its leaders need to realize that the costs of their top-down political model have surpassed its benefits. Without allowing greater civilian freedoms, Beijing would not be able to control the nation's rampant fraud, persistent human rights abuses, growing income gap, and environmental meltdown. The party, I said, needs to trust the people. Deng argued that most Chinese are too coarse—too "low quality" (*suzhi di*), a phrase often used in China—to be trusted with power. "We can't have democracy," he said as we tipped back one last shot. "The quality of the people is not yet high enough."

———

On the cloudy day that we transferred from the *MV Dragon* to our tour bus, the Three Gorges Dam seemed like a perfect metaphor for the party's authoritarian controls. The bus dropped us on top of a hill overlooking the mile-and-a-half-long concrete band. The rust brown reservoir backed up in a flat lake to the west. To the east, the river boiled with currents where the dam's turbines expelled plumes of water.

It started to rain, but my Chinese companions crowded around a monument advertised as the world's largest steel book. In giant English words, the book proclaimed that the "Three Gorges Project has made the long-cherished wish of the Chinese people come true. The great achievement is an embodiment of all participants of the work and will render benefits to the future generations with its comprehensive functions in flood control, power generation and navigation improvement."

An overgrown set of Olympic rings commemorated the 2008 Beijing Summer Games—another long-cherished desire that, a year later, had faded into memory. Nearby, a wide diorama depicted people using the river for agriculture, fishing, and transportation. At the sculpture's center was an image of three men holding each other in the center of the river's flow. Together, they formed the shape of a turbine, a symbol of China's age-old effort to impose human order on the natural world.

———

On our way back to the *MV Dragon*, our guide, Little Yu, asked if anyone had questions. I raised my hand: "There has been a lot of controversy about the dam," I started. "I mean, some people worry about its environmental costs, about the people who were relocated, about the danger of a possible earthquake. But you didn't talk about any of that. Do you think there are any concerns we should think about?"

As the only foreigner on a bus of tourists clearly impressed by the dam, I knew criticism, even the suggestion of criticism, could provoke anger, but I hadn't expected that the bus would become silent. I could hear rain tapping steadily against the windows.

Little Yu pursed her lips. "We aren't trained to answer questions about any problems," she said. "I heard there have been some landslides and some people didn't want to move to new homes at first, but those things have been dealt with. There isn't anything else."

"Anyway," she added, "only foreign friends ever ask those kinds of questions."

Back in Beijing two months later, I drove through a sticky August evening to meet Samuel Turvey, one of the world's top experts on the Yangtze's ecology. Turvey, who worked for the Zoological Society of London, had recently published a powerful testament about the Yangtze's degradation, a slim book called *Witness to Extinction: How We Failed to Save the Yangtze River Dolphin*.

Part history, part diatribe, the book recounts a six-week trip to search for *baiji* in 2006. A team of scientists had used boats equipped with sonar and high-powered binoculars to scour the river between Shanghai and Yichang but found nothing. At the trip's end, they declared the dolphin extinct, an event that created a brief uptick of global concern but should have caused outrage: as Robert Pitman, an NOAA ecologist who participated in the search wrote, the dolphin was the first large animal driven to extinction not because it was hunted but "merely as an indirect consequence of human activity: a victim of market forces and our collective lifestyle." Both Pitman and Turvey warned that its disappearance could herald an era when many more species would die out simply because, in a world dominated by man, there would be no space for them.

I liked Turvey's book because it took critical aim at a wide range of targets. Chinese fishermen had raced to catch fish in a classic case of an overused "commons." The Chinese Communist Party had continued to force nature into obedience with the Three Gorges Dam and other mega-projects. Chinese officials had created "among the highest amount of environmental laws and regulations in the world" but failed to build a court system that enforced them.[8] Scientists tasked with monitoring the *baiji* had dithered about how to save it, and while international organizations had pumped out publicity, they were slow to provide funding to see if any dolphins survived. "Instead of positive interaction on behalf of critically endangered species, I found to my disgust that the world of international conservation seemed at times to consist only of press releases and empty promises," Turvey wrote.[9]

After my time on the river, Turvey's cynicism struck a chord and the book's final sentences rang powerfully: "The last remnants of what was once the most magnificent river system in Asia are being washed away forever. And how many people are really doing anything to fight it?

"Somebody out there, please, prove me wrong."

———

Turvey had the sort of no-nonsense look and demeanor I expected after reading his book. He was wearing shorts and an orange T-shirt. His hair was buzzed close against his head. When we met in the lobby of a cheap hotel in Beijing's outskirts, one of the first things he mentioned was that something he had eaten the night before had disagreed with his stomach.

We sat in a garden by a highway and swapped stories of Yangtze degradation. I mentioned the pollution I had seen between Chongqing and Yichang. "Oh, that's nothing," Turvey replied. "You should take a boat from Yichang down to Shanghai. That's where it really gets depressing."

He was especially distraught that the passing of the *baiji*—the last confirmed sighting of which had been in 1985—hadn't created any commitment to rehabilitating the river or protecting species that remained. A finless porpoise, *Neophocaena phocaenoides asiaeorientalis*, might be the next Yangtze species to go. (Its wild population fell from twenty-seven hundred in 1991 to roughly one thousand in 2011, according to Chinese scientists.)[10]

"It's been very easy for both China and the world to ignore the *baiji*,"

Turvey said. "As far as I can tell, everyone's just gone back to doing what they were doing before its extinction."

———————

Perhaps because the world had moved on, we drifted late into the night drinking beer and talking about the Yangtze's past and what its deterioration says about the future. Turvey talked about a recent trip he had taken to a small strip of protected marshlands east of Yichang where critically endangered Siberian cranes still winter. He had also seen a Chinese water deer there, the only large wild mammal he had seen along the river.

"There was real biodiversity," he said, looking optimistic for the first time. "I mean, there was still this amazing beauty and it made me realize what the whole region had been like once."

We talked about how nations around the world were ramping up resource extraction and what that might mean for biodiversity, forests, and climate change. We agreed that China offers a warning about what the world might look like in a few decades, a world where more of us consume more of everything.

Turvey thought the Yangtze provided the best metaphor.

"The Yangtze is the most screwed-up ecosystem you can imagine," he said. "If you start with that, it actually gives you optimism because nothing could be as bad in terms of degradation, in terms of lack of interest, of the fact that you clearly can't say stuff there, that it looks god-awful and that it's soul-destroying."

The night had quieted and only a few cars rumbled past on the highway. We stared into the darkness and took swigs of our beers.

"That's what the rest of the world is in danger of becoming," he said.

PART II

LIFE ON THE BRINK

Ecologists warn us that we are now in the Earth's sixth great extinction episode. Plants and animals are apparently going extinct at a rate that is between one hundred and one thousand times the natural rate of extinction before human dominance of the Earth's ecosystems. The five earlier episodes were caused by massive natural disruptions of the Earth's ecological processes, including collisions with asteroids, changes to the Earth's climate through geological processes such as volcanic eruptions, and changes in the characteristics of the Earth's orbit. The current episode of mass extinction is the only one in which one species has pushed the others over the cliff.

—JEFFREY SACHS, *COMMON WEALTH: ECONOMICS FOR A CROWDED PLANET*

4

TIGER, TIGER, BURNING BRIGHT

It has been said that seeing a wild tiger is always like a dream, its appearance like a ghost that could fade into a haze of fact and fiction, into the memory of an animal that—like the passenger pigeon or the dodo bird—might once have lived but now requires a large dose of imagination.[1] I was reminded of that transient power as I pushed my way through New Delhi's Indira Gandhi International Airport on a warm January afternoon. Fighting between packs of travelers, I rounded a corner and suddenly found myself staring at an enormous photograph of a Bengal tiger. Across the bottom of the billboard, in large white letters, were the words "Incredible !ndia."

The image seemed both fortuitous and appropriate. India is itself an alpha-beast, a nation at once intoxicatingly beautiful and wildly chaotic, a place where a traveler is as likely to lose his mind as to find enlightenment, where he can swing from euphoria to horror and back again over a span of minutes. On my first trip to the country a year earlier, I had wandered out of my New Delhi hotel at dawn searching for coffee and approached a young man for directions. Just as I reached him, he tipped open a small nylon bag and—in a moment that put the exclamation point in the government's advertising campaign—a two-foot-long cobra fell to the ground beside my feet. It flared its neck and revealed what my stunned brain assumed were venomous fangs. "Mister, want to see a snake?" the man asked as I stumbled quickly away.

Later on that trip, I had been enthralled by what had seemed the fantastic world of a children's book: men rode elephants down sidewalks, monkeys swung from power lines, parrots perched on the roofs of restaurants—a profusion of life that highlighted an easy relationship between Indians and the natural world that contrasted sharply with China.

The tiger seemed fortuitous because I had flown to India in search of the beast. Several months earlier a friend had sent me a report showing how rising Chinese demand for tiger parts threatens the survival of arguably the planet's highest-profile species. Despite a worldwide ban on the international trade in tiger parts under the Convention on International Trade in Endangered Species of Wild Flora and Fauna—a law better known by its acronym, CITES—investigators from the Wildlife Protection Society of India and the London-based Environmental Investigation Agency had documented a string of Chinese traders openly selling parts and skins. In China's far west, they found scores of wealthy Tibetans wearing tiger-skin robes and using tents made from their pelts. In majority Han Chinese cities, they found shops offering skins to tourists looking for "prestigious gifts or home décor." One trader claimed that 80 percent of his customers were Han Chinese. Others reported that customers included local officials and army officers.[2]

The report laid out the scale of the trade. In 1993, the conservation world had awakened to the rising tide of Chinese demand for Indian wildlife when Delhi police caught a Tibetan smuggling 633 pounds of tiger bones, the remains of what might have been twelve adult animals.[3] A decade later, three men were arrested in western China carrying 31 tiger skins, 581 leopard skins, and almost 800 otter skins. Investigators tracked the tigers to India partly because a *Times of India* newspaper was stuffed inside the cargo.

Other seizures had turned up similarly large stocks of animal parts: thousands of tiger and leopard claws, dozens of skins, hundreds of pounds of bones. Tallying the pieces, the groups had estimated that nearly eight hundred Indian tigers were poached between 1994 and 2006, a figure that might have been equal to half of the wild tigers remaining in Incredible !ndia.

The report also sketched out the tiger's dismal state worldwide. In 1900, one hundred thousand tigers are believed to have roamed a region stretching from Turkey east to Siberia and south into the tropical rain forests of Thailand, Vietnam, and Indonesia. As human communities grew, however, they pushed and hunted tigers out of all but slivers of that range. Between 1875 and 1925, at least eighty thousand tigers were killed by hunters in India alone, many of them by British officials and aristocrats.[4] By 1950, the world's tiger population had fallen to forty thousand.[5] In 1970, the last Caspian tiger was killed in Turkey, and by the 1980s the species had been exterminated from the Indonesian islands of Bali and Java.

Today, between three and four thousand tigers remain in the wild and, according to the International Union for the Conservation of Nature (IUCN), the compiler of the Red List of Endangered Species, their habitat is just 7 percent of what it was in 1900.[6] Traffic, the world's leading organization dedicated to studying the trade in endangered species, believes that fewer than twenty-five hundred "breeding adult tigers" remain.[7]

———

I was also moved because I had seen the tail end of the tiger trade. Reporting at a warehouse-sized market in Chengdu, the capital of China's southwestern Sichuan Province, in 2003, a traditional medicine trader had offered to sell me tiger bone and promised it could cure a long list of problems. A relative, an American who did business in China, told me about a brick-sized piece of tiger bone a Chinese colleague had given him years earlier. Not wanting to offend his host, he accepted and then packed it away in a shoebox in his suburban American home. Browsing at a store in Wangfujing, Beijing's most popular downtown shopping street, I came across a book titled *Medicated Diet of Traditional Chinese Medicine*. Among entries describing the medicinal benefits of consuming turtle shells, human placentas, and pangolin scales was an entry for tiger bone:

TIGER BONE

ORIGIN The bones of Panthera tigris L. family Felidae.

NATURE, TASTE AND CHANNEL TROPISM Acrid and sweet in taste, warm in nature, and attributive to liver and kidney channels.

EFFICIENCIES Expel wind and alleviate pain, strengthen the bones and muscles.

INDICATIONS For rheumatism and flaccidity of the back and lower extremities caused by deficiency of the cold of the liver and kidney. Recently, its preparation of wine and injection are used for rheumatic arthritis and rheumatoid arthritis.

DIRECTION Decoction: 10–15g.[8]

A few months later, walking through another part of Beijing, I turned a corner and bumped into a stuffed Siberian tiger a shop had set outside to advertise alcohol steeped with tiger bones. On a shelf at the back of the store I found a few dozen bottles emblazoned with photographs of tigers and a paragraph stating that "Balsam Ussuriyskiy is made of extracts from the Ussuriyskaya Taiga," a region of eastern Russia that still protects several hundred wild tigers. A pharmacist swore the drink was made with the animals' bones.

In that case, a few phone calls had proved that the pharmacist was either confused or lying, probably hoping to convince me to pay $100 for a bottle of vodka. But there was ample evidence that Chinese citizens can buy real tiger-bone wine at hundreds of shops across the country despite laws prohibiting the trade. In 2005, a safari park near Beijing had openly advertised what it called North Big Storehouse Tiger Wine as containing bones from tigers that had "died from fight wounds."[9] A few years later, an official at the Shenyang Forest Wildlife Zoo in northeastern China told a Chinese newspaper that the production of tiger-bone wine was an "open secret" and that the zoo had given bottles to police officers and senior forestry officials tasked with enforcing China's wildlife laws.[10]

Across the country, roughly two dozen "tiger farms" bred animals in what appeared to be purely capitalistic ventures, and experts worried that the black-market trade could rapidly push wild tigers over the final edge. Traffic estimated that the fifty-five pounds of bones in a single adult tiger might sell for $160,000 while other experts put the value of a single pelt at up to $20,000.[11] Other parts—from penises, thought by some to boost virility, to eyeballs, traditionally thought to have medicinal benefits—might sell for a few hundred dollars each. Altogether, a single tiger could be worth hundreds of thousands of dollars and, because the illegal but overlooked sales meant that poachers might be able to pass wild animals off as farmed, experts worried that the trade could lead to increased poaching.[12]

———

As I learned more, I also began to see the plight of tigers as indicative of pressures on hundreds and perhaps thousands of species as China's economy grows. A report by the UN Office on Drugs and Crime would soon list China as the world's top consumer of smuggled wildlife products from Africa and Southeast Asia.[13] Investigations by other organizations found China to be a chief driver—sometimes *the* chief driver—of wildlife poaching and unsustainable harvesting.

With specific, high-profile species, the evidence was often overwhelming. Just as scientists worried that many of the world's wild elephants could be killed off within decades, the secretariat of CITES declared China "the most important country globally as a destination for illicit ivory."[14] The world population of wild elephants had fallen from 1.3 million in 1980 to fewer than 500,000 in 2010, and Samuel K. Wasser, a University of Washington biologist, estimated that between 8 and 10 percent of the world's elephant population were being poached annually.[15] An article in *Science* signed by twenty-seven experts stated that the "scale of illegal ivory trade demonstrates that most of Africa lacks adequate controls for protection of elephants."[16]

Rhinoceros were also increasingly threatened. Targeted for their horns, which have been used for millennia by practitioners of traditional Chinese medicine, it seemed likely that hundreds of animals were killed each year. Shaved or powdered, the horns could sell for up to $45,000 a pound—at times making them more valuable than gold, cocaine, or heroin. By conservative estimates, more than seventeen hundred pounds of the horns were sold in Asia each year.[17] Given that a rhinoceros horn weighs between eight and eleven pounds, the trade required at least 160 animals, almost 1 percent of the world's remaining wild rhinos.[18]

Sharks provided another high-profile example. Researchers estimate that 73 million sharks are killed each year for the lucrative trade in their fins, which are used to make soups served at top-end Chinese restaurants, weddings, and other special events.[19] According to the 2009 IUCN Red List, at least 17 percent of the world's 1,045 shark and ray species are threatened with extinction. WildAid and Oceana, two advocacy groups, reported that the demand for shark fins tripled between 1987 and 2004 and continues to grow: "A relatively obscure custom of the wealthy from southern China— using the needles of shark fin in soup as an ingredient to add texture, but not flavor—has burgeoned to the point where shark fin soup has become an almost ubiquitous dish at weddings, banquets and business dinners throughout the Chinese world," the groups stated in a report. "What was once eaten on a special occasion by the privileged few is now regularly eaten by hundreds of millions of people."[20]

Rising demand had also been partly responsible for attracting organized crime into the world's last great wildlife sanctuaries. Where poachers once wore flip-flops and used homemade snares, many were now armed with high-tech equipment. "We are now faced with criminal gangs deploying GPS devices, night vision equipment and foot soldiers to track rhinos for days," Cathy Dean, the director of Save the Rhino International, told a *Telegraph* journalist. "Highly trained operatives, possibly ex-soldiers, are then being flown into parks by helicopter, and armed with specialized veterinary drugs and darting guns, chainsaws, and automatic weapons."[21]

Lower-profile species face potentially graver risks, given that few organizations raise alarms about their slipping numbers. John MacKinnon, the former head of the European Union–China Biodiversity Program, has estimated that fifteen hundred varieties of flora and fauna are close to being wiped out in the wild due to demand for traditional medicine.[22] The non-profit group Traffic states that demand for Chinese traditional cures is growing at an annual rate of 10 percent and that between 15 and 20 percent of medicinal plants and animals are now endangered.[23] Jane Goodall, the primatologist and wilderness advocate, has written that the annual international trade in wildlife has grown to as much as 30,000 primates, 5 million birds, 10 million reptile skins, and more than 500 million tropical fish. A growing portion of that wildlife ends up in China, which some conservationists have likened to a giant vacuum cleaner of the natural world.[24]

———

The scale of China's impact, however, was driven home to me by Wang Song, a zoologist who pushed China's leaders to join the CITES treaty in 1981 and—over the next two decades—served as one of the country's chief negotiators to its secretariat. Now seventy-eight years old, Wang had watched the wilderness cleared across most of his country.

When we met at a coffeehouse in eastern Beijing, he did not mince words. "Overuse is the biggest problem," he said as we sipped Americanos looking out over a small man-made lake. "We use too much of everything: timber, water, animals, everything. The government needs to admit that a lot of our development has come at the expense of the environment."

Wang was particularly concerned that many Chinese show little concern for the well-being of wildlife and, despite lobbying by experts, that the government had yet to pass laws protecting animals against cruel treatment. In addition to China's tiger farms, businessmen had set up operations to breed and sell dozens of other species. Some farms raised bears to milk their bile, a traditional Chinese medicine that workers extract by punching holes in the sides of the animals' stomachs and then inserting painful catheters. Others raised a wide variety of unusual species with commercial value, among them scorpions, crocodiles, heron, musk deer, salamanders, and a range of turtles and snakes.[25] Some farms have claimed to be raising the animals for eventual release to the wild, but—like China's tiger parks—seem more interested in selling their parts, a fact revealed by their location: half are within easy driving distance of Guangdong and Guangxi, southern China's largest markets for traditional medicine and exotic food.[26]

"As a CITES negotiator I've been to thirty or forty countries over the years," Wang said. "I've met people all over the world. And I often tell them that I've never found a nation with a more selfish attitude toward wildlife than we Chinese have. This is not an exaggeration. If we're going to save any wildlife, we have to be honest about it. Traditional Chinese medicine and our traditional idea that we should eat everything are the problem. If we can't change our mentality, all of our wildlife and all of the wildlife in neighboring countries will be gone."

———

The more I learned, the more it became clear that on top of everything else threatening wildlife—climate change, habitat loss, invasive species, hunting, pollution, the list goes on—China's rise might mark the end for countless species, and I decided to travel to India to learn how Chinese demand has imperiled arguably the world's highest-profile creature: if we cannot save tigers, it seemed unlikely that less publicized species would fare any better.

But I was also motivated by a more primal urge: I wanted to see a wild tiger. Partly, I explained my desire in professional terms. Like other top predators, tigers are considered keystone species—species that reside at the summit of an ecosystem and, by regulating herbivore populations, are vital to its health. Starting in the 1960s, scientists had shown that removing predators from an environment often leads to collapse: pull starfish from a tide pool with a healthy collection of barnacles, snails, mussels, and limpets, for example, and the mussels crowd out everything else; remove wolves from American forests and deer begin to kill off favored plant species; eliminate sea otters from kelp beds and sea urchins take over, eventually destroying a once vibrant community of fish, seals, and seabirds.[27] To understand *why* wild tigers matter, I wanted to see *how* they protect healthy forests.

Mostly, however, I wanted to see a tiger for purely selfish reasons. For as long as I can remember, I'd been fascinated by the beasts. Growing up in Massachusetts and Kentucky, I sought out stories about tigers. One of my earliest memories was reading a book about an Indian boy forced to surrender his clothing to tigers and how he tricks them into chasing each other around a tree until they are somehow transformed into butter. When my parents took me to zoos, I always sought out the tigers, and I later found Rudyard Kipling's *The Jungle Book*, where I was enthralled by Shere Khan, the sinister tiger. For me, the quest was largely personal.[28]

On the morning after I arrived in New Delhi, I plunged into its chaos, flagging down a *tuk-tuk*, one of India's three-wheeled motorcycle taxis, and crossing myself as the driver swerved into a river of traffic: regal Ambassador cars built in the 1950s and held together with tape and wire; lines of trucks painted with bright rainbows, images of cows, and the large English words HORN PLEASE; all the cars, motorcycles, and tractors of the modern age. Within the stream of vehicles, scores of beggars eked out crude livings by tapping their bowls against car windows.

I had arranged my trip through Tykee Malhotra, a friend of a friend who had founded a nonprofit organization—named Sanskara—to better protect pockets of India's remaining wilderness. When I called from Beijing, she told me that she'd started the organization after learning that a close colleague was contemplating suicide. "Something just snapped," she told me. "I sat down on the floor and meditated and I reached a different consciousness. I realized life can have more meaning and everything can be more positive."

Tykee also struck me as a good guide because her story provided a baseline of the changes that have remade India's natural world over recent decades. She grew up in the 1960s and 1970s in the forested Himalayan foothills of Assam and Darjeeling, where her father managed a British company's tea plantation. Her family's house was surrounded by wildlife. Her sister's first word was *haathi*, Hindi for elephant, "because every evening there would be elephants around the house and she was told to be quiet so we could listen to them," Tykee explained. "We weren't afraid, but we had to be aware that they were there. That's what our whole life was like over there." Family pets included a slow loris—a small, docile primate with saucer-like eyes—a pangolin, and a gibbon that learned to fetch her father's slippers. After a poacher killed a tiger, they cared for its orphaned cubs for two magical weeks.

In the late 1970s, Tykee's father retired from the plantation and her parents set up a small tourist camp on the eastern edge of Corbett National Park, a sanctuary in northern India that rivals Africa for its wildlife. A set of animal trails ran just behind the resort, and into the late 1980s, they could hear tigers and elephants almost every night from their cabins.

———

Tykee had asked me to meet her at a restaurant abutting Lodi Gardens, a much-loved park built around the crumbling tombs of fifteenth-century shahs and sultans, and I arrived early to wander through its sprawling grounds admiring monkeys and trying to identify hundreds of colorful birds. The proliferation of life at the center of New Delhi, the capital of what will soon be the world's most populous nation (India's population is expected to overtake China's sometime around 2025), provided a sharp reminder of the importance of philosophy to the preservation of wildlife. Unlike in China, where wildlife is rare even in remote areas, Indians have maintained an easy relationship with animals for millennia, a fact that explains their proliferation today. Besides being home to half of the world's remaining tigers, India provides refuge to a majority of Asia's elephants (*Elephas maximus indicus*) and protects the only lions outside of Africa—four hundred Asiatic lions (*Panthera leo persica*), a distant relative of African lions that once ranged across Central Asia and into Greece and Italy.[29] More than 1,250 species of birds—more than twice the number commonly found in the United States—live within its borders.

Many of those species spend part of their time around people, and the willingness of Indians to coexist with animals provides a stark contrast to China, where, with few exceptions, there is almost no support for the idea that animals should have their own right to existence. Largely, India has maintained that natural estate because the protection of life is a key concept within Buddhism, the religion that originated in India and was important across the subcontinent from the third century BC until about 1000 AD, and Hinduism, the religion of eight of every ten Indians today.[30]

When I sat down with Tykee an hour later, she explained that the ideal of coexistence is deeply embedded in the Indian religions and that many animals are considered holy. The Hindu god Durga, for example, is sometimes depicted riding on a tiger, which some Indians believe can create rain and end drought. Ganesh, the Hindu god of wisdom and one of India's most popular deities, has the head of an elephant. Gray langur are considered incarnations of Hanuman, a deity who served as a disciple to Lord Sri Rama. "Traditionally Indians revered our animals," Tykee said as we picked at bowls of Tunisian stew. "For many Hindus, killing animals is actually forbidden."

But India's massive population, widespread poverty, and growing desire to modernize have begun to shift the balance away from such traditional concepts, and Tykee explained how the country's natural estate is under increasing pressure. With 17 percent of the world's people living on just over 2 percent of its land, habitat is rapidly disappearing.[31] With growing global demand for wild animals and natural resources, particularly from China, poachers have become increasingly sophisticated and pressure is rising to open protected lands. Many Indian agencies tasked with managing wildlife and wilderness have proven inept and corrupt.

The difficulties faced by India's ecology were a reminder of the complications of protecting wildlife. As captured by Edward O. Wilson's HIPPO acronym—habitat destruction, invasive species, pollution, population growth, and overharvesting—all species face a range of pressures, and as India's population continues to grow and its people are exposed to foreign philosophies, that millennia-long cohabitation between communities and wildlife is likely to degrade. Already, poor farmers and herders are pushing into protected habitat, cutting it into increasingly small pockets where animals are segmented into genetic pools that may prove too small to sustain coming generations. Conflict between farmers and animals is increasingly common, and with the problems, some Indians have begun to think of animals less as be-nevolent spirits than as obstacles to a richer life.

For tigers, however, overharvesting has proven the greatest threat. And—as with most of the world's commodities—the harvest of India's great beasts is driven largely by its northern neighbor.

A day before I headed north in search of tigers, I fought my way back through New Delhi's traffic to talk with Belinda Wright, the founder and director of the Wildlife Protection Society of India. Wright had become famous for her powerful advocacy for the protection of wilderness, earning her both committed friends and ardent enemies. She had blasted the govern-ment, calling conservation plans mindless and officials negligent, and her work had angered enough poachers and criminal gangs that she had been forced to protect her home with a tall steel fence and security guards.

I expected to meet a woman who was something of a tiger herself—powerful and regal but remote and aloof—but when Wright reached the hotel where we talked, I found a woman who reminded me more of a friendly house cat. Her golden brown hair was cut into a bob and her intense blue eyes looked playful and happy. When she talked, which she did almost without pause for two hours, she pumped her hands so rapidly through the humid air that she seemed to be conducting an orchestra.

When it came to tigers, she was blunt. As she saw it, India's *Panthera ti-gris* faced three threats: poaching, habitat loss, and rising conflicts with local communities. Of the three, only poaching could lead to their extinction within her lifetime, and she worried that such a tragic end was increasingly likely.

She was particularly concerned about the speed at which poaching had spread across India. Before 1993, when Delhi police caught a woman carry-ing the bones of what had probably been twelve tigers, few Indians had con-sidered the possibility that systematic poaching might be a threat.

"Everyone was just sort of shocked," Wright said as we sipped strong ma-sala tea. "We thought that there wasn't any serious poaching because there wasn't demand for tiger parts in India. People thought there was no way China can be having such an impact on our wildlife because traditionally China and India have been adversaries. But what they'd forgotten is that India and China have traded salts and spices and other things for thousands of years on the old Silk Road. The poachers were using the same routes and couriers to go into new products, and one of those products happened to be wildlife."

The increasing participation of criminal gangs had also modernized the industry. Even a decade ago, Indian poachers had hunted primarily with homemade snares and wooden spears. Now they were using high-tech weapons. "I'm just shocked by how efficient the poachers are, how knowledgeable they are, and that there is nothing in place by the government that can truly address this huge threat," Wright said. "It's terrifying what they know and how determined they are. For the most part these poachers are illiterate. They look impoverished. They dress in rags. They beg when they're traveling and things like that. But most of them have hefty bank balances and insurance policies and all sorts of things. That's how they operate. They're very, very smart."

The other problems—habitat loss and rising conflict with farmers—may prove more difficult to combat in the longer term, but because they do not directly target tigers, conservationists and officials have time to create wildlife sanctuaries and move problem animals. In contrast, "poaching is the one thing that can just wipe out an entire population over a very short period of time," Wright said. "It's just voom, and suddenly they're gone."

———

And, of course, the poachers are set in motion by consumers. When I asked Wright how China fit into the picture, she threw up her arms and, for the first time, looked unhappy. "If the demand from China for tiger bones doesn't stop, I have no idea how we're going to save the last wild tigers," she told me.

Together with a handful of other environmental groups, the Wildlife Protection Society of India had done more than any government agency to understand the dynamics of the trade, and they had found that almost every tiger poached in India was sent north. "In the 1980s, the tiger-bone trade hit India big time, but that was really just the beginning," Wright said. The next stage came in the 1990s as China poured money into its far western regions to develop infrastructure and industry and tamp down political unrest. As Tibetans became wealthier, they began to buy skins.

The Tibet connection often surprises Westerners, who tend to think of Tibetans as protective of the natural world because of their Buddhist beliefs. But historically Tibetans have both protected and appropriated the natural world. Many Tibetans refuse to kill animals but willingly wear skins and eat meat. Tibetan nomads, who have no history of using banks, buy expensive, easily transportable items as a way to store wealth. Even today, many Tibetan women wear large amounts of expensive jewelry, often gold necklaces and earrings fitted with valuable stones. For men, tiger skins had become similar symbols of power and stores of value.[32]

"The skin trade in Tibet was created just as Tibetans began to make more money and could afford them," Wright said. "It just became a fashion. It could have been Rolex watches but instead it was skins." By the time she traveled through Tibet in 2005, the trade had become widespread. Over six weeks she saw eighty-three fresh tiger skins, the remains of more tigers than she will ever see alive.

The trade shifted again after the Dalai Lama, a godlike figure to most Tibetans, called on his followers to discard robes decorated with the pelts of wild animals. Countless Tibetans burned such clothing. But the underground trade had been established and instead of shutting down, the criminal gangs began marketing in the much larger and richer communities in eastern China.

"The traders were very upset that skins had stopped selling in Tibet, so they went out and found Han who wanted skins for decorations and for expensive gifts to give their bosses and so on," Wright said.

India's creaking bureaucracy was the problem's third leg. As Wright and a dozen other conservationists I talked with saw things, the Indian government had proven incapable of effectively protecting its wilderness areas. Many pointed to an incident a few years earlier in Rajasthan, a state west of New Delhi. In late 2004, news broke that twenty-six tigers living in the Sariska Tiger Reserve, a sanctuary twice as large as California's Redwood National Park, had disappeared. A government official had reported a steep decline in a reserve census and called for stepped-up government protection, but the entreaty had been lost amid the endless paperwork of the Indian state. In the middle of the year, a local man gave authorities details about a gang of poachers operating in the park, but the information sat in the system for seven months. Only after scientists reported the absence of tiger signs— scat, claw markings, and pugmarks, the technical term for tiger tracks—and the press picked up on the story did the government act. But by the time the poachers were caught, they had killed all of the reserve's tigers.

"I just don't think India can protect its tigers," Wright said as she leaned across a tiny glass table. "The demand is too big. The price is too high. The tiger is too valuable dead. It has very little value alive.

"In India we have this philosophy that whatever's there will always be there. No one can actually come to terms with the fact that something might actually disappear. That's why Sariska was such a huge shock. It showed that, in the end, India is like a supermarket for the illegal wildlife trade."

5

THE SIXTH GREAT EXTINCTION

Future generations would be truly saddened that this century had so little foresight, so little compassion, such lack of generosity of spirit for the future that it would eliminate one of the most dramatic and beautiful animals this world has ever seen.

—GEORGE SCHALLER, QUOTED IN *TIGERS IN THE SNOW*
BY PETER MATTHIESSEN

In the center of Paris, a few blocks from Notre Dame and the Louvre, is a cathedral-like space that eulogizes the ultimate end of life. Outside its doors, the best-loved animals of today's world parade: stuffed tigers, lions, and elephants, zebras, chimpanzees, and orangutans. Whales, dolphins, and giant squids hang strangely in midair, gathering dust like discarded furniture. Scores of smaller creatures rappel from walls and railings: monkeys frozen mid-swing, birds caught forever in moments of liftoff.

Nearer to the doors is a cross section of a tree cut in 1999 from a forest in Fontainebleau, a favorite weekend getaway for Parisians. A small sign explains that during the tree's nearly four-century-long life, humans pushed more than one thousand species from Earth. A time line shows the rough dates of their extinctions.

First, in 1650, when the tree was just a sapling, went *Aepyornis maximus*, the elephant bird, a giant ratite native to Madagascar that had been the world's largest feathered vertebrate. It stood more than ten feet tall and weighed nearly a ton but—by common scientific consensus—was a chicken at heart since it never fought back against hungry islanders who hunted it out of existence.

In 1710, when the tree was sixty, came the icon of extinction, *Raphus cucullatus*, the dodo bird. A flightless creature endemic to the Indian Ocean island of Mauritius, it looked something like a gigantic pigeon perched on long, gangly legs. Full-size, it weighed thirty pounds and ate a diet of seeds, bulbs, and fallen fruit, much of which it swallowed whole. As David Quammen notes in *The Song of the Dodo*, his work about evolution and extinction, we know very little more about the bird, other than that it "thrived for a long time and then met disaster . . . caused, directly or indirectly, by *Homo sapiens*."[1]

In the 1840s, the last *Alca impennis*, the great auk, a flightless bird that once lived in huge colonies along the coasts of Europe and New England, was killed by a collector. The bird's rapid disappearance created enough concern that a handful of scientists had worked to protect its final nesting grounds, but demand for pillows made with its down proved too great, and in 1844 a fisherman sent to an island off the coast of Iceland smashed the last known egg under his boot.[2]

In the 1920s came the end of *Macropus greyi*, the toolache wallaby, an elegant and swift species of Australian kangaroo that was hunted to death by feral foxes introduced by British émigrés and by the émigrés themselves, who liked the wallabies' fine gray fur and, because they were fast, enjoyed chasing them.

In the 1960s there were nearly two dozen confirmed extinctions. Among them was the Caribbean monk seal (*Monachus tropicalis*), the last large mammal declared extinct prior to the Yangtze River dolphin.[3] In the 1980s we lost *Moho braccatus* and *Podilymbus gigas*, the Kauaʻi ʻōʻō and Atitlán grebe. The ʻōʻō, a black and yellow honeyeater with a long, curved bill and a song that sounded like a slide whistle, fell victim to invasive species introduced to Hawaii by immigrants and travelers: rats, pigs, and mosquitoes (which carried various avian diseases). The grebe, a dark brown water bird with a black head flecked with white streaks, was pushed out of Guatemalan lakes by bass introduced for fishing. The bass ate crabs and smaller fish the grebes relied on. Sometimes they ate young grebes.

When visitors move beyond the tree, they pass through the thick wooden doors into a dimly lit room with a sweeping ceiling and carefully crafted iron balconies. The air is cool, as in a stone church, and the space is silent. As their eyes adjust, they begin to make out the shapes of animals, each held in its own glass case and illuminated by a single light. Nearest to the doors is *Hippotragus leucophaeus*, the blue antelope. A simple sign reads: "Extinct. Victim of the colonization of Africa."

Behind the blue antelope is a small black and yellow honeyeater from Hawaii, a cousin to the Kaua'i 'ō'ō, that was declared extinct in the late nineteenth century, and down the row of glass cases, dozens of other species— most gone, some highly endangered—stare back with gray, olive, and black eyes. There is a south China tiger (*Panthera tigris amoyensis*), which is probably extinct in the wild, and an endangered North Island brown kiwi (*Apteryx mantelli*), a bird found only in tiny pockets of New Zealand. A thylacine (*Thylacinus cynocephalus)*, the world's largest marsupial carnivore until it was killed off in the 1930s, seems ready to bolt from its glass tomb. A Domed Rodrigues giant tortoise (*Cylindraspis peltastes*), a species that evolved and died out on one small island in the Indian Ocean, looks pensive behind its glass wall. Beyond them is the skeleton of a Steller's sea cow (*Hydrodamalis gigas*), an animal that was exterminated by hunters seeking food and skins, and the stuffed body of an *Equus quagga quagga*, a species with the head of a zebra and the body of a horse that roamed South Africa in herds numbering in the tens of thousands until it was hunted out of existence in the 1800s.

—————

The cathedral—an inner sanctum of the Grande Galerie de l'Evolution at Paris's Musée d'Histoire Naturelle—is perhaps the world's most poignant memorial to the destruction humans have wrought on the natural world. But to understand how humanity has rearranged the world's biodiversity, we have to return to the ecologist Daniel Pauly's concept of shifting baselines. In other words, to understand how humans have changed the natural balance, we have to compare how species have fared over recent decades with how they fared before humans began to dominate the planet.

To do that, scientists have used the fossil record to determine when thousands of species evolved and disappeared. The ballpark answer seems to be that, excepting massive natural disruptions to Earth's climate (through collisions with asteroids, enormous volcanic eruptions, and shifts in the planet's orbit, none of which have happened since *Homo sapiens* evolved), one out of every one thousand species died out every one thousand to ten thousand years. Put another way, the Earth's natural extinction rate over millions of years gave each species an average estimated lifespan of between 500,000 and 5 million years.[4]

Humans, of course, have shifted that balance. According to the Millennium Ecosystem Assessment, the UN-led study of the global environment, the rate of "known extinctions" over the twentieth century was between fifty and five hundred times higher than that natural baseline.[5] But even that estimate is likely conservative since it is impossible to prove that a species no longer exists and scientists tend to be conservative when making final pronouncements. The International Union for the Conservation of Nature, for example, lists the Yangtze River dolphin as "critically endangered" even though none have been seen for over a decade. Hundreds of species fit into the category of being neither here nor gone, but if we assume that they are extinct, or soon will be, the rate of extinction since 1900 jumps to one thousand times above the baseline rate, meaning that if a species were to emerge today, it could expect a lifespan of five hundred to one thousand years, if the present rates of extinction don't climb further, as they almost certainly will.[6]

The result has been a loss of biological diversity on a scale not seen since some 65 million years ago, when many scientists believe a six-mile-wide asteroid smashed into the planet and created a cloud of ash that blocked photosynthesis, killing much of the world's plant life and all of its dinosaurs. According to the IUCN's 2009 Red List, nearly one-third of the world's amphibians, more than one in eight species of birds, and nearly one-quarter of mammals are now at risk of imminent extinction.[7] For some plant groups, the situation is more serious. Among seed-bearing evergreens, 28 percent of conifers and 52 percent of cycads face a "high risk of extinction in the wild."[8] According to the group's analysis of almost 45,000 species, 869 are extinct or "extinct in the wild" and 290 others are "possibly extinct."[9]

Even those figures, however, are highly conservative. The IUCN estimates that scientists have only accurately measured 2.7 percent of 1.8 million known species. According to a press release the group issued in 2009, the tally is thus "a gross underestimate, but it does provide a useful snapshot of what is happening to all forms of life on Earth."[10]

––––––––

The next step in understanding our biodiversity crisis is gauging responsibility for the rapid increase in losses. The Musée d'Histoire Naturelle does not lay blame, but—reading between the lines—it becomes obvious that the Western world is largely responsible. The impact of today's wealthy states was to some extent a direct result of colonization and resource exploitation—the slaughter of species for profit and sport. But it also grew from a ratcheting up of the planet's economic metabolism: as people in London, Paris, and New York demanded tropical products, for example, land was cleared, roads were built, animals were hunted, and communities were pulled into the modern world, initiating additional sets of cascading change. Writing about the United States, Richard Tucker, a historian at the University of Michigan, argues that demands for imported products have constituted a dimension of American power that while "almost totally ignored . . . has surpassed all others in its grasp of Nature's global resources and thus in its worldwide ecological impacts."[11]

Over time, however, Western nations have become more aware of the environmental costs of our demands, and while Americans and Europeans remain among the world's top per capita consumers of almost everything, we have begun to protect wildlife in our own nations and (increasingly) to buy products made with sustainably harvested resources. Partly this is the result of our evolving laws: we have created penalties for importing protected wildlife and illegally felled timber. But it is also the result of a larger cultural shift: our education systems stress environmental science, making children the drivers of change in families; journalists and nonprofit organizations report regularly on environmental problems, making companies keenly aware that stewardship—or at least the perception of stewardship—is important to the bottom line; environmental organizations have become more successful at promoting everything from a shift to renewable energy to the sustainable global harvest of seafood.

At the same time, however, Western countries have passed the reins of growth to the developing world, and among developing nations, China, by dint of its rapidly growing needs, its ancient beliefs in natural cures, and its nascent environmental awareness, stands above all others in the damage it is causing to biodiversity.

Partly, the damage wrought by China is simply an unintended result of its rising demands. As with Western demand for now-mundane products like bananas, coffee, and tropical timber, growing Chinese desires have pushed resource exploitation into some of Earth's last untouched places. A list of headlines from only one month while I was researching this book— March 2011—helps drive home the scale of its rising impact.

At the beginning of the month, news broke that China would purchase 60 billion cubic meters of natural gas from Turkmenistan, a small Central Asian nation that borders Iran and where China was completing a pipeline that stretched across Uzbekistan and Kazakhstan. On the same day, a group of Chinese companies announced plans to invest $35 billion in African railroads "to transport copper and coal out of Africa and into the power plants of China and India." The investment was part of "Africa's biggest railway boom since the 19th century," *Bloomberg News* reported.

A few days later came news that a consortium of Chinese airlines would buy forty-three Boeing planes, a deal valued at roughly $10 billion, and that China—which was building half of all nuclear reactors under construction globally—would quintuple its nuclear capacity over the next six years.[12] On March 17, Sinopec, China's largest oil producer and refiner, said it would buy a

37 percent stake in a Saudi Arabian refinery, and a company in western China announced an almost $4 billion investment in a Tanzanian power plant.

Later in the month, the *Christian Science Monitor* reported that China had secured "some $65 billion in regional deals" across Latin America over the previous year—a surge in investments the correspondent called "an unprecedented energy grab in the oil- and mineral-rich region." The *Des Moines Register* reported that China was "on the market to buy 200,000 acres of farmland across Russia, Australia, Argentina, and several other countries." Lester Brown, the president of the Earth Policy Institute, a Washington, D.C.–based think tank, argued in an editorial that rising Chinese demands and shrinking farmland—making way for roads, cities, and encroaching deserts—had contributed to rapid global food price inflation: cattle and hog futures had hit all-time highs; corn and soybean futures had both more than doubled in price from five years earlier.

———

Over the long term, those indirect consequences of China's growth—the destruction of habitat to build roads and dams, the introduction of invasive species to newly opened forests, the increase in pollution from new factories, the general rise in our global economic metabolism—may prove most harmful to wildlife. But during the coming decades, the effects of direct Chinese consumption will be more serious, a fact driven home when a small ship stalled off the coast of China's southern Guangdong Province in early 2007. When Chinese coast guard officers boarded the abandoned boat they found hundreds of crates stuffed with endangered species. Included in the cargo were forty-four leatherback turtles, nearly three thousand monitor lizards, over a thousand Brazilian turtles, and thirty-one pangolins. Twenty-one bear claws were wrapped in newspaper.

Trade in each of the species was banned under international laws, but all of the animals and parts could also be found in Chinese restaurants, markets, and medicine shops. An investigation conducted the same year by Traffic and the China Wildlife Conservation Association found that half of markets and nearly half of luxury restaurants surveyed in southern Chinese cities sold wildlife.[13] Another survey found that 44 percent of respondents in six Chinese cities had consumed wildlife in the previous year and that most believed that eating wild snakes, sharks, birds, turtles, sea cucumbers, and abalone should be a personal choice. One in five believed that wild pangolin was fair game. A "small minority, ranging from about 2 percent to 9 percent, was receptive to eating" leopard, tiger, bear, monitor lizard, antelope, and Chinese sturgeon, and nearly half of respondents believed that wild meat was more nutritious than farm-raised animals.[14]

Multiplied by 1.3 billion people even a tiny minority can have a massive impact, and the report stated that "despite efforts undertaken by the government, the media, and nongovernment organizations, among other parties, to combat unsustainable wildlife consumption, China's consumption of high value wildlife products, including threatened species, has risen rapidly as its economy has grown. This consumer demand is increasingly placing wild animals and plants, and their ecosystems—both in China and abroad—at risk through unsustainable and often illegal wildlife trade."[15]

At first glance, the Hehuachi traditional medicine warehouse in Chengdu, the capital of Sichuan Province, looked like a bustling American farmer's market: crowds of shoppers jostled between hundreds of stalls selling piles of dried fruits, plants, and spices. On closer inspection, however, its offerings proved more exotic. I had arrived at the market on a cold winter afternoon in 2004 and slowly picked my way through the football field–sized space. Near where a taxi dropped me off, a woman sold bags of dried scorpions that she said could be eaten to relieve arthritis. The next stall offered dog kidneys the size of silver dollars and long, baton-like canine penises guaranteed, its owner promised, to cure impotence.

As I made my way along the aisle, I found hedgehog skins for rheumatism, starfish for diarrhea, seahorses for improved circulation, and deer hooves to relieve joint pain. Plastic tubs lined up on a countertop held thousands of desiccated snakes, each wound into a tight disk, that a saleswoman said would treat numbness, itchiness, and muscular convulsions. She pointed to a pile of shells stripped from turtles caught in the forests of western Sichuan—one of the few parts of China that preserves a vestige of its original wildlife—and said that, ground up and eaten, they would strengthen my kidneys. A few nearby stalls sold what looked like large dried prunes but were in fact human placentas, an ingredient traditional medicine doctors believe improves both lung function and virility.

I'd visited the market to research the impact of traditional Chinese medicine on endangered species, and I made my way to a stand covered by pale, almost translucent horns that I recognized as once belonging to saiga antelope, a species recently decimated by an upswing in Chinese demand. As rhinoceros became endangered in the 1980s, conservationists suggested the horns as a possible substitute, and between 1993 and 2003, poaching had cut their wild population from over a million to fewer than thirty thousand.[16] Abigail Entwistle, a zoologist from Fauna & Flora International, a British nonprofit, had called the extermination "the most sudden change in fortune for a large mammal species recorded in recent times." At the Hehuachi market, a kilogram of their horns sold for the equivalent of $200.

The saiga story was powerful, but the sale remained legal, and I was looking for tiger bone and rhino horn, both of which were banned under China's 1998 Wildlife Protection Law. I approached a stall where a man in a cheap-looking gray suit stood behind an array of animal parts. When he looked up, I told him that I was visiting China and that my elderly Chinese teacher had asked me to buy him small amounts of both.

The seller, whom I will call Li Xiao, was middle-aged and had a squat, compact face, like everything had been squeezed together in a vice. He looked me over and seemed to size up my story. And then, rolling the dice, he nodded: yes, he said, he could get either. He leaned closer and explained that a kilogram of tiger bone would take a day and cost 30,000 yuan—then $3,600. Rhino horn was more expensive at 60,000 yuan per kilogram. I mentioned that my teacher had asked me to ensure that whatever I bought came from wild animals, and Li nodded: the tiger bones had come from

India; the rhino horn was from Africa; both had been bought in the 1970s, when the trade was legal.

I replied that I would have to ask my teacher about the prices but wanted to see the rhino horn first, to make sure it looked real. Li told me to wait. He asked a neighbor to watch his stall and then biked away down a busy street. Ten minutes later he returned, pulled me to a quiet corner, and dropped a plastic bag in my hand. Inside was a dark gray cube with sides measuring roughly one inch: black rhino horn.

In 2004, foreigners were still rare in Chengdu and Li clearly believed my story. With the number of journalists and conservationists who have since visited China's biggest traditional medicine markets, I would now be unlikely to convince anyone to show me contraband products, even if I fed them a believable story. Li, in particular, is unlikely to trust another foreigner. After he put the bag back in his jacket pocket, I told him that I had misrepresented myself: I wouldn't report his name, but I hoped he would answer a few questions.

For a long moment Li looked stunned and ready to bolt, but then, perhaps realizing that I had written down his name and phone number, he agreed. He leaned closer and explained that he was forty-three and had worked as a traditional medicine wholesaler for over twenty years. The year before he had earned 45,000 yuan—$5,500—and estimated that one-fifth had come from the sale of illegal products, a percentage he considered common at the market. There was still demand for contraband parts but, at least for him, it had grown smaller.

"Hospitals and doctors don't buy the illegal products much anymore," he said. Most of the sales were to individuals who hoped to cure terminal conditions. Often they had tried remedies that hadn't worked.

"People want to live," Li said. "If these things didn't work, the price wouldn't be so high." Eventually I ran out of questions and Li biked away through the rows of stalls selling a dried wilderness.

*   *   *

To understand Chinese demand for wildlife, one needs to look back at the country's perplexing history of traditional cures. Under the larger Confucian rubric that called for taming and using the natural world, early Chinese thinkers developed a medical system that relied on natural products. Partly, the system—now known as traditional Chinese medicine—shares the Western medical belief in testing and improvement: for at least four millennia, generations of doctors prescribed cures and discarded ones that didn't work.

But the system is also rooted in a more mystical concept of yin and yang, opposing forces considered essential to Chinese cosmology that doctors believed could be balanced by consuming a bewildering assortment of minced, ground, boiled, or cooked minerals, plants, and animals. The earliest book about the field was composed somewhere between 2600 and 1000 BC and stuck to then-common foods.[17] By 1597, when a scholar named Li Shizhen published one of the most extensive catalogs ever made of traditional cures, however, China's pharmacopeia had grown to incorporate thousands of rarer species.

Called *The Compendium of Materia Medica* (*Bencao Gangmu*), the book listed more than eighteen hundred possible ingredients, four hundred of them animal parts, or, occasionally, entire animals. Included among the natural treatments were pig epiglottises (flaps of elastic cartilage attached to the larynx), nose flesh from buffaloes, porcupine urine, and the meat of any animal killed by lightning.[18]

Rhino horn and tiger bone were considered particularly useful. The book prescribed rhino horn as an antidote to poison, demon possession, feverish colds, carbuncles, fear, anxiety, melancholy, and, in what seems like obvious overkill, bloody noses and the overproduction of phlegm. It prescribed almost every part of the tiger: tiger blood could be used to strengthen willpower; tiger eyeballs—after being soaked overnight in sheep's blood and then dismembered, dried, and powdered—were said to treat malaria, fevers, and crying; flesh from a tiger's nose could help cure epilepsy and convulsions; whiskers could be used to ease toothaches.

The entry on tiger bones was particularly long. After being "broken open and the marrow removed," dabbed with butter, vinegar, or urine, and then "browned over a charcoal fire," they were said to cure ulcers, sores from rat bites, rheumatic pain, typhoid fever, malaria, nightmares, swollen feet, "devil possession," dysentery, hemorrhoids, and "bones which have become stuck in the gullet."[19]

More recent handbooks have listed both rhino horn and tiger parts. A 1993 text listed pulverized tiger bone as helpful for "stiffness and migratory pain in the joints" and capable of strengthening sinews and bones.[20] The book I found in a Beijing bookstore in 2005 stated that tiger bone was capable of eliminating "dampness from the muscles, . . . tendons, and bones."

———

Despite such cookbooks of the natural world, it is sometimes hard to believe that Chinese—and other Asians influenced by centuries of traditional Chinese medicine—still use such medieval potions. Rhino horn is composed of keratin fibers, the same protein found in hair and fingernails. Consuming it is "just as efficacious" as drinking "a potion made of powdered fingernails," Richard Ellis wrote in *Tiger Bone & Rhino Horn*, a book about Chinese demand for traditional cures. The Swiss pharmaceutical firm Hoffmann–La Roche conducted a series of tests on rhino horns in 1983 and declared that they have no effect on the human body.[21]

Tiger parts have likewise been shown to have little or no medicinal value excepting the psychological placebo effect for people who already believe they will help. While scientists have found that pulverized tiger bone can produce an anti-inflammatory effect in animals with arthritis and an analgesic effect in rats, a number of studies have shown that bones of more common species—including pigs, dogs, cows, and mole rats—have the same impacts.[22] Modern Western medicines available over the counter are more effective.

Yet Chinese demand for animal parts seems to be growing. Partly this is simply a reflection of China's growing wealth: older Chinese—who grew up with traditional medicines—now have more money to spend on expensive treatments. As they face death, some are willing to spend thousands or tens of thousands of dollars on anything they think might save them. Within a generation—as science further debunks ineffective cures and Chinese accept Western medicine—that demand is likely to fade. But, until then, it will probably increase.

Wang Song, China's early CITES negotiator, was particularly scathing of the use of animal parts. "There is no scientific basis to most traditional Chinese medicine," he said when we met at a Beijing coffeehouse. "It's just unscientific traditional ideas about wildlife. We need to educate people. We need to break this concept."

That process, he said, could take decades: "We have to start with young children and with teaching our officials so they understand the need to protect the wilderness, why wilderness and wildlife matters," he said. "I guess this will take a generation or two, but if we don't do it, if too many people believe in traditional Chinese medicine and they have money, what wildlife will survive?"

———

As I was finishing my interview with Wang, he introduced another major driver of biodiversity loss with an often repeated Chinese joke. "You know," he said, "in southern China people eat everything on four legs except tables, everything that flies except planes, and everything in water except boats."

I had heard the saying before and already knew that China is arguably the world's most adventurous culinary destination. Over the decade that I had lived in China, I had learned that almost everything that moves is considered edible. I had been served snake soups and tiny pigeons roasted on long skewers. At a banquet in Sichuan Province, the host had placed a heaping mound of fried bees in front of me. I once reluctantly joined two friends for a boiling hot-pot meal that included the genitals of various animals. I had passed countless restaurants displaying a wide array of unusual food: in backwater towns, restaurants commonly displayed the skinned carcasses of cats and dogs, their muzzles frozen in permanent snarls; in wealthier cities, seafood was more common—giant shark fins, sometimes tied in red bows and always bearing outlandish price tags, held prominent space in front windows; everywhere, turtles and fish peered out of dirty glass tanks.

And I had seen more exotic fare. At the edge of a national park in Hunan Province, a restaurant owner had shown me a thick black snake that she called the "three-step": one bite and the victim would take three steps before collapsing. Separated from its fangs and boiled, it cost a few hundred yuan. Outside a nature sanctuary in Sichuan Province, an official happy to be hosting an American guest presented me with a plate of what he said was wild local deer: it had been killed in the park and was healthier than farm-raised animals, he explained. A Chinese friend described being served meat from wild pangolins and monkeys at an expensive restaurant in Guangdong Province. My wife, a food writer, met a self-described Chinese gourmand who boasted of eating bear bile.

Such eccentric fare is rare, but Chinese do eat probably the world's greatest diversity of beasts. For his book about Chinese medicine, Richard Ellis found evidence of Chinese diners consuming a variety of unusual species, among them porcupines, foxes, badgers, boars, squirrels, mongoose, leopard cats, raccoon dogs, rats, civet cats, chipmunks, gerbils, peacocks, cobras, pythons, salamanders, water monitors, and nutria, a large, semi-aquatic rodent indigenous to South America.

Wang believed that China's open-minded culinary attitude was rooted in its beliefs in traditional medicines. "Because we have this idea that every animal part has medicinal benefits, we eat everything," he said. "What's so good about pangolin? Why do people want to eat it? But they do and now there are no pangolins left in China. If only a small portion of us get rich, we can eat out most of the world's wildlife."

The scale of China's—and, in the larger picture, Asia's—demand for wild species was driven home to me by Peter Paul van Dijk, the deputy chair of the IUCN's Tortoise and Freshwater Turtle Specialist Group, the scientists responsible for monitoring the health of the world's terrapins. I had contacted van Dijk after coming across a document titled "Emergency Rulemaking Request to Repeal Arkansas' Turtle Collection Law." Signed by a half dozen environmental groups (including the Audubon Society of Central Arkansas), the report petitioned the Arkansas Game and Fish Commission to restrict the commercial harvest of wild turtles, some species of which the organizations worried faced imminent extinction due—strangely enough—to Chinese diners. "Over the last decade, conservation biologists have cautioned state wildlife agencies that freshwater turtles in North America are being increasingly targeted to supply food markets in Asia, particularly in China, due to depletion of wild populations of Asian turtle species," the petition stated, adding that although U.S. turtle harvest records were poor, the few existing data points were worrying: Arkansas government figures showed, for example, that licensed collectors had removed more than half a million wild turtles from the state between 2004 and 2006; data from the Dallas–Fort Worth, Texas, airport alone showed that "more than 256,638 wild caught adult turtles" were exported to Asia between 2002 and 2005. Overall, the experts estimated, the total trade in U.S. turtles likely added up to "thousands of tons per year."[23] After mystifying trips halfway around the world, most of the animals probably ended up in the stomachs of Chinese diners.

In one sense, the wild turtle trade was just another example of how China's rise was reconfiguring local ecologies globally. But it also struck a personal chord. Growing up in Kentucky, I had frequently found box turtles in various stretches of woods and rural areas. Occasionally, I adopted one as a short-term pet. Unlike with tigers or elephants, the stakes seemed imminently graspable: few people will ever be lucky enough to see a wild tiger, but almost every American can find a turtle.

And, like the reopened coal mine in Trinidad, Colorado, the burgeoning trade surprised me: I had seen turtles for sale at hundreds of Chinese restaurants. But it seemed improbable that decisions by Beijing or Shanghai residents could contribute to the extermination of entire American species. Yet that was at risk of happening.

*   *   *

Van Dijk directed Conservation International's tortoise and freshwater turtle program, and on an unusually muggy August morning, I made my way to the group's headquarters in Arlington, Virginia. Like Washington, D.C., Arlington has the feel of bureaucratic blandness: white bunker-like buildings were ringed by manicured yards and carefully pruned trees. Inside, however, Conservation International celebrated the natural world: dozens of posters showed elephants, birds of paradise, sharks, and other wildlife.

Perhaps because the office conveyed that sense of the natural world, van Dijk struck me as vaguely elfin. He had a tight-cropped reddish-brown beard flecked with white and moved with quick efficiency that hinted at years spent looking for turtles across Southeast Asia. When we met, he handed me a business card emblazoned with a photograph of a monarch butterfly and the sentence, "People need nature to thrive."

As we started talking, his elfin appearance was enhanced by his obvious love of the natural world. A Dutchman by birth, he had been eight when he adopted his first turtles from a couple "looking for a place to get rid of four turtles because they had grown too big and one had bitten the finger off of their daughter, or something like that," he told me. From there, he had enlarged his collection until he had a greenhouse full of the animals and soon enough he graduated to studying them, earning a doctorate by tramping through the forests of western Thailand. (His dissertation was titled "The Natural History of the Elongated Tortoise, *Indotestudo elongata* (Blyth, 1853) (*Reptilia*: *Testudines*) in a Hill Forest Mosaic in Western Thailand, with Notes on Sympatric Turtle Species.")

Roughly halfway through a decade in Thailand, however, van Dijk noticed that he was having a harder time finding wild tortoises and began to hear stories about traders buying large numbers to ship to China. In 1999, he attended a meeting with other Asia-based experts and realized that what he had thought were "individual, localized occurrences" weren't individual or localized at all: "I realized we were seeing the same massive, continent-wide process at different places and different times," van Dijk told me.

While the trade hit Vietnam first, it quickly emptied their forests and then spread to Laos, Burma, and Indonesia. "You just saw a pattern of ex-panding concentric circles over the years. Every couple of years, the trade moved further. And that's when I said, 'Okay, I can spend the rest of my career chronicling the extermination of turtles or I can try to do something about it.' So I decided to do something about it."

————

The first thing van Dijk did was take a job with Traffic studying the impact of the turtle trade on wild populations, a task that turned out to make inter-esting science. Like sturgeons, orangutans, and elephants, turtles take many years to reach sexual maturity—on average, fifteen to twenty years is a good ballpark. They also experience what scientists refer to as "low juvenile sur-vival" and "high adult survivorship": only a few hatchlings survive their first few years, but those that do reach maturity almost always live human-length lives. A common box turtle found in the woods of the United States could easily have lived through World War I.

That combination makes turtles particularly vulnerable to collapse when people start carrying a few away. One recent study found that taking only two female turtles from a population of two hundred can halve the total population in fifty years.[24] "By removing an adult turtle from its environ-ment, you're not just taking one turtle, you're taking thirty years of eggs," van Dijk explained. "When you're harvesting turtles, you're not harvesting sustainably. You can hit bottom before you even realize what's happened."

Before humans, that wasn't a problem since adult turtles are basically indestructible. "The only things that can kill an adult tortoise is a human with a knife or getting caught up in a catastrophic forest fire," van Dijk said. Which is precisely why China had become important.

When I asked van Dijk about the impact of rising Chinese demand for turtle meat, he replied with a short history lesson: "The person who I con-sider the single most influential person on Asian and therefore global wildlife conservation of the last couple decades is Deng Xiaoping," he said. "In 1989, after the Tiananmen Square uprising, the Chinese Politburo decided that they needed to liberate the economy but retain the political structure and that's what they've kept for the last twenty years. The most important thing they did was make the Chinese yuan convertible. So now people could buy things on the open market, and since China had eaten its way and polluted its way through its own biodiversity, they basically started bringing in biodiversity to meet its demands. The market was there and the market was pretty insatiable."

The sudden influx of demand was met by what van Dijk called "vast numbers of people in Southeast Asia who are perfectly willing to spend a day tramping through the forest to come up with a few turtles they can sell for a dollar to a trader who makes a few more dollars selling it to China."

"It's just a vast network of people willing to scour the countryside for biological resources," he said. "It's turtles. It's pangolins. You name it. If it has trade value, it will be found and shipped."

————

As with all species, Chinese consumers do not bear full responsibility for what experts have taken to calling the "Asian turtle crisis," but—as with tigers, rhinoceros, elephants, and dozens of other creatures—they bear much of it. Turtles have existed since the Late Triassic period, roughly 220 million years, outlasting the dinosaurs, but today half of their species are listed as threatened by the IUCN, putting them on par with sturgeons and primates as the world's most at-risk families.[25] Three species—including the Galapagos giant tortoise, which was hunted to near extinction by hungry nineteenth-century whalers, a reminder of the impact of the West's era of rapid development—are listed as "extinct in the wild." Twenty-six more face "an extremely high risk of extinction in the wild in the immediate future," according to the IUCN.

Partly because of its proximity to China, Asian species are particularly at risk: only four Red River giant soft-shell turtles, a terrapin that historically inhabited the Yangtze and Red Rivers of China and Vietnam, are known to survive; the Northern River terrapin, an Asian turtle that changes color during its breeding season, is thought to survive only because a wild-caught male was found—slaughtered—in a Bangladesh market in 2010.[26] A 2011 report by the world's top turtle experts stated that the "regional pattern of high extinction risk for Asian species is primarily because of the long-term unsustainable exploitation of turtles and tortoises for consumption and traditional Chinese medicine, and to a lesser extent for the international pet trade." The report, simply titled "Turtles in Trouble," concluded that without "concerted conservation action, many of the world's turtles and tortoises will become extinct within the next few decades."

———

Van Dijk explained the speed at which Chinese demand has decimated Asia's turtles by how long it takes to find wild turtles in Asia. In the early 1990s, finding two or three turtles a day was unexceptional. Now, "if I go out into a random piece of land and walk around for a week, I'll be lucky to find two," he said.

As wild turtles have become rarer, the trade has been pushed further afield, and while van Dijk didn't expect American species to be wiped out by collectors, he worried that depleted populations could succumb to other problems, most notably pollution, climate change, and habitat fragmentation. "If collection reduces a population by 60 percent, that remaining 40 percent needs optimal conditions if it's going to survive," he said. "If that doesn't happen, they might never recover."

I had been trying to fit Chinese wildlife demand into the context of other threats facing global biodiversity, and after we finished talking about turtles, I asked van Dijk how nonspecialists should think about China's impact more generally. He leaned forward in his chair and rubbed his beard. "China's just doing what the world has done before," he said. "Even the Mayans overexploited nature. The big difference is the speed of the change.

"It took Europe a couple of centuries to destroy its environment. It took the U.S. about a century to get from a frontier mentality to where we are now. China is doing this whole process at breakneck speed. It's doing it in just a few decades. And because of the globalization of trade, they can impact the environment globally. Wherever we look, we see that China is a major driver of wildlife loss.

"We're going to lose species, no doubt about that," he added. "I say to my friends that the next fifty years are going to be very interesting, but they're not necessarily going to be enjoyable."

6

CORBETT NATIONAL PARK

The last word in ignorance is the man who says of an animal or plant: 'What good is it?' . . . If the biota, in the course of aeons, has built something that we like but do not understand, then who but a fool would discard seemingly useless parts? To keep every cog and wheel is the first precaution of intelligent tinkering.

—ALDO LEOPOLD, *ROUND RIVER*

Emotion." That, as Belinda Wright, the director of the Wildlife Protection Society of India, saw it, is the greatest reason the world should invest in saving its last tigers.

At the end of our conversation in New Delhi, before we each ventured back into the sticky afternoon heat to fight through the thickets of diesel-belching trucks, tired-looking cows, and tiny zigzagging *tuk-tuks*, I asked Wright the question that had been gnawing at me for days. Hundreds of species had gone extinct without provoking a serious shift in how societies protect the natural world. I had seen the probable end of the Yangtze River dolphin and, in the wild, of the Chinese sturgeon. The world hadn't blinked.

The tiger was higher profile. Conservation groups and governments had invested hundreds of millions of dollars in its protection, setting aside wilderness sanctuaries, training park rangers to fight poaching, and educating consumers about the importance of avoiding tiger products. In 2008, the World Bank had partnered with forty conservation and scientific organizations with the goal of doubling the world's wild tiger population by 2022.[1] Former Russian president Vladimir Putin, an ardent tigerphile, had organized a campaign that would culminate with a five-day summit during the Chinese Year of the Tiger, the highest-level meeting ever held to protect a single species.

But the effort seemed to be coming too late. During the decade between 1997 and 2007, the range of wild tigers had been cut almost in half.[2] Why would the world behave differently to the risk that tigers might soon be found only in zoos? Given a history of neglect, what would change our response? To this, Wright's answer reminded me of a sentence George Orwell had used— for different effect—in *Animal Farm*: "All animals are equal, but some animals are more equal than others."

"The tiger is the most charismatic mammal on this planet," Wright said, staring at me with her steely blue eyes. "If you look at it historically or culturally or in art, it has been such a dominant force in many countries for centuries. Even in the United States, where no wild tigers ever lived, there isn't a child who doesn't know tigers. It was voted the most popular animal on this planet in a recent survey. Little children eating their cereal in California know what a tiger is. This is not just any old animal. So, if we can't persuade China to take its hands off wild tigers, then I think it's shameful. If we cannot save the tiger, which is such a powerful presence, then what can we save? What hope is there for mankind?"

———

The argument that tigers are a kind of test for humanity—that if we fail to carve out space for them, we will necessarily fail to protect the rest of the world's natural estate; that they are as important as symbols of our intentions as they are for their biological roles—was powerful, and I was thinking about it as I walked into the heart of tiger country a few days later. I had traveled with Tykee Malhotra to Corbett National Park, tracing India's overcrowded roads north from the capital through tiny farm villages and ramshackle towns, across the Ganges River and then into low Himalayan foothills. At Tykee's parents' tourist lodge, she had introduced me to Deep

Contractor, a young Indian biologist she had recently hired to work for her nonprofit. And then Deep had invited me to join her for a walk.

Without thinking much, I agreed, but as we made our way into the forest, I began to have second thoughts. More than 160 tigers lived in Corbett National Park—probably the densest population of wild tigers on the planet—and Deep estimated that 7 or 8 occasionally wandered through the managed plantations surrounding the sanctuary. I had also been reading *Man-Eaters of Kumaon*, a book by Jim Corbett, the British Indian Army officer after whom the park had been named. Told as a culinary chronicle of the Champawat man-eater—a tiger that arrived in the region "as a full-fledged man-eater, from Nepal, from whence she had been driven out by a body of armed Nepalese after she had killed two hundred human beings"—the work fit well into a genre that David Quammen, the nature writer, describes as "predator pornography . . . toothy porn [that] gives a skewed impression of the fraught, ancient relationship between large carnivores and the ubiquitous primate that, in moments of reckless desperation, they sometimes turn upon as prey."[3]

Intellectually, I knew my fears were exaggerated. Even a century ago, when India had many more tigers than it does today, Corbett had noted that most of the animals showed little interest in humans. ("It is only when tigers have been incapacitated through wounds or old age that, in order to live, they are compelled to take a diet of human flesh," he wrote.) But the instincts early humans developed to avoid becoming lunch remain strong, and as I followed Deep into the forest, I felt a powerful surge of adrenaline.

The forests around Corbett National Park are designated as borderland sanctuary, meaning that they can be used selectively with government permission, and the area where we walked had been logged many years earlier. Where native species once lived, loggers had planted sal trees, a species that grows quickly and straight and that works well as railroad ties and telephone poles. Eventually, they would be cut again.

Still, the forest provided a better wildlife show than anything I had seen in North America. Near where we turned off a dirt road, we found four-foot-tall termite mounds that looked like the weathered stones used in Japanese gardens. We broke off small pieces to peer into straw-shaped tubes that descended into a dark insect underworld: somewhere in the blackness, a fat queen engorged herself among her writhing family. We paused to watch a troop of two dozen Hanuman langur—large monkeys with jet black faces ringed with gray fur that puffed into pompadour-like crowns—swing through the canopy. Rounding a hill, we surprised a sambar—a large deer the color of well-steeped Darjeeling tea—that bleated and charged away. As we walked, Deep and a local guide named Nursing, a thin man with soft, friendly features and a quick eye for wildlife, listed a wide variety of animals they had seen in the forest: elephants, pythons, sloth bears, cobras, leopards, and several varieties of deer.

Deep also tried to calm my nerves about meeting a tiger. As a graduate student at the Wildlife Institute of India, the country's top school for conservation biology, she had spent several months setting camera traps in the national park and, on foot, had encountered tigers three times without being mauled. On the first encounter she had needed to replace the batteries in a camera trap forty feet from a resting tigress. "I was really nervous, but she didn't mind me," Deep recalled. A few months later she was counting pugmarks in a riverbed when she startled a tiger. The animal growled and began to approach, but when Deep and a colleague climbed a tree, he stalked off. "I realized that unless you approach a tiger or scare him, he won't attack you," Deep said. "Really they aren't so different from housecats in their behavior."

―――――

The afternoon was dry and the temperature of a New England fall day and after an hour I began to relax. But then Deep bent down and picked up a small, fuzzy white lump. "Tiger scat," she said matter-of-factly. "I guess it's twenty days old." She pointed to head-high scars on a nearby tree where the animal had sharpened its claws on the bark.

As anyone who has ever rounded the bend of a trail to find a bear loping through the forest or, scuba diving, has witnessed a shark slide effortlessly from the dark distance knows, the presence of great animals makes the natural world more poignant, our experiences more meaningful, and I recalled a line from David Quammen's book *Monster of God*: the alpha predators, Quammen wrote, "allow us to recollect our limitations. They keep us company. . . . If we exterminate the last magnificently scary beasts on planet Earth, as we seem bent on doing, then no matter where we go for the rest of our history as a species—for the rest of time—we may never encounter any others."[4]

As I peered into the darkening forest, I felt a surge of euphoria. Suddenly everything seemed more alive.

Unless they've traveled to the great spaces of Africa, India, or Brazil, Westerners have difficulty imagining what healthy wilderness looks like. Largely, that is because the developed world emptied our great spaces of their largest species hundreds of years ago. In Europe—which like much of China has sustained a dense population for centuries—almost all of the lowland forests were cleared for farming more than a millennia ago.

In North America, the change came later and more suddenly as settlers pushed across the continent in the eighteenth and nineteenth centuries and began to slaughter wildlife. First to go were species that, like sturgeon in American waterways, could be harvested easily. An estimated 50 million bison lived on the Great Plains in the 1600s—once traveling in herds so thick that they were described as robes covering the land. But settlers hunted them for their skins and meat, and by 1890 fewer than a thousand survived.[5]

The impact on North America's predators—wolves, mountain lions, and grizzly bears—was as extreme. In the early nineteenth century, a million wolves may have roamed the continent, and when Lewis and Clark journeyed from Missouri to the Pacific Coast between 1804 and 1806, they encountered thirty-seven grizzlies, after polar bears the world's largest terrestrial carnivore.

Over the nineteenth and twentieth centuries, however, hunting, trapping, and a government-led eradication campaign decimated their ranks. By the 1970s, gray wolves occupied less than 4 percent of their former range in the contiguous states. Its southeastern cousin, the red wolf, was extinct in the wild. Today, grizzlies are rarely seen, living only in a few isolated pockets of wilderness.

The result is that North American and European national parks are what one Indian conservationist called "green deserts"—spaces that preserve faint reminders of their former diversity. When I first heard the term, I did not understand, but as I drove with Deep into Corbett National Park the next day, I began to see how wildlife can shape and color a landscape.

We had set out early that morning for Ramnagar, a city just outside the park's southern border where Deep collected permits and we met our driver, a tall, regal-looking Sikh named Honey Prabhujot Singh. From Ramnagar, Singh guided us through the crush of Indian humanity—past overflowing shops, rainbow-painted trucks, alleys full of women squatting beside butane stoves—and half an hour later we arrived at a rickety checkpoint at the edge of the park. Deep showed our papers to a young guard, and after he scrutinized them for several minutes, he swung open a metal gate and we entered an entirely different world.

———

Part of what makes Corbett among the world's best places to see wildlife—a window into a natural realm now mostly gone—is that it was established early. In 1936, the British colonial government declared the park India's first government-funded wildlife sanctuary, and it has remained one of the country's best-managed reserves ever since. Despite scattered poaching—including two tigers killed in and around the park in the years before I visited— Corbett is India's only reserve that has maintained a steadily growing tiger population, and it protects dozens of other species: Indian elephants, jackals, langurs and macaques, rock pythons, wild boar, sloth bears, Eurasian otters, monitor lizards, 4 species of deer, 580 kinds of birds, and a highly endangered crocodile called the gharial (*Gavialis gangeticus*) that is the only surviving member of an ancient family with long, slender snouts.

Like China's national parks, India's sanctuaries are designed like matryoshka dolls, the Russian wooden figurines with progressively smaller replicas inside of them. First there are the managed perimeter forests that are heavily used, typically by timber companies that lease the land but—because they are rarely patrolled—also by herders and locals looking to collect wood and other useful things.

The forest at the edge of the national park was an example of this outer ring, and we drove through a landscape similar to where Deep and I walked a day earlier. The sal trees rose as straight as rulers and, because monocultures planted at the same time don't allow spaces in the forest canopy, there was little undergrowth. Still, the wildlife was greater than anything found in the United States, with the possible exception of untouched sections of Alaska. Singh stopped to point out a sambar and a pair of chital—delicate-looking small deer with soft white spots—feeding from a low bush beside the road. A stork-billed kingfisher slept on a tree branch above them, its purple-red beak tucked under midnight black wings.

The second level of protection in Indian sanctuaries is what Westerners would recognize as a national park: hunting, logging, and collecting are banned and the land is richer. Instead of plantations, the forests support a natural diversity of plant life and as we crossed into that zone, the landscape became denser, creating the base for greater animal numbers. Singh pulled our open-topped jeep to the side of the road to watch a troop of langur swing through the canopy of an Indian gooseberry tree. A large female from the clan sat on a nearby branch and slowly poked leaves into her mouth, her copper eyes staring out from beneath a flamboyant tuft of fur.

Farther in, the forest opened into a wide floodplain around a tributary of the Ramganga River. Fueled by the warmth of the winter sun and the safety provided by large, open spaces, the valley provided a greater accounting. A troop of macaques paraded through the top of a mimosa tree. An elephant pulled saccharum grasses from the riverbed and beat them against the ground to clean their roots before using her trunk to push the meal into her soft, pink mouth. Muntjac—animals more commonly called barking deer because, when alarmed, they emit canine-like yelps—picked their way warily along the edge of a road, pausing to eat from low bushes. A crested kingfisher, a beautiful bird with a striking black-and-white mantle, rested on a rock in the strong afternoon light.

––––––––

For Deep, the profusion of life was a perfect illustration of why predators should be protected. "Some people argue that we don't need tigers," she said as we pushed farther into the park. "They don't care if they go extinct. Some people even think they should go extinct. But they don't understand the importance of biology and that it took eons to achieve this natural balance."

Without tigers, she added, the carefully balanced environment would quickly spin out of control. Each tiger typically requires about thirteen pounds of meat each day and will kill an animal roughly once a week. If herbivore populations spike, as might happen after a series of wet years, when foliage is plentiful, hunting would become easier and tiger numbers would rise in a similar arc. If the tiger population grew too large, some would leave to seek new hunting grounds and—as food became scarce—mothers would produce smaller litters.

That cycle is central to healthy ecosystems: without tigers, the herbivores would begin to consume their food base at an unsustainable rate, eventually stripping accessible plants of their leaves until they began to starve. Their population would crash and the few survivors would start the more extreme cycle again as the plants that remained regained health.

"If you don't have tigers, the natural cycle will be destroyed," Deep said. Eventually, such changes would damage not only the ecosystem but the services it renders for nearby communities, like regulating climate and providing clean water. "A deteriorating ecosystem creates negative changes that can ricochet for centuries," she added.

––––––––

The importance of top predators has become clear to science only over recent decades. One of the earliest studies to highlight their often critical role was done in the early 1960s by a young ecologist named Robert Paine. Over several years, Paine regularly visited a stretch of rocky coast on Washington's Olympic Peninsula. Once there, he made his way to a tide pool and meticulously cleared it of large orange starfish.

Capable of growing as large as a foot and a half in diameter, the starfish, formally called *Pisaster ochraceous*, were the small ecosystem's dominant predator and, without them, the pool's ecology changed. *P. ochraceous* are able to eat a variety of prey but prefer a large mussel named *Mytilus californianus*. Without *Pisaster*, *Mytilus* flourished: within a year the mussel had taken over half of the tide pool; in time, it pushed out every other species—barnacles, limpets, snails, anemones, sea sponges, and other creatures—that had shared the space. All that remained was a blanket of dark blue *Mytilus*.

The paper Paine wrote about the experiment—"Food Web Complexity and Species Diversity"—became one of the most cited works in the history of ecology. He summed up its hypothesis in one sentence: "Local species diversity is directly related to the efficiency with which predators prevent the monopolization of the major environmental requisites by one species." A follow-up paper introduced the concept of "keystone species": like the keystone of an archway, some species—including *Pisaster ochraceous* in the tide pools of the Olympic Peninsula—are crucial to the health of entire ecosystems; removing them can lead to rapid collapse.[6] (In short, George Orwell was right: even if all animals are equal, some are more equal than others.)

Later studies added weight to Paine's findings. In 1974, two graduate students published a paper showing that the extermination of sea otters from an island near Alaska—to use their skins in clothing—had led to a proliferation of sea urchins that ate kelp, ultimately leaving barren pavements of algae that supported little diversity. Twenty-seven years later, a group based at Duke University published a paper titled "Ecological Meltdown in Predator-Free Forest Fragments." The scientists spent nearly a decade studying small islands formed by a reservoir in Venezuela and found that the loss of predators— including harpy eagles, jaguars, armadillos, and army ants—had led to an explosion of herbivores. Over time, howler monkeys and leaf-cutter ants killed off many trees, leaving only thickets of thorny, inedible plants.

"The end point in this process is a nearly treeless island buried under an impenetrable tangle of liana stems," the group wrote. In little more than a decade, green, species-rich jungle was reduced to a brown wasteland, and they added that their observations "are warnings because the large predators that impose top-down regulation have been extirpated from most of the continental United States and indeed, much of Earth's terrestrial realm."

———

Late in the afternoon, at the edge of a floodplain of the Ramganga, I saw my first tiger. Because India's wildlife is ever vigilant for its alpha predator, we had known for over an hour that she was nearby: in the late afternoon heat, everything had become strangely quiet. A chital looked up from a low bush, its ears twitching nervously. A sambar with large horns suddenly lifted its head toward the riverbed and then cocked its front leg, as if preparing to sprint. A pack of macaques at the top of a tall tree carefully scanned the valley for movement.

The animals knew that somewhere a tiger padded quietly, its legs pumping like soft pistons, its shoulders rising into a muscular hump like a Brahmin bull's, its colors—more rust and charcoal than orange and black—blending into the tawny grasses and dry shrubs. Without seeing her, we knew she was there, her mouth hanging open to reveal a wide, pink tongue wedged between scimitar teeth, her ears tipped forward, listening through the electric stillness for movement—the snap of a branch, the faint click of a hoof striking stone— her tail curled into a question mark that seemed to punctuate the forest.

We had also seen pugmarks. Half an hour earlier, Deep had found two sets of paw prints pushed into thick dust at the edge of a dirt road. One of the tigers was male, a fact obvious to Deep because its toe pads left almost perfect circles above a large, leathery palm. The other left longer, oblong impressions—a female. Tigers generally mate during the winter, when they can find prey more easily, and Deep speculated that the male was pursuing the female. Pulled to the side of the road, we joined the wildlife in their taut vigil, scanning the thick grasses for movement, listening intently for sounds.

As we waited, Deep whispered a brief explanation of why *Panthera tigris* is one of the most finely built killing machines ever to evolve. Adult tigers can weigh six hundred pounds yet need only a few seconds to accelerate to a thirty-seven-mile-per-hour sprint. They are capable of the same acrobatic feats that housecats perform—leaping dozens of feet, climbing trees, cornering sharply, crawling into small spaces. Yet they generally hunt by stealth. Their coloration makes them a perfect match for the Indian winter grasslands. Their soft footpads allow them to stalk noiselessly.

Deep explained those adaptations as part of the perfectly balanced Indian forests. Despite their power and speed, tigers hunt prey that is faster and has more stamina. Nine times out of ten, tigers fail to catch a target. If they're noticed before reaching striking distance, they will often abandon a hunt.

———

Sound is the warning of the Indian forest, and a few minutes later, as the sun began to drop toward distant hills, a macaque high in the canopy began to howl—a rising call that sounded like a loud squeaky door. A moment later a second macaque joined as it spotted the tiger.

As their screams reverberated through the valley, other animals abandoned what they were doing. The sambar stared intently upstream. A muntjac swung its head toward the riverbed and began to make cackling, canine yelps. Looking in the same direction, the sambar took several steps backward and joined the chorus with a series of low, agitated cries.

And then I caught sight of my first tiger. She emerged from behind a large stone that blended with her autumn colors; if she stood still, I would not have seen her. At first, she seemed unreal: I had imagined she would appear with a sudden burst of speed and color to tackle some ruined victim, but instead she was moving slowly, her head down, mouth agape, seemingly indifferent to the warning calls that reverberated through the forest. She placed each paw purposely, stepping between clumps of grasses and then climbing a shallow bank toward the road.

She crossed in front of our jeep, her colors contrasting sharply with the pale dust, and I was struck by her combination of power and grace. Her neck was a pillar of muscle. With each step, her body seemed to contract and then expand outward, yet she moved lightly around stones and fallen trees. She seemed strangely weightless.

As she approached a gnarled tree and squatted against it, Deep leaned over to whisper that she was marking it with urine. The male would smell her elevated hormones and follow the scent to mate with her.

The explanation had the technical precision common to science, but I was content to play the philosopher. The tiger rubbed her head against the mottled bark of a fig tree, crossed the road again, and then, for the first time, looked at us. Her two-foot-long tail almost perpendicular to her back, her left paw extended, her head down, ears cocked forward, each a patch of white ringed with woolly black, she stared up the dirt road with what appeared to be contempt: I imagined that she was disgruntled but also flattered by our intrusion—we had disturbed her walk, but she was queen of this land and we had come to pay homage. Eventually she flicked her tail, turned, and stalked into the forest.

After her colors had faded into shadows, I paused to evaluate my euphoria. I had seen one of the world's great beasts, and although tigers stand on the edge of extinction, their existence had suddenly become real: no longer were they confined to television pixels, children's stories, and zoos. We waited half an hour hoping she would reappear, but our desires meant nothing, and eventually we drove slowly back through the park past the vigilant muntjac and chital and sambar.

———

On my final morning in the national park, I put away my notebook and simply enjoyed the forest. We set out at dawn and quickly spotted a hawk surveying the forest floor in the red-orange light. Then starlings began to hunt, their dark wings cutting circles through the brightening sky.

As we drove north, the sun crested the canopy, silhouetting the trees. A heron skimmed the top of the braided, low Ramganga River and two peacocks strutted along the edge of a dirt road, their plumage tucked neatly behind them. A pair of jackals cut through a burned-over field with long loping strides.

After the sun had warmed the forest floor, we stopped to admire rock pythons sunning themselves. Each was more than six feet long but I almost missed them: their skin perfectly matched the dried leaves and twigs of the forest floor; only their heft—as round at the middle as my thigh—and their flicking black tongues gave them away.

And as we were driving out of the park, it offered one last treasure. Near noon we were stopped at the edge of a road overlooking the river when a macaque hidden in the canopy sounded an alarm. A barking deer joined and a moment later a sambar standing downstream backed up and began to make its deep, guttural call. I drew a bead from where it was staring to where a tiger stalked out of dry grass beside a thin arm of the winter river.

She padded to the river's edge and stepped into it, her rust and charcoal power reflected in its still water. As she crossed, submerging herself to her shoulders, two otters swam the other way, seeking momentary refuge. She looked healthy and full and paid them no attention.

A moment later—only a few seconds after she emerged—she reached the other side and disappeared into the dark forest.

Two years later and half a world away, I made my way past the Washington Monument and the neatly trimmed White House rose gardens to meet Thomas Lovejoy, one of the founding voices of conservation biology. Over a forty-five-year career, Lovejoy has held a series of jobs at the intersection of science and policy, serving as a biodiversity adviser to three U.S. presidents—Reagan, H. W. Bush, and Clinton—and the president of the World Bank, but also continuing field research, and I wanted to ask him how China had changed his thinking about global biodiversity. How had China's rise shifted the picture?

Lovejoy kept an office at the H. John Heinz III Center for Science, Economics, and the Environment, a nondescript building near the center of Washington, D.C., and we met in a conference room without any of the mountains of papers and lab equipment common to most researchers. In dress, however, he had the no-nonsense demeanor of many scientists I had talked with: he wore an orange short-sleeve shirt buttoned open to midchest and a battered plastic Timex watch; his wispy sand-colored hair was disheveled; in a city where language and meaning often part company, he spoke with the measured cadence of someone who says precisely what he means.

His big-picture response was that China had hit the conservation community suddenly and hard. He had only begun to think that China could become a problem "five or six" years earlier, but by mid-2011 it had become *the* problem, and while quantifying China's impacts was difficult, they were also obvious. "In terms of Africa alone, I am sure China has increased the pressure on biodiversity by many times over the state before they got engaged," he told me. "There was a very slow, almost dawdling economic trajectory in many of these countries and then, boom, China comes in and things get snapped up and before you know it, most of the story is already foreordained.

"Suddenly they are a new driver of problems because they are buying up all kinds of land and mines and forests and stuff like that, and it's happening in a snap of the fingers."

———

Lovejoy's comments were poignant partly because he has spent most of his life trying to get the world to realize what it could lose. In 1979, he made one of the boldest predictions about the damage man might do to the natural world. In "about half a human life span . . . hundreds of thousands of species will perish," a reduction of "10 to 20 percent of the earth's biota," he wrote in a frequently quoted essay.[7] Starting from 1979, half a human lifespan takes a person roughly to 2020, and I asked him to evaluate his prognostication three decades in.

"It's not too far off," he said. "In fact, I think it's going to be worse than that in the direction we're now going." A report he had worked on for the UN Environment Program (UNEP) seemed to confirm his pessimism. The report was blandly titled *Global Biodiversity Outlook 3*. But if it had a boring name, its contents were anything but: the United Nations set out to evaluate progress on a target, set in 2002, to "achieve by 2010 a significant reduction of the current rate of biodiversity loss at the global, regional and national level," a goal that had grown from the Convention on Biological Diversity. That treaty had been endorsed by the UN General Assembly as one of eight millennium development goals and, in theory, involved a commitment from almost all of the world's governments.

But like most of the millennium goals, the world had missed the target by a wide margin. Of twenty-one "biodiversity subtargets," none had been achieved globally. Some had been abject failures: most habitats in most parts of the world ended the first decade of the twenty-first century "declining in extent"; invasive species had become more common; genetic variety had dropped; the risk of extinction "for many threatened species" had increased. The details were often more frightening, and the ninety-four-page report offered a variety of other depressing numbers, graphs, and pie charts: the populations of wild vertebrate species, for example, had fallen by an average of nearly one-third between 1970 and 2006, with rivers, lakes, and tropical areas hit particularly hard; bird populations in North American grasslands fell 40 percent between 1968 and 2003; 42 percent of all types of amphibians were declining in number; globally, almost one in four plants was threatened with extinction.[8]

Lovejoy, however, was more worried about what could happen as China and the rest of the developing world continue to get richer. "Everybody's basically mimicking what America did, but the reality is that in the end, there's just not enough world to go around for everyone to live a top-of-the-food-chain

American or European lifestyle," he said. "When somebody like me is look-ing at the world and where it's going, what I can see is we've already reached the stage where we are seeing ecosystem failure. There's bleaching of tropical coral reefs—which is mostly about elevated temperature; the incredible mor-tality of coniferous trees in North America because summers are longer and bark beetles get the upper hand. Then you see the Amazon clearing and die-back and coastal estuary dead zones that are doubling in size every five to ten years.

"What I'm trying to say here is that biodiversity loss can look sort of like a stream—and with the addition of China it's a much more rapidly flowing stream now—but we have to realize that there are going to be some big thresholds that are crossed and there'll be huge chunks of biodiversity lost. And some of that we can predict, but others we'll only know about when they happen."

The overall message was that with the addition of China's demands—and behind China the rising demands of the rest of the developing world—time to stem the losses is running out: "Somehow the message has got to get through to China," Lovejoy said. "The issue is, how much do we want to shoot ourselves in the foot?"

PART III

OUR SHRINKING FORESTS

If China consumes paper at the same rate we do, it will consume twice as much paper as the world is now producing. There go the world's forests.

The point of these conclusions is simply to demonstrate that the Western economic model is not going to work for China. All they're doing is what we've already done, so you can't criticize them for that. But what you can say is, it's not going to work.

And in some way it will not work for the industrialized countries either. . . . The bottom line of this analysis is that we're going to have to develop a new economic model. If we want civilization to survive, we will have to have that. Otherwise civilization will collapse.

—LESTER BROWN, PRESIDENT, EARTH POLICY INSTITUTE

7

A FOREST LAID FLAT

Somewhere in the canopy above me, hopping between moss-covered branches, was an animal synonymous with wonder. It was dawn in New Guinea—a time locals more poetically refer to as bird-singing hour—and a jungle of green separated us: enormous ferns with prehistoric-looking fronds, pencil-thin bamboo with emerald leaves, dangling vines as thick as my legs, broad-leafed epiphytes wedged into paper-thin cracks, palm trees that dropped roots like floating mangroves. I could make out the creature's small whitish shape only occasionally. But its song was clear. It announced itself to the waking forest with a call that sounded like a lilting Southeast Asian language. A moment later its voice morphed into a seagull's plaintive echo. Then it laughed like a kookaburra.

I had hiked into the forest with a twenty-eight-year-old guide named Fidelis Kimbeng, and he tilted his head to one side and whistled. A moment later the bird replied with a long descending note. "A bird of paradise," Fidelis whispered. "I don't know the name of the species, but it's the one with no feathers. It's trying to attract a female."

It had taken me a week to reach that patch of forest. I had flown from Beijing to Singapore and then overnight to Port Moresby, the capital of Papua New Guinea. From there, a twin-propeller plane had then taken me over a wild mountain range to Madang, a sleepy city on New Guinea's northern coast, and I had driven through a fractured landscape of logging concessions. Finally, I had spent two days hiking through the densest jungle

I had ever seen. After the effort, I was looking for some kind of destination, and I claimed the bird as my reward.

A light rain tapered off and as the sky brightened from tangerine to yellow, the jungle became animated: hundreds of birds began to call, a daily ritual of greeting and boundary setting. Fidelis had grown up in what Papua New Guineans call "the bush," and he identified a half-dozen species by their songs: a hornbill's deep baritone honks; the airy whistles—like someone just learning the skill—of a cuckoo; a soft cooing from a bird known in Pidgin, the English derivative spoken in Papua New Guinea, as *balus*: airplane. "We call it *balus* because it flies like an airplane, with its wings straight," Fidelis said.

————

I had traveled to New Guinea—after Greenland, the world's second-largest island—hoping to see a bird of paradise, and for the next hour I continued to stare through the curtains of greenery. Preparing for my trip, I'd read *The Malay Archipelago* by Alfred Russel Wallace, a contemporary of Charles Darwin, and learned that birds of paradise had been New Guinea's top attraction for centuries. Today, Wallace is best known for explaining the central concepts of evolution before Darwin wrote *On the Origin of Species by Means of Natural Selection,* but in his own time, Wallace was more celebrated as a field biologist, and he had devoted long sections of the book to ruminations on various animals. (Wallace's paper, "On the Tendency of Varieties to Depart Indefinitely from the Original Type," compelled Darwin to put two decades of notes in order.) I had learned that when the first European traders reached Southeast Asia in the sixteenth century, locals presented them with dried skins from birds they called *manuk dewata*—God's birds. Portuguese traders gave the birds another name: *passaros de col*, birds of the sun. European scientific elites changed their name again. They wrote in Latin, calling them *avis paradiseus*, paradise birds.

The hyperbolic-sounding names were a reaction not to the vocal range of the various species but to their plumage. New Guinea is among a handful of islands where few native animals hunt birds, and its thirty-eight bird of paradise species have tails that open into bright trains, fans, and—like peacocks—shields of shimmering feathers. Some have elegant wirelike tails the metallic blue-green color of Northern Hemisphere hummingbirds. Many biologists argue that the plumage developed to impress mates, but it is unnecessary for survival, raising—at least for me—the possibility that the birds simply appreciate beauty. Wallace seemed to suggest as much when he wrote that their "exquisite beauty of form and colour and strange developments of plumage . . . furnish inexhaustible materials for study to the naturalist, and for speculation to the philosopher."[1]

I stared into the canopy hoping to catch a clear view of the bird but constantly being distracted by other things. A large, black rhinoceros beetle seemed lost as it picked its way along the edge of a saw-toothed leaf. Fidelis pointed to a hornbill that lifted off from a low branch with the sound of a train leaving a station, each beat of its wings creating a deep baritone thump. A small, beautiful insect with wide emerald spots and giant, drooping antennas made a precarious ascent of my boot.

After two days in the forest, I already knew that its whole is more interesting that any of its constituent parts. In a world that has been largely developed and rearranged by man, the forests of New Guinea protect a biological time capsule, one of a few places left where large swaths of land have never met a chainsaw, bulldozer, or paved road, a wilderness where it remains possible to imagine the planet as it looked millennia ago. Largely, that isolation is a product of geography. The island—today split almost evenly between Papua New Guinea in the east and the Indonesian state of Papua in the west—is covered by rain forest–clad mountains, sprawling swamps, fissured caves, and whitewater rivers. Like Australia, with which it was once connected in a single landmass called Meganesia, it is home to a wide range of deadly creatures: its poisonous snakes include both death adders and banded sea kraits; saltwater crocodiles can grow large enough to flip small boats; black widows are only slightly less appealing than bird-eating spiders (which, although not deadly, deliver an enzyme strong enough to liquefy a bird); mosquitoes—most dangerous of all—carry two strains of malaria. When a group from the British Ornithological Society set out in 1910 for a mountain range they could see in the distance, they managed to cover only forty miles before giving up—on day 408.[2]

More indicative of the difficult geography were the communities that never left the interior. People have lived in New Guinea for at least 45,000 years and, at some point, a group made it to the higher, malaria-free mountains at the island's center. The rest of the world discovered their existence only in 1935, and as recently as 1961 anthropologists were able to make first contact with a group of highlanders, almost certainly the last time such a vast, previously unknown civilization will be pulled into the modern world.

That isolation has preserved New Guinea as what Wallace called "the greatest terra incognita that still remains for the naturalist to explore," a place that contained "more strange and new and beautiful natural objects than any other part of the globe," and reaching it was the highlight of an eight-year trip he made to Southeast Asia between 1854 and 1862.[3] During the trip he amassed a collection of more than 125,000 plant and animal specimens, many of them new to science, and New Guinea protected an oversized amount of that biodiversity: it covers only 0.5 percent of Earth's landmass—an area equivalent in size to two Californias—but protects 6 percent of all species.[4]

Given the global loss of forests since Wallace's trip, the island is even more important today. Harvard University's Edward O. Wilson, probably the most famous modern-day naturalist, claims New Guinea as one of five "last true wildernesses on land."[5] Norman Myers, an influential British environmental writer, puts its forests among "less than 5 percent" of the tropics that still harbor "pristine wilderness."[6] When Jared Diamond, the environmental historian, first explored a remote section of its interior in 1974, he encountered animals that almost certainly had never seen a human. Not knowing fear, they were entirely tame: birds of paradise performed mating dances in front of him; unrecorded species of tree kangaroos sat and stared at the strange intruder.

* * *

Fidelis was tall and as chiseled by hard work as any model in an Abercrombie and Fitch catalog. He had a mop of spiky black hair and quick eyes that seemed to catch the jungle's many nuances: a hidden bird's nest, an edible plant, signs of wildlife that had moved on long before. He had grown up in a tiny village two days' walk to the east but had studied in Port Moresby, and, a few years earlier, a group of Western scientists had hired him as a para-ecologist, a scientist trained to do tasks graduate students typically do in the West: collect specimens, run experiments, tabulate results. He had spent part of a year working with a Czech lepidopterist—an expert on butterflies and moths—and could identify dozens of species as they flitted through the canopy. The day before he had pointed out his favorite—*Papilio ulysses*, a large black-and-metallic blue butterfly named after the Greek hero of the *Odyssey*.

Like everyone who grows up in the forest, Fidelis also had a deep, almost intuitive, knowledge of the natural world. As we waited, he showed me a palm tree that can be used to make bows and the arrowhead-shaped leaves of a plant that can be eaten to break fevers. He told me how to find wild pigs and explained that drinking their blood helps set broken bones.

He also helped me parse the jungle's unique aroma. After the sun had risen and the birds had quieted, saving their strength in the tropical heat, I commented on the thick smell of the forest, a combination of damp earth and decomposing leaves that seemed to define fecundity—the very scent of life. Fidelis stopped and sniffed their air, perhaps the way an American would if someone said a shopping mall's odor defined commerce.

"Do you smell that sweet smell?" he asked.

I had noticed a pungent fragrance, like crushed fruit.

"Wallaby sperm," Fidelis said.

Wallabies look like small kangaroos, and although they're native to New Guinea, it struck me as odd both that something kangaroo-like would live in the jungle and that their sperm would have a rich, pleasant smell. I must have looked skeptical because Fidelis proceeded to explain in Pidgin-inflected English: "When it sleeps with its girlfriend, it spreads out its sperm so it smells like this," he said. "They will make a new wallaby."

* * *

Just beyond where Fidelis caught the wallaby's scent, he stopped at the base of a huge tree with coffee-colored bark. Seven feet around at the bottom, it rose sixty or seventy feet in an almost perfect pillar and then began to throw out thick, dark branches. Nearer the ground, we examined an epiphyte kingdom clinging to its sides: long looping vines wove their way between patches of fungus, mushroom plateaus, and mats of light green moss; armies of insects marched within the miniature forest: jewel beetles that glowed metallic red, orange, and yellow; a dusky walking stick with paper-thin folded wings; tiny red ants with menacing pincers. Tilting our heads back, we peered through the understory at its wide canopy, a sprawling expanse lit yellow-green by the rising sun.

"Kwilla," Fidelis said. "This tree is very valuable."

Kwilla goes by other names—*merbau* in Indonesia, *idil* in the Philippines, *komu* in Thailand, *Intsia bijuga* in botany departments—and I had seen it before. Four years earlier Greenpeace had held a press conference in Beijing to publicize how kwilla had been reduced from a range that once stretched across Africa, India, and Southeast Asia to small pockets, most of them in New Guinea. The International Union for the Conservation of Nature had listed the species as "facing a high risk of extinction in the wild in the near future," and Greenpeace estimated that if logging continued at its recent pace, kwilla would face commercial extinction within several decades.[7]

The sudden decline made the tree an arboreal version of tigers—its existence suggested a healthy forest; where it was gone, the forest was almost certainly degraded—and Greenpeace compared its exploitation with the demand for mahogany in the 1980s and 1990s. "Viewed by the wealthy as highly desirable for the production of expensive furniture, pianos and boats, mahogany in the Amazon was targeted by the logging industry to the point where it became officially considered endangered," Greenpeace noted in a report. Because selective removal of a single species often results in clearing a vastly larger area, with as many as forty or fifty trees cut to remove one that is sought, "the over-exploitation of a single species can have knock-on effects for entire ecosystems," the authors added. In the Amazon, "vast areas" of rain forest had been cleared to remove a single, valuable tree.[8]

The chief difference between mahogany and kwilla was that the logging was driven by demand on different sides of the planet. For mahogany, it had come from Western, often American, consumers. With kwilla it was driven by the world's new rising superpower: "During the last decade, unprecedented economic growth, coupled with a shortage of domestic forest resources has driven China to become the world's largest importer of tropical logs . . . (and) largest market for merbau products," Greenpeace stated.

Many of China's kwilla imports were also illegal, often funneled through a complex network of loggers who falsified documents, merchant ship captains who overlooked suspicious cargoes, and corrupt customs officials happy to let contraband slip through if their pockets had been sufficiently padded. In 2006, Chinese customs data recorded the import of thirty-six thousand cubic meters of Indonesian logs, one-fifth of it kwilla, despite an Indonesian law prohibiting all log exports.[9] "Despite the stringent measures adopted by the Indonesian government to combat illegal logging, destructive and illegal logging operations are pushing the valuable . . . species to the brink of extinction," Greenpeace stated.

A few months after Fidelis and I stood at the base of the kwilla tree, I was three thousand miles to the north staring at a forest that offers a unique warning about the future of the world's remaining wilderness. I had flown from Beijing to Shanghai and then ridden two hours through an industrial landscape of looping highways, sprawling factories, and cookie-cutter suburban towns. A bus dropped me off in a town called Golden Port and I took a taxi from there to a small park where, on a hazy February morning, I climbed a long flight of stairs through a forest of stunted pine trees. A government banner at the top of the hill read, "Everyone should have a civilized attitude and maintain a harmonious environment everywhere."

A friend had suggested the park as the best place to see a forest that—if it were living—would be among the world's most stunning, and I made my way to the edge of a monument with a clear view east. There, stretched out before me, I caught my first view of what he had called the "horizontal wilderness," a place that in an area the size of a small university campus offers more spectacular tree species than any nation. Reaching along the Yangtze River's southern bank were Mongolian scotch pines, Cambodian rosewoods, and Indonesian teaks. Ten-foot-diameter kevazingo trees from Gabon brushed against Douglas firs from British Columbia and white tulip pines from New Guinea. Malaysian Pacific maples pushed against Cameroonian boumas, a tree that can throw a canopy of flowers sixteen stories into the air. All together, there were at least 221 species.

The log depot was called Zhangjiagang and I sat on the edge of the monument and squinted into the haze: in the distance a ship loaded with logs pushed its way up the Yangtze's rust-colored water. Closer in, tall orange cranes swiveled to pluck logs off a larger boat and deposit them on the river's concrete bank. Front-end loaders took over from there, lifting each log and carrying it through twenty- and thirty-foot-tall mountains of wood.

Nearer in, I could make out the next step of the trade: young men arrived on bicycles to count the logs and paint numbers on each—lot numbers, merchandise numbers, phone numbers. Buyers arrived and wandered through the piles. When they found something they liked, they pulled out cell phones and tried to close deals.

If I had stayed long enough, I would have seen the trade's back end: long, flatbed East Wind trucks would carry the trees away, out the port's gate and past the karaoke bars and snooker halls of downtown Golden Port. They would pass countless no-frills factories that make any of the million made-in-China things we buy and finally pull to a stop at one of them. There, workers would unload the logs, cut them into planks, and stack the rough-hewn timber inside industrial drying ovens. If it were possible to see that far, I would have witnessed parts of the world's last great forests slowly become everything that trees are made into: furniture and floorboards, window frames and moldings, toys and instruments.

* * *

After my trip to Papua New Guinea, I had arrived in Golden Port with the same morbid fascination that draws people to view the aftermath of earthquakes, fires, and floods. As a journalist covering Asia, I had seen other examples of how China's rising fortunes were damaging the world's forests. In 1998, I was traveling in Tibet when heavy rains and glacial melting—exacerbated by record global temperatures—flooded the Yangtze, inundating millions of acres of farmland, killing thousands of people, and costing the state billions of dollars in damages. Over several days in Lhasa I watched television footage of People's Liberation Army soldiers frantically trying to shore up dikes against the rising river. When the Yangtze finally subsided, a panel of experts convened by the central government blamed chronic deforestation in China's far west—the legacy of Mao Zedong's science-bereft policies and rapid industrialization unleashed by Deng Xiaoping—for raising the toll. With the authority vested in its single-party state, the leaders passed the National Forest Protection Program, a regulation that forbid logging in more than half of the country's forested areas.

That decision set the stage for the next chapter of damage as Chinese companies began to import large amounts of timber. Between 1998 and 2010, both China's total consumption of wood and its timber imports roughly tripled.[10] At first that growth was driven largely by Western demand: Chinese exports—roughly a third of them to the United States—grew ninefold; by 2009, China had captured roughly one-third of the world's total furniture trade.[11] By the end of the decade, however, China's domestic market had become more important. In 2005, RISI, one of the world's largest timber market research firms, estimated that 92 percent of wood products made in China were sold in China. Five years later, that figure had risen to roughly 94 percent.[12]

As with other commodities, I could personally see China's growing material desires. In Beijing, upper-class families covered their floors with slow-growing tropical hardwoods. A friend's husband spent the equivalent of $100,000 outfitting his office with redwood furniture, some of it probably made with kwilla. Before the 2008 Summer Olympics, the central government created a brief stir when it tiled the interior of Beijing's new National Center for the Performing Arts with Brazilian rosewood, a species that had been listed as threatened in 1992 and, according to CITES law, could be traded only in "exceptional circumstances."

China's rising demand for paper and plywood was more important. The *China Daily* reported in 2005 that Shanghai residents used twice as much tissue and toilet paper as the international average, a sign that—as far as bodily needs go—Chinese aspired to the same double-ply comforts enjoyed in the West. Sino-Forest, a Chinese timber company, estimated that China would need roughly 1 billion cubic meters of wood—nearly three times China's total demand in 2010—to build, decorate, and furnish new housing units over the next five years.[13]

China's growing hunger for meat and processed foods also reverberated globally. As China moved from being a marginal player in the world's soy and palm oil markets to their biggest buyer, farmers responded by clearing large areas of rain forest to plant soybeans and oil palms. The rate of deforestation in the Amazon, the world's largest rain forest, spiked after years of slow improvement. Josef Kellndorfer, a forestry expert at the Woods Hole Research Center in Massachusetts, called a sudden rise in clearing centered on Brazil's Mato Grosso state, the nation's soy farming heart, a "wake-up call" for the conservation community. "There was this hope that [Amazon deforestation] would continue to go down and might even slow to zero by 2020, but now we see it won't easily work out that way," he told me.

As China's demands rose, environmental groups began releasing regular reports tracking the country's impacts. Forest Trends and the Center for International Forestry Research, two of the world's most respected international forestry think tanks, warned in 2006 that—at recent deforestation rates—most of the last old-growth forests in Cambodia, Myanmar, and Indonesia would be gone by 2020.[14] Chinese demand for Russian logs grew by a factor of twenty-one between 1997 and 2005, and the groups warned that

Russia's far-eastern forests—the world's largest boreal wilderness—could be heavily degraded by 2025.[15]

Greenpeace held a press conference to point out that—in less than a decade—China had gone from importing a small amount of wood to importing *half* of all tropical trees globally, a large, if uncountable, portion of them felled illegally.[16] Among a series of frightening statistics, the activists stated that China's consumption of "industrial wood products"—a catchall for everything factories make with wood—had risen 70 percent in a decade. Yet the average Chinese citizen still used a fraction of the Western average. Numbers in the global timber trade are confused by varying definitions, but the group estimated that, on average, Chinese consumed one-eighth as much paper as Americans. If Chinese demand ever reached the U.S. level, China alone would require what was then the world's total timber harvest.

––––––

As I learned more, I realized that China's demand is surging even as the world's forests have dwindled to a shadow of their former selves. Since humans became the planet's dominant force of ecological change, we have cleared or damaged nearly half of the world's forested areas and—looked at over centuries—the speed of change has accelerated rapidly: more than half of that clearing has occurred since the beginning of the Industrial Revolution, and most took place after World War II, when peace in the United States, Europe, and Japan led to a consumer boom.[17] During the last two decades of the twentieth century, 15 million hectares of forest—an area the size of Illinois or Croatia—were cleared each year, most of it in the tropics: since 1950, the world's rain forests have shrunk by more than 60 percent; two-thirds of what remains is fragmented.[18]

As I thought about our growing planetary demands, it seemed unlikely that more than scraps of the last great forests would survive China's rise. I came across a study by the World Resources Institute, a Washington, D.C.–based environmental think tank, that found that less than a quarter of the planet's remaining forests were large and "ecologically intact."[19] WWF warned that one-tenth of the world's forests had disappeared since 1986 and that "at current rates of deforestation" more than half of the Amazon rain forest could be gone by 2030.[20]

I called Bob Flynn, the international forests director at RISI, the timber consultancy, and asked how much Chinese demand could grow. Flynn replied that China's "timber supply deficit"—the amount of imported wood (logs, panels, pulp, chips, and lumber)—had grown at an average annual rate of 16 percent from 1997 until 2010, considerably faster than its overall economy. He didn't expect that Chinese citizens would ever use as much wood as typical Americans do, but only because there aren't enough trees. "If we plug the numbers in for China and India reaching U.S. averages, our numbers would look so ridiculously high that no one would believe us," he said.

But, he added, all of his previous forecasts about Chinese growth had been too conservative: "I think, yeah, we can't have demand going up that much because something will slow it down. But then it does grow."

A sentence in a Greenpeace report particularly caught my attention: "If developed countries do not curb their wood consumption and, similarly, if China does not slow down the growth of its wood consumption, future generations will be living on a planet without ancient forests."[21]

At the end of my first full day at the Zhangjiagang port, outside a hotel that had been taken over by timber traders, I met a young broker whom I will call Wei Sicong. I was looking at a bulletin board covered with advertisements for various exotic species when Wei walked up to ask if I was looking to buy. He handed me his card. On one side it gave the name of his company. On the other, "Services: Every kind of wood."

I had traveled to Golden Port to learn about the tropical timber trade, but after a day and a half, I'd had little luck. Environmental groups have written dozens of reports about the illegal wood moved through Zhangjiagang, and because most brokers avoid journalists, foreign reporters sometimes pose as timber buyers. I hadn't wanted to misrepresent myself, but, tired after a day of trying to explain myself, I split the difference. I told Wei, whose name I have changed, that I was a writer. But I also said I had an uncle who *might* be interested in setting up a furniture factory. Since I was in Shanghai for the week, I'd decided to look into the business. Except for leaving a technical loophole with "might," this was untrue.

But it also worked. Wei invited me into a cluttered office, poured me a cup of tea, and told me that if my uncle did decide to build a factory, he could supply the wood. He was twenty-four and had worked at the port for two years, and he laid out an instant business plan. For starters, he suggested my uncle should rent a nearby factory. Carpenters would be easy to hire since migrant laborers flock to Golden Port for jobs. He could supply the raw materials. He handed me two sheets of paper: the first listed 80 species of Malaysian trees; the second contained the names of 148 species from Papua New Guinea. He could get any of them.

I pointed out that under a 2010 amendment to an American law called the Lacey Act, exporting to the United States requires legally sourced wood. I had heard that much of what arrives in Golden Port might not be legal. But Wei waved off the concern. "Everything is possible here," he said. "I have friends in the government, so we can get any paperwork you need." As he saw it, the bigger problem was my uncle's interest in furniture. "It's very easy to make money, but you really should think about wood flooring," he said. "That's where the real money is."

———

By the end of a few cups of tea, I had convinced Wei to take me with him when he inventoried his company's stock, and he picked me up at my hotel early the next afternoon. We began our tour by driving through downtown Golden Port, which looked like most up-and-coming Chinese industrial cities. We drove along wide streets flanked by shops that testified to the country's inequality: street-side stalls sold cloth shoes and shirts for a few dollars; just beyond them an office advertised services for wealthy locals seeking foreign visas and to enroll their children in boarding schools, part of an increasingly large wave of outwardly flowing Chinese wealth.

We passed through a large gate bearing the characters "Welcome to the Zhangjiagang Free Trade Zone," turned up a smaller road, and, suddenly, were inside the horizontal forest. Small mountains of wood rose on either side of the car, each of the logs painted with a phone number and name. Closer now, I could see that most of the trees had also been marked with a three-letter code that identified its species: TUL for tulipwood, ASS for silver ash, SIL for silkwood maple. We stopped to photograph an African kevazingo tree with a diameter taller than me. Traders had recently created a significant bubble in its price: a single thirty-foot-long section could sell for the equivalent of $600,000, and Wei explained that buyers typically used the wood to make sculptures that might sit in corporate headquarters or the homes of newly minted millionaires.

Wei's job that afternoon was to paint numbers on a stack of logs owned by his company, and as he worked I wandered through a pile of tan and cherry trunks. I knew from talking with experts that many of the trees had been felled in intact old-growth forests—generally the only places where loggers can still get such large-diameter logs—and I imagined them crashing through spaces that had never been cleared before. As bulldozers cut roads and men fired up chainsaws, countless animals would have retreated. Others would have become confused or hungry and wandered into newly established fields. Years earlier, I had seen dozens of juvenile orangutans taken from loggers in Indonesian Kalimantan: as workers cleared the forest for new palm oil plantations, they had killed the animals' mothers and kept the infants as exotic pets.

I was thinking about the orangutans when a small yellow-and-white plastic tag caught my eye. It was stapled to the end of a bloodred log and emblazoned with the image of a bird with outstretched wings and an enormous tail that I recognized immediately as a bird of paradise, the symbol of Papua New Guinea's exports. Next to the tag, scrawled across the wood, were three letters: KWI, kwilla.

Wei had told me the night before that kwilla was his most profitable product. Good, thick logs sold for as much as $800 per cubic meter and, depending on a salesman's bargaining skills, a single tree could be worth $5,000. "Kwilla is the tree I can really get rich off," he said.[22]

As Wei worked, I stood transfixed by the sight of hundreds, perhaps thousands, of kwilla logs that might have come from near where Fidelis and I had listened to a real bird of paradise four months earlier. The forest we hiked in was ringed by logging concessions, and on my way back to the local capital I'd followed a line of trucks to a much smaller port. Near where fishing boats bobbed on the Bismarck Sea, I'd asked a worker where piles of logs would be shipped.

The man wore a T-shirt that read "I only drink beer on days that end in Y." He'd smiled widely and pointed across a soft, white beach, as if casting a stone into the Pacific.

"China," he'd said.

8

NEW GUINEA

In March 1858, Alfred Russel Wallace caught his first glimpse of New Guinea. He had endured many hardships to reach the island—bouts of malaria, storms at sea, attacks by bandits, long stretches of loneliness—and he later wrote that upon spotting its northern coast, not far from the Bismarck Sea, he "looked with intense interest on those rugged mountains, retreating ridge behind ridge into the interior, where the foot of civilized man had never trod."

Getting to New Guinea is easier now, but in a world where a traveler can begin a day in New York and end it in Tibet, South Africa, or Chile, the island remains one of the most remote places on the planet. For me, the trip began when I locked the door of my Beijing apartment on a cold November afternoon. As the wind hit me, I pulled a scarf over my mouth to protect against the city's gritty pollution. Two days earlier, air quality monitors installed on the roof of the U.S. embassy recorded PM 2.5 (particulate matter with diameters smaller than 2.5 millionths of a meter) at levels the Environmental Protection Agency terms hazardous. In U.S. cities, air-quality managers would have warned citizens to avoid outdoor activity, but Beijing didn't publicly measure the pollutant and, for most city residents, the haze was just another bad day.[1]

I adjusted my backpack and walked down my lane, past two women playing badminton and a line of small shops. A woman wearing a face mask walked a poodle with ears dyed bright pink. I hailed a cab at a crowded intersection and, protected within its small interior, finally took a few deep breaths.

Only after my plane climbed above Beijing's pollution bubble was I reminded of how skies are meant to look. In clear, high air, we flew south over China's arid eastern plains, much of the land appearing from above like patches of dry skin. At sunset, we crossed into Guangdong Province, China's industrial heartland, its sprawling factories reflecting the last rays of light from their roof-tops, and then bent west along the scimitar edge of Vietnam, over Nha Trang and east of Ho Chi Minh. We slipped into Malaysia near its southern tip and dropped toward Singapore, a billion-watt light at the end of the world's largest landmass. Hundreds of container ships anchored in the South China Sea burned like fires, and streetlights cast orange-gold pools on asphalt highways.

From Singapore, my next flight headed east over the thousand islands of Indonesia: over Borneo's troubled orangutans and north of Bali's five-star resorts, past Flores, one of the world's top scuba sites, and Timor, where fight-ing between separatists and pro-Indonesian militias left hundreds dead in the 1990s. Wallace had called the Indonesian archipelago "the largest and most luxuriant islands which adorn our earth," but today he wouldn't recog-nize them. Since China's awakening, Indonesia's forests have fallen at among the fastest rates globally. In 2002, the UN Environment Program warned that most of Indonesia's lowland jungles could be gone within three de-cades.[2] The Jakarta government responded by banning log exports, but envi-ronmental groups estimate that illegal shipments could comprise as much as 80 percent of its trade. According to a recent study of satellite images, Suma-tra and Kalimantan—two of Indonesia's largest islands—lost nearly 10 per-cent of their forests between 2000 and 2008.[3]

As dawn broke we were crossing New Guinea. I pushed open my window shade and peered out at the healthiest land I am ever likely to see: the entire world below my thirty-five-thousand-foot window was deep green. A few emerald rivers cut loops through the jungle, but otherwise nothing broke the canopy—no towns or villages, no roads, no pillars of smoke. I finally felt like Wallace, a naturalist on my way to discover the world as it once had been.

*   *   *

A few hours later I was sitting on the balcony of the Binatang Research Center, a small collection of laboratories and bunkhouses on Papua New Guinea's northern coast. Below me, a British graduate student peered into hundreds of plastic bags hanging from clotheslines. Each contained a leaf or twig impregnated with insect larva—one of the first-ever methodical studies of "gall-inducing insects," thousands of almost entirely unknown bugs that have evolved the ability to force plants to build edible walls (called galls) around their eggs. Inside the building, researchers identified other insects and then carefully pinned them to trays. A few, like the Queen Alexandra's birdwing (*Ornithoptera alexandrae*)—the world's biggest butterfly, with a wingspan a foot across—were well studied, but most had never been classified. The researchers filed many in wooden drawers marked "Unidentified Families XXXX."

I had arranged my visit through a string of contacts that ended with Vojtech Novotny, a Czech ecologist who is arguably the world's top expert on New Guinea's forests, and we met for coffee overlooking a bay where three boys were splashing loudly. Novotny was forty-six and looked like Wallace might have after a few months in the forest: he was spare, with a lean face, and he dressed casually in shorts, a short-sleeve shirt, and plastic sandals. Like Wallace, he wore large glasses and had grown a substantial beard. (A picture of Wallace near the end of his life shows him with a bushy white Santa Claus–like beard; Novotny's was just as big but red and flecked with only hints of white.)

Other things about Novotny also reminded me of Wallace. Both, for instance, kept unusual pets. Wallace raised a string of animals, including an infant orangutan and several birds of paradise. Novotny had an ornery hornbill named Kokomo that hopped around the center's yard and pecked at the fingers of anyone, except Novotny, who tried to pick it up. Both men had also dedicated large parts of their lives to field research. Wallace spent eight years in Southeast Asia and five years in South America. As a way of introducing his work, Novotny explained that he had gotten hooked on New Guinea during his first visit in 1995; he sent an email to his university in then-Czechoslovakia saying he needed another six months and ended up staying for a large part of every year since, enough time that he had learned to self-diagnose impending bouts of malaria.

For me, a more important similarity was that Wallace and Novotny shared interests both in the precise answers demanded by science and in larger questions that can be addressed only by philosophy, literature, or religion. *The Malay Archipelago* became a bestseller in Britain (and, reportedly, Joseph Conrad's favorite book) partly because Wallace approached the natural world with awe and curiosity and partly because he addressed greater social and cultural issues. Novotny had written an equally appealing book, *Notebooks from New Guinea*, and he seemed the perfect person to answer my broadest questions: Why should the world care that, if current trends continue, a generation from now the planet will look much more like China and much less like New Guinea? Why, in short, should we protect our last old-growth forests?

———

Scientists have a number of stock answers to that question. First, they say that forests are important providers of what they call eco-services. For local communities, that means everything from maintaining healthy soils that purify water and prevent flooding (by holding rainfall and releasing it slowly) to moderating weather by slowly transpiring moisture. Because they protect the world's richest biological environments, they also provide communities with food and building materials. In Papua New Guinea that is particularly true: a 2000 government census found that more than 80 percent of the nation's citizens remained directly dependent on the natural world and many continued to live entirely on things they found in the jungle; if all commerce were to cease—if, say, the world suddenly ran out of fossil fuels—they would be among a small group of people for whom life would hardly change.[4]

More recently, scientists have begun to focus on forests as carbon storehouses. As plants grow they trap carbon, and while mature forests are generally carbon-neutral—absorbing as much carbon as they release—when they're cleared, most of their carbon escapes to the atmosphere. Deforestation now contributes roughly 15 percent of global carbon emissions, and if forests are cleared more rapidly, that percentage could rise.[5] (The world's forests are thought to contain 638 billion tons of carbon, more than is currently stored in the atmosphere; the Amazon alone holds roughly one-sixth of that, more than a decade's worth of the world's fossil fuel emissions.)[6]

Experts also point to the high biological diversity of forests as a good reason to save them. While old-growth forests cover only about 10 percent of the planet's land, they provide habitat for roughly 80 percent of terrestrial species.[7] Tropical forests are particularly important, together sheltering more than half of Earth's terrestrial life.[8] And only a tiny part of that diversity is better understood today than it was when Wallace visited New Guinea in the middle of the nineteenth century.

If preserved, that untapped knowledge may prove to be of great practical value. Many modern products and concepts—from engineering to psychology—are based on natural structures, but medicine is most frequently cited. Nearly 40 percent of all medical prescriptions dispensed in the United States are derived from wild plants, animals, and microorganisms (or are synthesized to mimic naturally occurring chemical compounds), and scientists generally point to a handful of widely used examples, among them morphine (a powerful analgesic that was based on chemicals found in opium poppies), quinine (an antimalarial drug derived from the bark of the South American cinchona tree—*Cinchona ledgeriana*), and erythromycin (an antibiotic first found in a fungus from the Philippines).[9] Thousands of similar cures are still used by forest communities and most have never been tested in Western laboratories.[10]

―――――――

Novotny saw value in all those arguments. He'd spent most of his career studying intact, healthy New Guinea forests. But he'd also looked at logged-over sections, and he described the resulting grasslands and monocrop plantations as "biological deserts," places where the world's most complicated, diverse ecosystems had been almost instantly reduced to some of its simplest environments. More than fifteen thousand plant species have been identified in New Guinea, and in one hectare of healthy rain forest—an area roughly the size of two American football fields—it is common to find more than three hundred unique kinds of trees. (By comparison, a healthy old-growth forest in New England or northern Europe generally contains no more than fifty species per hectare, a factor, largely, of colder weather.)

Like everywhere in the world, New Guinea's large mammals and birds receive most of the attention: ornithologists visit with hopes of glimpsing birds of paradise and cassowary—man-size animals that, with hornlike crests and Big Bird–esque feet, resemble giant prehistoric turkeys; hikers search for tree kangaroos, the result of Australian wallabies moving into the jungle.

Both groups should, however, be looking at the island's insects. So far, scientists have identified more than 10,000 species and the number of drawers marked Unidentified Families XXXX has piled up. Novotny estimated that some 250,000 species probably live on the island, and while some, like butterflies, are well understood, most have never been classified.[11] "For example, with certain groups of parasitic wasps, you can be sure that at least 95 percent of them are unknown," Novotny said as we looked across the shimmering bay.

Clear-cutting—when loggers take every tree regardless of age or species—creates a cascade of changes. After loggers leave, farmers move in to burn debris and take advantage of open land. Increasingly, companies buy the tracts to plant oil palms.

Even when loggers leave fragmented forests, the damage is acute. When particular trees are removed, their absence sets off chain reactions as reliant species move elsewhere. And changes in physical space also have long-term consequences. In natural rain forests, sunlight hits the forest floor only when old trees fall. But after loggers clear an area, more light penetrates, giving quick-growing species an advantage. Even after careful selective logging, where only specific species are taken, the large amount of sunlight stimulates the growth of vines and—just as kudzu has overrun woodlands beside many American roads—two vine species, beach knickers (*Caesalpinia bonduc*) and merremia (*Merremia peltata*), have choked large areas of logged New Guinea jungle.

In a century or two, selectively cut forests might recover enough to look pristine. But they will still lack the diversity of untouched forests. "Those fragmented and logged-over forests can sustain some part of the species bio-diversity, but it's very hard to say how much," Novotny explained. "They're a bit of a messy ecosystem."

————

For Novotny, the fact that large areas of the world's last biologically intact forests can be so degraded in a decade or two is reason enough to invest in saving remaining old-growth rain forests. "The value of having a complex, evolved ecosystem is that it can be studied to understand how complicated biological systems evolve and work," he said as we sipped strong local coffee. "The biological diversity can be used and finally will be used if it's preserved. These are products of evolution so they're very sophisticated and we don't really understand them yet. It's about preserving things which are the prod-uct of millions of years of evolution and can't be re-created."

Novotny, however, was new to advocacy. Like many scientists, he shied away from activism, preferring to explain rather than interfere. But over two decades, he'd become disturbed by the rising speed of Papua New Guinea's deforestation, and in 2010 he published a journal article called "Rain Forest Conservation in a Tribal World: Why Forest Dwellers Prefer Loggers to Conservationists." In the article, he noted that almost a quarter of Papua New Guinea's forests were cleared or degraded between 1972 and 2002. More recent studies had shown that over 90 percent of the country's ex-ported logs are shipped to China, where demand is rising rapidly. The "grow-ing intensity of logging . . . raises some intriguing questions," Novotny wrote, "notably why so many tribal communities apparently prefer loggers to conservationists, and what conservationists might do to endear themselves to indigenous forest owners."[12]

Then he went on to offer answers. One of the paper's central arguments was that New Guinea's forests weren't saved by enlightened thinking but because, until recently, locals couldn't do much damage. New Guinea's lowlands have the highest malaria incidence outside of Africa, keeping the population small, and people armed with Stone Age tools couldn't clear many trees: "The limited damage done by forest-dwelling populations to lowland forests . . . appears to be a consequence of technological impotence [rather] than of free choice," he wrote.

The arrival of the modern world had changed that. Finally presented with chainsaws and bulldozers, locals had decided to trade trees for televisions, roads, cars, hospitals, and schools. "Despite decades of investment in conservation, I am not aware of a single large rain forest in Papua New Guinea that has been successfully protected when a choice between logging and conservation was available to its landowners," he wrote.

As Novotny explained it, the problem was simple. Like the rest of the world, New Guineans want better material lives, and if conservationists want to save forests, they should start paying competitive rates. In one community where the Binatang Research Center had begun to work, that rate seemed to be about $2 per hectare per year, plus a simple school and some antimalarial pills. Given that 12 million hectares of old-growth forest remain in Papua New Guinea, the cost of saving intact areas would be around $24 million each year, plus some bricks and mortar and a few industrial-size trash bags of antimalarial pills.[13]

That seems like a small amount given what could be lost. In 2011, New York City and a city-based nonprofit group spent $42 million to manage the 341-hectare Central Park, certainly a beautiful and much-enjoyed space, but not much compared to the wonders of New Guinea's jungle.

Sitting on the balcony of the research center as evening fell, I asked Novotny if he thought the world would react quickly enough to save significant parts of what remained.

The boys had finished playing and Novotny gazed across the quiet bay. "When I came here in 1995, we were writing proposals about how New Guinea had one of the lowest deforestation rates in the world and how great that was," he said. "Now New Guinea's right in the middle of typical rates of deforestation for tropical forests and the trend is getting worse. The status quo is pretty good, but the forest will not last if all these trends continue," he said. "It could go either way."

L ooked at over a longer time line, Papua New Guinea is rapidly going the way of patio furniture and living room floors. In 2008, scientists at the University of Papua New Guinea released a report about the state of the country's forests. By comparing aerial photographs taken in 1972 with satellite images from 2002, they were able to measure how much of its tree cover had been lost and damaged.

The 1972 images show what looks like an uninhabited country. New Guinea was still a blip on the world's forestry map. (Australia, its next-door neighbor, didn't need its timber and Japan had yet to begin importing significant quantities.) According to the report, 82 percent of the nation was covered by intact forests, leaving it "perhaps the most forested land in the world," and looking at the photographs, one gets a sense of how the planet looked without humans: other than a few coastal plantations and highland meadows, the country was blanketed with trees.[14]

The 2002 images show the rising mastery of man. Nearly a quarter of Papua New Guinea was cleared or degraded during the three intervening decades, and the images reveal rectangular blocks of farmland and timber plantations with amoeba-like arms spreading along valleys. In areas with new logging, roads appear in fishbone patterns, the first stage of what will become greater clearing as locals build houses and carve out farms. Over time, the addition of a single road, possible only because a logging company arrives with heavy equipment, can set off a chain reaction of smaller, individual reclamations, and, according to the study, almost a quarter of the nation's logged land had been converted to "non-forest cover."[15]

Assigning responsibility for those losses is as difficult for forests as it is for tigers and turtles. The arrival of loggers starts the process, but it is driven by both consumers and landowners. Papua New Guinea's population had risen from 2.7 million in 1972 to 5.6 million in 2002, and the report finally drew a line down the middle, attributing the losses almost equally to logging and the expansion of subsistence farming.

Given Papua New Guinea's growing population—in 2011, it reached 6.7 million—and China's timber demand, it is, however, clear that the speed of deforestation could easily rise, and the report found that if trends continued, more than three-quarters of the country's accessible forests would be gone or degraded by 2021. "It will not be long—perhaps in the lifetimes of the country's current leaders and policy-makers—before the ecology of large portions of the country has been degraded permanently, with major consequences not only for terrestrial and marine biodiversity and timber and non-timber production, but also for the livelihoods, health and development prospects of large numbers of Papua New Guineans," the authors wrote.

———

Two weeks after I talked with Novotny, I flew to Port Moresby. Spread haphazardly between patches of spotty forest, the city epitomized a colonial-era banana republic. Expensive homes were ringed with barbed wire to protect against packs of unemployed men who wandered the streets. Locals gossiped about corrupt officials selling the county's natural resources and parking the earnings in offshore bank accounts. When I visited the national botanical gardens, the front office dispatched a security officer, in case anyone tried to rob me. (Aside from a tree kangaroo that kicked at the door of its small cage, everything was quiet.)

I caught a taxi to the Papua New Guinea Forest Authority—a bunker-like building with broken air conditioners and mismatched plastic chairs—to meet Goodwill Amos, the director of an office tasked with studying the relationship between Papua New Guinea's wilderness and climate change. A friendly man with a Buddha-like stomach and an Einsteinian bush of gray hair, Amos explained that pressure from environmental groups had forced Japanese timber companies to slow their buying in the 1990s. After the Yangtze River flooded in 1998, however, China had more than filled the gap:

within a year, China had become Papua New Guinea's top customer; in 2010 it took more than 90 percent of the country's log exports.

Chinese firms had also proven more ravenous: in 2003, Papua New Guinea's log exports broke 2 million cubic meters—roughly the amount of wood in 2 million full-grown New England maples or 1 million Douglas firs—for the first time; by 2007, they reached 2.8 million.[16] Amos believed the trade was limited only by the speed at which loggers could cut. "Before China, the trade was flat," he said. "Now they take everything we harvest."

For Amos, China's demand was problematic because Papua New Guinea's government had proven incapable of managing the nation's resources. According to national laws, loggers are allowed to take only mature trees— trees with diameters of fifty centimeters or more—and to log only once every thirty-five years, enough time to allow forests to recover, providing citizens with sustainable incomes. But companies routinely ignored the laws, taking everything or taking only the biggest, most valuable trees and then returning a few years later for more. "The biggest problem is that the companies only take what the market wants, and when that changes they come back again and do more damage," Amos said. "We'd like them to go in once and not come back for thirty-five years."

The government had also failed to meet the basic needs of most Papua New Guineans. Logging companies offer many communities their first opportunity to enter the modern world: "In most places where landowners decide to log, there is no infrastructure," he said. "The people decide that if they need services"—roads, health clinics, and schools—"they need logging."

And he found fault with the international community. China had refused to ban illegally sourced timber, and Chinese buyers seemed to care only about getting the lowest price. While environmental activists had been able to shame many Western firms into buying timber from sustainably managed plantations—for example, toy maker Mattel pledged to avoid companies that "are known to be involved in deforestation" after a Greenpeace campaign that included the slogan, "Barbie, it's over. I don't date girls that are into deforestation"—the groups had found no traction among Chinese companies.[17]

At the same time, rich, developed nations had failed to provide promised funding to protect New Guinea's forests. At the Copenhagen climate change conference in 2009, the United States and a group of other nations offered to raise billions of dollars to help developing countries reduce emissions. Scientists suggested that some of that money could be used to protect blocks of healthy rain forest, trapping their carbon (a program known as REDD—Reducing Emissions from Deforestation and Forest Degradation). But few countries had actually received much funding.

Papua New Guinea's forests store roughly 5 billion tons of carbon—the amount emitted by the world in just over seven months of burning fossil fuels—but its government had received only a few million dollars to study conservation, and Amos wasn't holding his breath for more.[18] When I asked if he thought rich nations would provide enough aid to counter loggers, he shook his head: "Here we say NATO stands for 'no action, talk only.' For me, I don't think the wealthy countries will put up the money."

As I was leaving the office I noticed a cartoon pinned to a bulletin board. An overweight man leaned out the window of a car marked "Developed countries" to yell at a poor farmer cutting down a tree. "Yo! Amigo!!" the man shouted. "We need that tree to protect us from the greenhouse effect."

Amos didn't find it funny. "The problem is that we use the forest as a cash cow, just taking the resources without managing them properly," he said. "It's greed."

———

My final stop was with Phil Shearman, the director of the University of Papua New Guinea's Remote Sensing Centre. Shearman had led the team of scientists who compiled the country's state of the forests report, and I wanted to hear him prognosticate. Forest Trends and the Center for International Forestry Research (CIFOR) had recently warned that at "present cutting rates," Papua New Guinea's natural forests would largely be logged out by 2022. Amos told me that less than 13 million hectares of healthy, intact forest remained, half of what Shearman's team had found in the 2002 satellite images. I wanted to know what he thought Papua New Guinea would look like in a decade or two.

We met at a resort hotel and drank South Pacific beers by a swimming pool. Shearman had not looked closely at how forest cover had changed since 2008, but he believed the rate of clearing was similar to what he had seen earlier in the decade, somewhere in the ballpark of 1.4 percent each year.

"The primary forest here is falling very fast, very fast," he said. "The quicker they can get the timber to China, the quicker they can make it liquid and make more money."

Like Amos, he considered the national government incapable of stemming the pillage and was skeptical that wealthy nations would prove generous enough to outbid loggers. "The history of understanding deforestation is not so much a gradual thing," he said. "It's a punctuated equilibrium model, like warfare or evolution. There are long periods where not much happens and then, bang, you get a year with huge losses. Papua New Guinea is entering one of those periods now."

For anyone who finds beauty in wilderness, the value of a forest is not, of course, solely a function of its ability to store carbon, provide cures, or moderate flooding. There are greater meanings: the intuition of a more powerful intelligence in the intricate symphony of wilderness; the sense that we are part of a larger, immortal whole; the understanding of our shared history; the feeling, simply, of restfulness. Our greatest environmental writers have tried to capture those deeper values, and their writings often sound hyperbolic until we realize that they are also honest. John Muir, one of America's first great wilderness advocates, wrote about feeling at one with the natural world in California's Sierra Nevada: "We are now in the mountains, and they are now in us, making every nerve quiet, filling every pore and cell of us," he wrote. "Our flesh-and-blood tabernacle seems transparent as glass to the beauty around us, as if truly an inseparable part of it, thrilling with the air and trees, streams and rocks, in the waves of the sun—a part of all nature, neither old nor young, sick nor well, but immortal."[19] Henry David

Thoreau described the untouched land around Maine's Mount Katahdin as "a specimen of what God saw fit to make this world."[20] Rachel Carson, the author of *Silent Spring*, found "symbolic as well as actual beauty in the migration of birds, the ebb and flow of tides, the folded bud ready for spring" and advised that those "who contemplate the beauty of the earth find reserves of strength that will endure as long as life lasts."

I found a wellspring of that strength at the base of the tree where Fidelis identified the bird of paradise. Looking through the dense canopy at its small darting shape, listening to the symphony of New Guinea's waking forest, I was overcome with a sense of well-being. Everything seemed right.

I caught moments of that feeling over the five days we spent together. On our first night, I slept in Fidelis's village, a community named Wanang, and began to understand how New Guineans have carved sustainable lives from the forest for thousands of years. With a population of 163 people, Wanang truly was sustainable. Locals drank spring water and bathed in a river. For food, they practiced swidden (slash-and-burn) agriculture that required no industrial fertilizer: like their ancestors, they cleared small patches of jungle and, after several years, abandoned them to decomposing leaves and branches that replenished their nutrients. For construction, they used jungle materials: Fidelis had built his home from palm fronds, bamboo, sago grass, and kunai leaves. For entertainment, they told stories: other than a small solar array the Binatang Research Center used to power a radio receiver, Wanang had no electricity and people gathered each night to tell tales that reminded me of medieval ballads—*Beowulf* and *The Canterbury Tales* and *Piers Ploughman*.

On our final day together, I visited Fidelis and his family for a meal cooked with locally grown and wild-harvested ingredients. Up to then, our food had been atrocious. I had arrived in the village on Thanksgiving, and because I was a guest, one of the local chief's sons had cooked what villagers considered a sign of respect: he mixed a store-bought can of Globe "new improved recipe corned beef," two bags of Maggi "chicken flavor 2-minute noodles," and what looked like two pounds of white rice. As he cooked, he asked if I knew Jean-Claude Van Damme and if it was true that "you can

just put food in a box in America and then push a button and in two minutes, it's done?"

After several more days watching me force down tinned corned beef peppered with hunks of skin and fat, Fidelis had become concerned that I was
not eating enough. "We thought white people preferred packaged food," he
said. "Maybe our local food is better."

So I ended up eating local in the rain forest. When I arrived at his house—a
one-room hut built on stilts—Fidelis introduced his wife and three children:
his eight-year-old daughter, Ulysses (named after his favorite butterfly), his
three-year-old son, Sylvester (named after his favorite actor, Sylvester Stal-
lone), and a six-month-old boy, Legi, who was asleep in a bag his mother had
woven from tree bark. After Fidelis showed me a bow he had crafted from a
palm stem, his wife served a string of dishes that would be welcome at any
Thanksgiving table: there was a rich pumpkin soup served with cubes of
sweet potato, collard green–like leaves from a wild tree called melinjo (*Gne-
tum gnemon*), a chicken stewed with potatoes, and a plate of sliced bananas,
watermelon, and pineapple. At other times of year, she would have served
fruit from the palmetto family that Fidelis said "tastes like a lolly," wild man-
goes, galip nuts, and something Fidelis called "wild woman's breast fruit"
because it "looks like a breast and tastes nice." After some animated discussion we decided it is better known in English as papaya.

————

The longer I spent with Fidelis, the more I appreciated how closely attuned
he was to the natural world, how he drew meaning from its changes and
lived comfortably within its boundaries. Dropped into the middle of a rain
forest, I might survive a few weeks, but, if he wanted or needed to, Fidelis
could live his entire life within its sanctuary.

That intimate relationship became clear when Fidelis talked about his
deeper spiritual beliefs. On our first day together, he mentioned that his ancestors' spirits live on his family's land—a stretch of forest large enough that
he needs a day to walk across it. Partly, he believed, they act as protectors: if

strangers enter the land, perhaps to hunt wild pigs, "bad things will happen to them," he explained. In recent years, two trespassers had, in fact, died violently. When villagers found the first man, "his whole stomach had come out through his asshole. He had no stomach left."

The belief in forest spirits became most apparent, however, when I asked about movies. Western scientists from the research center had begun to show occasional films in Wanang by stringing up a sheet and using a battery to run a projector. So far, they had shown a dozen films, including some of the Indiana Jones series, *Apocalypto* (the story of a declining Mayan kingdom), and several natural history documentaries. But the most popular film had been *Avatar*, James Cameron's story about a mining company that wages war on a jungle-living species of tall blue beings called Na'vi on a planet called Pandora.

Avatar had resonated for multiple reasons. Like the villagers, the Na'vi live in near-perfect harmony with their forest, hunting and harvesting wildlife and drawing energy from Eywa, a power that can best be equated with the Western concept of Mother Earth. They also faced a similar problem: foreigners—in remote Papua New Guinea almost as strange as creatures from another planet—had recently arrived with bulldozers and chainsaws to exploit natural resources. And, as in the film, the Wanang villagers had chosen not to sell their forests and were increasingly ringed by villages that had.

The final similarity could be the thesis for an anthropology dissertation: like the Na'vi, Wanang's villagers believe that the natural world—or perhaps the spirits that reside there—has free will and, if disturbed, will act. When the topic of *Avatar* came up, Fidelis and I were sitting by a stream where thousands of blue-and-yellow day-flying moths basked in the sun. Fidelis turned to me and said, "It can really happen. Now, already, our land is under attack."

As it happened, we were hiking with a teenage villager named Matthew whose family owned the land we were on. Matthew said his ancestors' spirits lived on top of a nearby hill. "If anything disturbs the forest, they will fight," he said. "If loggers ever come to this forest they can be killed or get sick and die. Their medicines can't save them. The medicines are nothing to the spirits."

During the *Avatar* showing, the villagers had become most excited when the forest decided to join the war against the greedy company, which is called the RDA Corporation. In the movie, RDA stages a full assault on the Sacred Tree, the Na'vi's link with Eywa, and is winning handily until Eywa decides to throw the whole forest against them. Cheers erupted when Triceratops-like creatures mauled human soldiers and huge flying crocodiles destroyed gunships. "We know it can be like that," Fidelis explained. "The forest spirit will fight."

————

In other ways, however, *Avatar* suffered from the typical oversimplification of Hollywood blockbusters. In it, for example, no Na'vi appear to suffer from tropical diseases. The human invaders are also less astute than real-world loggers. In *Avatar*, the RDA Corporation makes no attempt to show the Na'vi the thrills of space travel, let alone American movies. But the main force driving Papua New Guineans to lease their land is the belief that people are happier somewhere else and that logs can buy them a place in that better world.

In Papua New Guinea, logging companies have learned to amplify that envy by taking village leaders on all-expenses-paid trips to Port Moresby and Australia. Sometimes they give them cars. More often they provide them with what locals call "talk-yes money" or "happiness money"—large, one-time payments to convince them to sell rights to their forests, to get them, in the clear logic of their language, to "talk yes."

In areas like Wanang, that is generally easy to do. The nearest paved road is a long day's walk and the government had provided almost no services. Until the Binatang Research Center built the area's first school in 2008, the isolation had left it almost entirely detached from the modern world. At the beginning of my trip, I asked a group of twenty villagers if they had heard of Barack Obama, and they shook their heads. One man had heard of the September 11 attack but knew only that "some terrorists hit America and some people died, but not too many people."

As modern life has begun to creep into the area through visitors and trips to cities and movies shown by foreign scientists, however, villagers have begun to feel trapped, and many want to leave, if only to see what the world offers. For Fidelis, the choice was simple: even though he believes his family land is sacred, he hoped to lease part of it, perhaps to a company that will drill for oil. (He had seen oil bubbling from a small pond.) He had lived in Port Moresby as a teenager and was impressed by urban life, and he wanted to buy a car and a modern house with an indoor kitchen. He also hoped to send his children to good schools and needed to pay his father-in-law 3,000 kina, the equivalent of $1,400, for what New Guineans call "bride price," a dowry.

If he came by a lot of money, he wanted to see Australia and the United States. "When I got to Port Moresby, I thought it was a huge city," Fidelis told me on our last day together. "Then I saw TV for the first time and it was a show about Sydney. I couldn't believe Sydney was even bigger than Port Moresby." More recently he had heard about New York, Beijing, and London, and he wanted to see them all.

For me, time was rushing back at the end of the hike: I was beginning to think about the hundreds of email messages I would have and the onward travel arrangements I needed to make, and I wished I could return to the base of the tree where we listened to the bird of paradise. But Fidelis saw the lure of the greater world.

"I wish I could be just like you," he said.

9

OUR FUTURE FORESTS

A few months after I left Papua New Guinea, I drove south from Boston and then east to Woods Hole, acre for acre one of the most eco-aware communities in the United States. Perched on Cape Cod's fishhook end, the tiny community is home to three research institutes: the Marine Biological Laboratory, the Woods Hole Oceanographic Institution, and, in the next town, the Woods Hole Research Center. Driving in, I passed mansions hidden by groves of oak, maple, and beech trees. A sign at a traffic light advertised an "eco-toilet summit" being held at a local elementary school. Downtown, shops sold coffee made from organic, shade-grown beans, and as I waited at one of them, I overheard a conversation about ways to improve calculations of greenhouse gas emissions.

I had been drawn to Woods Hole because the best general report about the world's forests over the last decades—a study by a group of scientists, politicians, and bureaucrats called the World Commission on Forests and Sustainable Development—was organized by the Woods Hole Research Center and I arrived at its beautiful shingle-tiled headquarters on a clear July morning. Because I was early, I sat outside by a slowly spinning wind turbine and flipped through the commission's report.

Published in 1999, the study warned that the world was rapidly drawing down its "natural capital," and that continued growth of both population and per capita timber demand could "potentially overwhelm the world's forests." As in other reports I had read, the study was filled with worrying statistics:

during the 1980s and 90s, the world had annually lost nearly fifty-eight thousand square miles of forest, an area slightly larger than New York State; forests had "virtually disappeared" in twenty-five countries and twenty-nine more had lost more than 90 percent of their woodlands; many nations that continued to have large forests had seen a decline in quality due to droughts, invasive pests, and mismanagement—fewer than half of Europe's trees, for example, were "completely healthy."

"The decline is relentless," the authors wrote. "We suspect it could change the very character of the planet and of the human enterprise within a few years unless we make some choices."[1]

———

For Richard Houghton, a center expert on forests and carbon, the picture twelve years after the report's publication was just as bleak. Houghton is one of the world's top specialists in how people use land, a man whose forty-five-year career began with studies of single oaks and has gone on to embrace multiple ways of studying the planet's total forest cover. His most consistent research, however, has been on the relationship between land and climate change, particularly how much carbon is stored in plants.

That connection is made most obvious by the Keeling curve, the measurements of carbon dioxide in air blowing across Hawaii's Mauna Loa volcano. The Keeling curve is famous—it is probably the most widely reprinted set of scientific data ever gathered—because it shows in a simple way how quickly the atmosphere is absorbing the gas: in 1959, the first full year that a chemist named Charles David Keeling measured carbon dioxide at Mauna Loa, the atmospheric mean was 316 parts of carbon dioxide per million parts of air. By 2010, the mean had risen to 390.

The Keeling curve is also interesting, however, because it shows the world's plants breathing. Printed as a graph, the data looks like the business edge of a saw, with each tooth representing a single year: the valleys measure the Northern Hemisphere summer, when trees take in carbon dioxide for photosynthesis; the peaks capture winters, when most trees are dormant.

(Because there are fewer trees in the Southern Hemisphere, the graph tracks the Northern Hemisphere seasons.)

THE KEELING CURVE

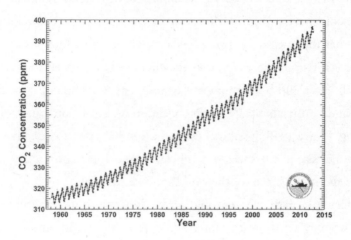

Source: Scripps Institution of Oceanography, U.C. San Diego.

Houghton has spent his career trying to understand the dynamics of that deceptively simple-looking cycle, and he showed me a manuscript he'd been writing. Titled "Historic Changes in Terrestrial Carbon Storage," the paper was an attempt to calculate how human activity has changed where the planet's carbon exists.

To think about this problem, it helps to remember two high school science lessons. First, all living things are composed primarily of carbon: if you dried out either a human body or a tree, nearly half its weight would be carbon. Second, as expressed in the law of conservation of mass, in any closed system, nothing goes away.

Starting with those principles, Houghton had pulled together various research to show how, by clearing land for farms, pastures, and everything else, humans have shifted terrestrial carbon into the atmosphere. Cropland and pastures now occupy as much as one-third of Earth's land and one-third of its remaining forests are under some kind of management, much of them as logging concessions. In all, Houghton estimated that nearly half of the planet's "productive land surface"—all land excluding sand, snow, ice, and rock—has been commandeered by people.

Most often that has meant replacing forests with fields. Referring back to high school science, we know that crops contain much less carbon than trees do and that the lost carbon had to go somewhere: Houghton estimated that over the last two or three centuries the changes have moved somewhere between 100 and 200 billion tons of carbon from Earth's land into its atmosphere and, until about 1950, deforestation was the top cause of global warming. (Since 1950, fossil fuel consumption has risen so quickly that, despite an increase in the speed of land clearing, deforestation today accounts for only about 15 percent of the world's total emissions.)[2]

Besides deforestation's contribution to global warming, another problem is that we may need healthy forests to reverse the trend, and, as we clear them, we lose the nutrient-rich soil they depend on. Houghton suggested that halting deforestation, combined with a "massive program of reforestation," could reduce carbon emissions by as much as 3 billion tons a year. Since only about 4 billion tons are currently being added to the atmosphere each year (the rest is being absorbed by the oceans and other natural processes), that reforestation, together with a slight reduction in our fossil fuel emissions, could "stabilize the concentration of CO_2 in the atmosphere immediately," Houghton wrote. The solution was refreshingly simple: as the trees mature they would capture billions of tons of carbon that escaped when they were first cleared.[3]

The problem, of course, is that since we continue to clear forests, adding hundreds of millions of acres "would require a reversal of the global trends . . . that have accelerated over the last 300+ years," Houghton wrote. Such reversals have happened in individual countries as they became richer and could afford to import wood—as China began doing in 1998—but, overall, the global trend has been toward fewer trees, and Houghton ended the paper with two questions that were beyond the scope of his research: Can such reversals become global? And can they become global even as demand for land and natural resources is rising?

Those seemed like the kinds of questions that shouldn't be shrugged off, and, sitting in his office, I asked them.

Houghton leaned back and looked out a window at Cape Cod's pretty regrowth forest. "You have to think about what we're starting with," he said. "When Europe came along, there were places for them to expand. There was the New World. So, what's available now? Well, I guess there are pieces of the tropics: Southeast Asia, Central Africa, and Brazil. I worry about the fact that society is just doing what it's always done, but much faster and on a bigger scale."

We talked for a while longer about what China's rise could mean for the environment, and as I was leaving, he reiterated that while China is "just doing what we did," from a planetary perspective, its rise was "really scary."

"You could argue that the world was already full by 2000," he said. "As a state, China now has the opportunity to set the limits of global growth or just grab everything they can. It's their choice."

———

I spent the rest of the day talking with other scientists at the center, and each had his own concerns. Eric Davidson, an expert in the nitrogen cycle, worried that growing demand for food (largely driven by China) will require more man-made fertilizers, causing more dead zones in lakes and estuaries and releasing more nitrous oxide, the third most important anthropogenic greenhouse gas after carbon dioxide and methane. "In terms of nitrogen, China and India are where most of the action is," he said.

Scott Goetz, a specialist in satellite imaging, worried about China's rising impacts on Africa. China displaced the United States as Africa's top trade partner in 2010, and its demand for resources has since spiked. Goetz had just returned from the Democratic Republic of the Congo, where China had recently agreed to build and renovate thousands of miles of roads, allegedly with the aim of establishing massive oil palm plantations, and reported that Congolese scientists were concerned that "the Chinese are going to come in and take all the forests." (Chinese demand for logs, many illegally felled, is so great that African journalists have begun to refer to the trade as the "Chinese takeaway.")[4]

Josef Kellndorfer, an expert on Brazil's forests, worried that Chinese demand for soybeans—largely used to feed the nation's growing taste for meat—could reignite Amazon deforestation. Since 2004, when an area the size of Belgium was cleared, Amazon deforestation rates had dropped sharply. In 2010, less than half of that amount was lost, largely because of new Brazilian antilogging polices. But two years of unusually large forest fires—probably related to global warming—and a spike in clearing had tamped down optimism. Brazil's environmental minister had recently called a crisis cabinet meeting to discuss an almost sixfold rise in clearing.[5] A former editor of a São Paulo newspaper warned that Brazilian agribusiness was "pushing for a new forestry law that would condemn vast areas of the rain forest to extinction."[6]

Kellndorfer worried that pressure will continue to grow: "People were pretty optimistic, but now they're realizing that it's the same old story," he said. "When there's increasing demand and prices go up, people clear forests."

––––––––

As at the end of Houghton's paper, bigger questions hung over the conversations: How much will Chinese demand grow? Where will clearing for timber and land happen? To what extent is China's growth the harbinger of a larger wave as India and other nations follow its lead?

The answers, of course, hinge on hard-to-predict variables: how closely, for example, will China follow the American path of suburbanization? If it does, will the Chinese want wooden homes instead of the ubiquitous concrete-and-steel structures they live in today? Will they continue to tile their floors, or will they want kwilla, mahogany, and teak? Will demand for meat reach American levels? If it does, what will those billions of cows, pigs, and chickens be fed?

Some experts have begun to speculate about answers. In 2009, the

London-based Environmental Investigation Agency reported that deforestation in Indonesia and Brazil was increasingly driven by "export-led commercial agricultural expansion." Between 2000 and 2007, Indonesian exports of palm oil more than doubled. Brazilian beef and veal exports grew almost tenfold, while soybean exports doubled. "Commercially produced timber, agricultural and livestock commodities are now the number one cause of deforestation and degradation worldwide," the group stated. "As developing countries' middle classes expand, this will only be more the case."[7] In 2006, Forest Trends and CIFOR stated that if China's wood imports continued to grow as quickly as they had for the previous nine years, by 2015 the nation would require an amount of industrial timber equal to roughly a third of what the world then used.[8] The author of a report for the UN Environment Program told journalists that if demand for wood continued to grow at "current trends," Asia's supply of "millable timber" would be gone by 2038.[9]

Bob Flynn, the international trade expert at RISI, was particularly clear. He expected China to blow past the United States as the world's top timber consumer sometime around 2015: "You build these models and the numbers are going up like a ski slope and you think, well, rising prices and inflation and other things will slow China down, but then somehow it keeps going up," he said.

As an "interesting theoretical exercise" he suggested that I see how much timber China would import in 2025 if their demand continued to grow at 16 percent annually. When I finished the math, the number was over 1 billion cubic meters, two-thirds of the world's total current demand.

"That would be a pretty scary number," Flynn said.[10]

Living in China, the calculations seemed simpler. Life for my Chinese friends had improved dramatically since I first arrived in the country in 1996. Most of my former students had moved into progressively larger apartments. New gated communities reminiscent of American suburbs sprang up around Beijing. For a newspaper story, I visited a villa complex called Palais De Fortune where million-dollar mansions came with indoor swimming pools, movie cinemas, and separate Western- and Chinese-style kitchens.

In early 2011, I spent a few hours touring the China (Beijing) International Building Materials and Interior Decoration Exposition. Amid hundreds of booths selling everything from heating systems to wine refrigerators, a dozen companies promoted wooden houses. A salesman for a company selling what looked like a Nordic cottage said Chinese were quickly turning to wood because they believed it was healthier and, with construction costs figured in, was often cheaper than concrete.

The company had set up a model, and I could see why Chinese families would prefer it. The house was built from Russian pine, and its rooms smelled like a forest. While concrete demands boxy shapes, it had a peaked roof and gables. "A lot of Chinese have never seen a house like this," the salesman said. "When they do, they want to live in one."

————

What became clear is that regardless of how one does the math, the world's forests are going to be under increasing pressure, and *where* wood comes from—how the world manages what remains of our forests—is going to be as important as how much we use. Estimates vary, but it is likely that the global community could sustainably meet its timber demands by harvesting 20 percent of its forests.[11] That, however, would require an end to clearing old-growth areas, something no one seems able to do. According to the Food and Agriculture Organization, the world's total forest area shrank by at least 52 million hectares—the size of Spain or Thailand or, incidentally, a little more than Papua New Guinea—over the first decade of the twenty-first century.[12] Four-fifths of those losses occurred in primary forests. (This figure also underestimates the damage because the FAO defines a forest as any land with more than 10 percent tree cover; other groups offer higher estimates.)

A rising tide of illegal logging further complicates the picture both because no one knows precisely how large the trade is and because even when governments want to act, stopping deals is difficult. What is clear is that many of the contraband logs end up in China. According to WWF, between 30 and 45 percent of China's timber imports have been felled or imported illegally. Global Witness, a London-based nonprofit, has put the figure at 50 percent, much of it illegally harvested in Russia.[13]

Studies of individual exporting nations show higher percentages of illegally felled trees. According to Global Witness, almost all of the wood shipped to China from Myanmar a decade ago was illegal. Other estimates have put China's illegally felled imports from Indonesia, Brazil, and Gabon at 80 percent, from Tanzania at 90 percent, and from Papua New Guinea at nearly 70 percent.[14]

The illegal trades generally involve loggers cutting in restricted areas, exporting without permits, breaking environmental regulations, or avoiding taxes, but companies have used various other underhanded methods. A decade ago, Russian firms could purchase logging licenses more cheaply if land had been damaged by fire. So many companies started fires: in 2003, 22 million hectares of spruce, larch, fir, Scotch pine, and oak—some of the trees five hundred years old—were burned. On a single day, U.S. government satellite photographs showed 157 fires stretching across 11 million hectares, enough that a plume of smoke reached three thousand miles to Kyoto, Japan.[15]

––––––––

Such problems have prompted action by some Western governments. In 2008, the United States amended the Lacey Act, a law dating to 1900, to ban the transport of any "plant product" harvested illegally. The law applies from "stump to shelf," making it illegal to "import, export, transport, sell, receive, acquire, or purchase" almost any plant harvested in violation of American or foreign laws.[16] Two years later, the European Union passed a similar law, to take effect in 2013.

But China, which imports more illegal lumber than any other nation, has done little to stem the trade. Chinese officials have argued, correctly, that the country is doing nothing that Europe and the United States have not done themselves and that, as a general policy, Beijing does not interfere in the domestic affairs of other nations. "China is just buying on the international market," Chen Yong, a top official in China's State Forestry Administration told me on the sidelines of a Beijing conference. "We can't go into a country and determine if the wood has been cut legally. If it has the proper paperwork, we have to accept it as legal."[17]

Bob Flynn, however, explained China's inaction differently: "In terms of environmental impact, the most important thing is that at least historically the Chinese really don't care where their wood comes from, as long as it's cheap. If you're talking about illegal logs from Indonesia or cutting down the last tree in the Solomon Islands, they apparently have no issues with that."

———

In a world of global supply chains, with fraudulent documentation and unenforced laws, the details of how China's rise will affect the planet's forests are messy, but it is clear that as demands grow, we will have increasingly less time to save what's left. Only 12 percent of the world's forests are protected and—as I saw on the outskirts of India's Corbett National Park—only a fraction of those lands are actually patrolled. "In a worst-case scenario, all of the world's readily accessible remaining forests outside those protected areas would be destroyed by unsustainable harvesting within the next several decades," Jared Diamond wrote in 2005.[18]

At the end of my conversation with Bob Flynn I asked him to speculate about where things could go.

"It's sort of the story we've been talking about," he said. "When you have so many people with rising incomes and they have aspirations for more consumption, it's an exponential, multiplying effect. The impacts, they're a bit frightening. And India's coming right behind China and they're in exactly the same situation with a large population and rapid economic growth."

Flynn was quiet for a moment. Then he laughed.

"Yeah," he said. "It's kind of staggering."

I followed a trail from Fidelis's village through a forest thick with massive trees and then onto an abandoned logging road that offered a sickly substitute. Without shade, the air was brutally hot and for several hours I saw no birds or even butterflies; trees along the road's edges were engulfed in kudzu-like vines.

I walked to where a bridge built years before had collapsed, a common occurrence after loggers leave, and then to a village named Manamaging that had recently opened its lands to logging. From a distance, the village looked like Wanang: a few dozen palm-and-bamboo buildings stood together atop a small hill. But as I approached, details pulled the community closer to the modern world: behind one hut several pairs of blue jeans dried on a clothesline; someone had replaced the grass roofs of several houses with corrugated iron sheets; a Michael Jackson song blared from a radio; when I arrived, a woman offered me instant coffee.

The villagers had also used their "talk yes" money to buy a used pickup that they operated as a taxi, and the next day, I rode back to the Binatang Research Center with a carful of villagers. In the logging concession, we passed huge insect-like front-end loaders lifting hundred-foot trees onto trucks. Each log was painted with numbers and letters—KWI for kwilla, CEP for pencil cedar, WAL for walnut—and tagged with the same yellow-and-white squares I would see a few months later near Shanghai.

We drove north through areas that had been burned over to plant corn and then turned onto a paved road. As we approached Madang, the modern world began to take shape: a market sold both betel nuts and Coca-Cola, packaged hot dogs and what Fidelis called "wild woman's breast fruit"; a line of cars waited at a Mobil gas station; guards patrolled outside the glass-and-steel headquarters of a new Chinese-financed nickel mine.

*   *   *

The driver's name was Benny Francis and after he dropped off the other passengers, I hired him to take me to the city's only log port. When I first met him, Francis struck me as someone who didn't have much to say. His head was covered by a mop of uncombed gray hair and his teeth were stained bright red by years of chewing betel nuts. Because he was short, he sat on two pillows to see over the truck's steering wheel. One of the first things he told me is that he didn't have a driver's license.

As we drove toward Madang, however, Francis impressed me as an acute social critic. He told me that he had been born "in the bush" in 1957 and learned English from Baptist missionaries. He drove a bulldozer in a cemetery for sixteen years and was then hired to build trailers for Kenworth trucks. The company had paid him a good salary, but when he retired he moved back to his family's forest, an unlogged tract of land a long day's walk from Manamaging. "Young people today want the town life," he said as he peered over the dashboard at an oncoming car. "They think it's better. But they don't know. In the town you can make some money but you spend all your money and you don't have freedom. In the bush we have our families and everything we need."

As Francis saw things, the arrival of a modern, more material-based lifestyle was eroding Papua New Guinea's clan-based society in negative ways. In 1986, Kenworth had sent him to Brisbane, Australia, to study welding, and while he was impressed by the city's comforts, he found its people strangely discontented. "Australia was a good place, but Papua New Guinea is different," he said. "White men I knew there had good educations. They had lots of money. But many weren't happy. Their thinking wasn't good. They always wanted more. They didn't know how to enjoy what they had."

His comments reminded me of a statement written by a committee that had drafted Papua New Guinea's constitution in the early 1970s, when the country achieved independence from Australia. The group had cautioned that the shift away from traditional communities toward an economy dominated by large-scale industries could damage "the social and spiritual fabric of our people."[19]

"We see the darkness of neon lights," the committee wrote. "We see the despair and loneliness in urban cities. We see the alienation of man from man that is the result of the present machine oriented economy. . . . There is overwhelming evidence to suggest that a significant number of people who live by the fruits of multimillion-dollar multinational corporations live in misery, loneliness, and spiritual poverty. We believe that since we are a rural people, our strength should be essentially in the land and the use of our innate artistic talents."

———

There is evidence that most Papua New Guineans have, in fact, fared poorly by opening their land to loggers. A series of studies by the World Bank between 2000 and 2005 found that "few lasting benefits are reaching landowners." In many cases villagers felt that "logged areas were made worse off by logging."[20]

The problems noted in the reports were legion: in some areas logging had led to increased crime and corruption; locals spent some of the windfall on alcohol, leading to fights and violence; the majority of logging concessions were found to be "ecologically and economically unsustainable," with frequent damage to rivers and little effort to replant tree species that could be logged in the future; laws protecting worker health and safety were routinely overlooked and companies sometimes failed to provide promised infrastructure; logging company payments "in most cases resulted in an increased dependence on shop-bought foods, especially rice, tinned fish, and soft drinks"; in communities not used to having money, little was invested. "The overriding conclusion drawn is that the full costs associated with logging projects reviewed appear to outweigh the benefits," the report stated.

For Francis, a bigger problem was that locals were getting obviously unfair deals for their forests. With a population of several hundred, the villagers of Manamaging had received a talk-yes payment of just over 10,000 kina (the equivalent of just under $5,000) and were getting another 50 kina ($24) for each cubic meter of kwilla taken out.[21]

"In China, I hear they get two thousand or three thousand kina for a cubic meter," Francis said. "I told people here those numbers, but they want the quick money. They just say yes, yes and take the money." (When I visited the Zhangjiagang port near Shanghai, traders were selling kwilla for up to $800—1,700 kina—per cubic meter.)

————

We arrived at the port—a muddy dirt lot the size of a few football fields—as Francis was explaining his frustrations, and we got out to look around. A squat two-story building was ringed with barbed wire. Across from it, the Bismarck Sea lapped quietly against a white sand beach. Between them, a few thousand logs were piled according to species, and we found a small hill of kwilla. Newly cut, the trees were the color of dried blood.

A few men were resting under a palm tree, and I wandered over to them. The logs would be shipped to China, one said. I asked about their work, and he said each man was paid the equivalent of $95 for every ship they loaded.

"With every boat, someone gets hurt," a second man added. A day earlier, a man's leg had been crushed when he slipped between two rolling logs.

There were no boats that day, so Francis and I snapped a few photographs and then walked back to the truck.

As we were leaving, Francis slapped the steering wheel. "All the things is fucked up," he said. "The trees are gone, the land is spoiled, it is all gone. It will come. But they don't think about that, only the money."

Early in 1857, Alfred Russel Wallace arrived at a small island on the south coast of New Guinea. As he normally did, he bargained with the head of a local village for the use of a hut—paying one "chopping-knife" as a week's rent. Then he began collecting. For the first few days it rained and he found little, but as he was preparing to leave, his assistant returned from the forest with a specimen that, he wrote, "repaid me for months of delay and expectation."[22]

The bird was small ("a little less than a thrush") but was so ornately ornamented with colors and feathers that Wallace pronounced it "one of the most perfectly lovely of the many lovely productions of nature." Its body was "intense cinnabar red, with a gloss as of spun glass." Its head feathers were "rich orange." Its breast was white and banded with a "deep metallic green." Its feet were cobalt blue. Long, slender wires protruding from its short tail ended in button-like spirals "of a fine metallic green."

"These two ornaments, the breast fans and the spiral tipped tail wires, are altogether unique, not occurring on any other species of the eight thousand different birds that are known to exist upon the earth," Wallace wrote. The specimen was a king bird of paradise (*Cicinnurus regius*), a bird still almost unknown in Europe, and holding it drew him into a philosophical mood. He thought of the "long ages of the past, during which the successive generations of this little creature had run their course—year by year being born, and living and dying amid these dark and gloomy woods, with no intelligent eye to gaze upon their loveliness; to all appearance such a wanton waste of beauty."

The idea that such beauty had not been appreciated by Europeans excited "a feeling of melancholy" until Wallace realized that the "wild inhospitable regions" were critical to the birds' survival: "Should civilized man ever reach these distant lands, and bring moral, intellectual, and physical light into the recesses of these virgin forests, we may be sure that he will so disturb the nicely-balanced relations of organic and inorganic nature as to cause the disappearance, and finally the extinction, of these very beings whose wonderful structure and beauty he alone is fitted to appreciate and enjoy," Wallace wrote. "This consideration must surely tell us that all living things were *not* made for man. Many of them have no relation to him."[23]

In an era of European colonization rooted in the belief that all living things *were* made for man, the statement was both radical and prescient. Wallace had already formulated the core ideas of evolution and he recognized that the natural world not only exists independently from humans but that it is threatened by the arrival of "civilized man." Looking at the beautiful bird,

Wallace wrote that for much of the natural world, "existence . . . is disturbed or broken by every advance in man's intellectual development."

————

I was thinking of Wallace's enlightenment as I picked my way up a ridge high in New Guinea's cloud forest. After hiking with Fidelis, I'd wanted to see the island's interior—the country that Wallace could only dream about as the world's "greatest terra incognita"—and bought a seat on a tiny missionary Cessna. The plane dropped me on a grass airstrip high in the Finisterre Mountains, and in a village named Yawan, I hired two local guides, teenagers named Semcars and Junior, and started for the top of a mountain a long day's walk away.

I'd been attracted to the highlands partly because they're markedly different from New Guinea's lowland jungles. They provide habitat to most of the island's endemic mammals—notably tree kangaroos, cassowary, echidna, and cuscus, the world's largest possum—and provide an even richer study in nature's endless varieties of green. Yawan sits at just over five thousand feet, putting it at the lower end of New Guinea's montane forests, and the jungles reaching from there to roughly nine thousand feet, where they give out into scrub brush and grasses, are also called cloud, or sometimes mossy, forest. In the intense heat of the tropical sun the forest begins to transpire each morning: plants open microscopic pores to pull in carbon dioxide and, in the process, lose water to evaporation. By midday the water has cooled and condensed in the higher atmosphere and the forests are generally bathed in moisture.

By noon we were inching our way up a spine of the mountain in the middle of a thick cloud. The first thing I recognized is why much of Papua New Guinea remains accessible only by foot or plane (the country has only one foot of asphalt per capita): the route felt more like climbing a ladder of unevenly spaced rungs (hidden beneath a mat of rotting leaves) than hiking. For most of the morning I stared at the ground, trying to pick handholds that wouldn't disintegrate and to avoid thorns that seemed to cover every third plant.

When I finally paused to look around, however, I saw that the cloud forest presented a world as bizarre and beautiful as anything Hollywood might dream up. The steep slope allowed more light to hit the forest floor than in the lowland jungle, creating a study in levels. Along the ground, ferns with twenty-foot-long fronds pushed against the boat sail–sized leaves of wild bananas. Above them, a wide diversity of trees rose toward a sprawling canopy, each supporting its own hanging garden. Mosses engulfed their trunks and created a base for a variety of epiphytes: a clump of pink-and-white orchids climbed down the side of a conifer; nearby, delicate red funguses grew like shelves from a pandanus palm; long, tendril-like vines plunged earthward from above.

Since the highlands remain remote, its wildlife is also relatively intact, and as we walked Semcars pointed out animal signs: a half-eaten papaya a cuscus had dropped, claw marks left in soft bark by a tree kangaroo, bits of fruit discarded by a cassowary.

Semcars spoke broken English, and he peppered me with questions about the United States. He knew almost nothing about the country but had heard of New York, and he wanted to know how tall the city's buildings were. When I explained that the biggest were as tall as seven of the forest's tallest trees stacked together, he and Junior, who spoke only a local tribal language, expressed admiration by making a series of noises that sounded like chicken clucks.

They wanted to know more and, searching for something to say, I mentioned that there is a "small forest" in the middle of New York where people sometimes go for a "walkabout," the local Pidgin English word for hike. At this, they became more excited. Semcars asked if tree kangaroos live in the forest. Junior wanted to know if it was possible to hunt cassowary. When I explained that neither tree kangaroos nor cassowary live in Central Park and hunting is not allowed, they looked skeptical, as if a forest that could not provide calories wasn't a real forest.

Finally, Semcars asked how long it would take to walk across "the New York forest." When I replied that crossing takes about an hour, he looked at me sternly and said, "That is not a forest."

*   *   *

The next morning we started hiking shortly after bird-singing dawn. The sky was still tangerine orange, and when we finally broke clear of the tree line, only the wispy beginnings of clouds marred the deep blue sky. I sat on a clump of ferns and looked north across a valley blanketed by trees. Behind it, ridges folded into a tight accordion of canyons and peaks, all green except where waterfalls cut thin white lines through the foliage.

Dozens of tiny black-and-navy blue sparrows darted along the edge of the meadow and, like John Muir in the Sierra Nevada, I felt immersed in the natural world. Like Muir, I sensed that I was "part of all nature . . . an inseparable part of it, thrilling with the air and trees, streams and rocks, in the waves of the sun."

Throughout the trip I had been trying to understand the value of intact wilderness. Few people will ever travel to New Guinea. The carbon its forests store is important, but it could be taken up by lesser, regrowth woodlands. Its biodiversity is irreplaceable, but it is unlikely that scientists will use it to solve the problems faced by today's humanity.

Instead the answer seemed to be the simple truth that only the natural world offers a space where everything is at peace with itself. As we—humanity—have walled off wilderness, we have lost touch with the sense of belonging to that greater whole, and looking out over the ocean of green, it struck me that the protection of such places might provide common cause in an increasingly crowded world competing for resources.

If we lose such places—the final pockets of Earth that remain largely as they were before "civilized man" brought "moral, intellectual, and physical light" into its most remote recesses—we might lose one of the final threads that binds our uniquely capable species. Without reminders of our shared past, it seemed possible that we would begin a race to the bottom: instead of sharing and protecting our dwindling, finite forests, we might fight over their final scraps.

PART IV

OUR WARMING SKIES

When we consider the fate of the planet as a whole, we must be under no illusions as to what is at stake. Earth's average temperature is around 59° F, and whether we allow it to rise by a single degree or 5° F will decide the fate of hundreds of thousands of species, and most probably billions of people. Never in the history of humanity has there been a cost-benefit analysis that demands greater scrutiny.

—TIM FLANNERY, *THE WEATHER MAKERS*

10

TIME TRAVEL

In the Chinese countryside, killing a pig is a bloody but quick affair. A few days before the Year of the Tiger gave way to the Year of the Rabbit, I stood in the yard of a wood-and-tile house and watched Zhang Dejun, a sixty-four-year-old farmer, slide a metal hook into the mouth of a two-hundred-pound pig.

Zhang lived in a village that epitomized an aesthetic that might be called "classic China": a few dozen farmhouses punctuated steeply terraced fields where locals planted wheat, rice, potatoes, and corn. A thin trail wound up the side of a valley covered with oaks and pines. Smoke curled from distant kitchens into heavy, low-hanging clouds.

Before Zhang began his work, the only sounds were a haphazard cow bell and the rustle of a breeze through dry grasses. But pigs are capable of prodigious vocalization, and as Zhang dragged the animal from its sty, it emitted a long, high-pitched wail that echoed from nearby hills.

Zhang had enlisted the help of three relatives, and after he had the pig in the open, they began their efficient, age-old work: each grabbed one of the animal's legs and they lifted it over a simple wooden bench. Zhang was wearing thin rubber-and-canvas shoes, dirty black slacks, a blue jacket with worn-out sleeves, and an old People's Liberation Army hat with long woolen ear flaps. A cigarette dangled from his lips. He kicked a plastic tub under the pig's head, and his nephew—a middle-aged man named Xiangyang—slipped a foot-long knife into a soft, fatty fold of skin on the animal's neck. When he pulled the knife out, a stream of bright red blood followed, and for a long minute the men remained frozen in place, holding the animal as its life ebbed away.

When the pig finished kicking, the true work began. Xiangyang poured boiling water over the animal. Using a razor, he shaved off its bristles, which Zhang would sell in town for a few yuan. (Eventually, craftsmen would use them to make brushes that outlast the plastic variety.) He cut off its head with a small ax and then used the knife to make an incision up its belly. He pulled out its intestines, which he would wash and stuff with meat. Zhang's wife carried the blood into the kitchen to cool and clot. That afternoon, she would slice it into cubes and cook them with bean sprouts.

As Xiangyang slowly dismembered the pig, Zhang hung its various parts to dry: a maroon liver and bubble-gum-pink lungs; thick rib slabs; leg bones with their feet—a Chinese delicacy—intact; two woolly ears that he would slice into cartilage snacks; its clean-shaven head. In the end, almost nothing was discarded. Even blood that spilled on the ground became fodder for a flock of chickens pecking their way across the yard.

The village was named Tuojia and the slaughter was a reminder of the efficiencies of rural Chinese life. I had arrived a day earlier with Zhang Chao, a friend from my days as a Peace Corps volunteer, who had shown me around the community. We had stopped to watch a couple plant potatoes by hand and to examine a scooter built from bits of scrap wood. We watched an elderly man pound rice to make glutinous rice balls, a traditional Chinese New Year sweet, and examined racks of drying hand-pulled noodles.

Zhang Chao—whom I knew by his English named, David—had grown up in the village, and we followed farm trails to a ramshackle building with boarded-over doors. Small trees poked through the roof. "This is where I lived as a boy," David said. "No one wants it now."

Two decades earlier, the community had been multigenerational, and David had grown up thinking he would also farm. But as China grew richer, distant cities became magnets for youth and Tuojia's population had fallen by half. Most remaining villagers were too old to find urban work or too young to leave, often just small children entrusted to grandparents while their mothers and fathers labored in factories far away.

Both groups were destined to go within a few decades, and David expected that within a generation, Tuojia would be empty. As we gazed across a landscape that looked like a classical Chinese scroll painting, he said that he enjoyed returning home but never wanted to stay more than a week or two. "It's very peaceful here but also boring," he said as we peered through cracks in the door to his former house. "This is not our future."

———

Even so, I'd traveled to Tuojia looking for hints about the future. While half of China's 1.3 billion people now live in cities, the other half—often ignored, sometimes forgotten—remains in the countryside. Most live in ways approximating life in Tuojia, and the differences between China's rich coastal cities and its countless tiny hamlets carries a profound message about how China's rise will remake the planet over the twenty-first century.

That message was not immediately obvious as I sat in my Beijing office months earlier. I wanted to understand China's growing impact on the world's climate and, at first, thought I should focus my reporting on the country's most modern, fast-paced cities—Shanghai and Shenzhen.

I'd visited Shenzhen half a dozen times over the years and knew that it represents the pinnacle of China's incredible growth. Little more than a small fishing village in the 1970s, it had taken off in 1980, when Deng Xiaoping declared it one of China's first "special economic zones," pockets of the socialist country where the government began to experiment with capitalism. Between 1980 and 2007, Shenzhen's economy grew at an average rate of 28 percent annually, possibly the fastest sustained economic growth of any city anywhere ever. As its fortunes rose, its population swelled to 18 million, almost twice the size of Los Angeles, and large downtown areas began to resemble New York and London.

Shanghai, on the other hand, represents the peak of China's growing consumerism. While Shenzhen's origins lay with China's top leaders, Shanghai has deep capitalist roots. After defeating the imperial Chinese army in the Opium War of the mid-nineteenth century, Britain forced the emperor to open a series of treaty ports where foreigners could trade with Chinese merchants. Shanghai became the most important, growing into Asia's largest city—the so-called Paris of the East—by the 1920s. Under Mao it suffered for its early riches: as happened across China, its businesses were taken over by the state and its numerous bars, brothels, and casinos were closed.

But in Deng-era China, Shanghai returned with a vengeance: private entrepreneurs thrived and foreigners flocked back, attracted by the city's pro-capitalist, grande dame history. As China's economy grew, it was remade: across the Huangpu River from the Bund—the row of stately financial institutions and hotels built with nineteenth-century money on the river's south bank—a new city emerged in seemingly endless rows of apartment blocks and skyscrapers.

As it regained its wealth, Shanghai embraced the nation's emerging consumer ethic faster than any other city. The average household in Shanghai today owns more consumer goods than households in any other part of the country: two air conditioners, almost two color televisions, a refrigerator, 1.3 computers, more than two mobile phones. In 2010, the disposable income of the average city household was almost $5,000, two-thirds higher than the country as a whole, and Shanghainese had developed carbon footprints larger than residents of the United Kingdom, finally surpassing the country that laid its cornerstone more than a century earlier.[1]

The more I thought about what would drive China's carbon emissions—in 2010 equal to one-quarter of the world's total—however, the more I realized that I needed to spend time among its quieter half, the 650 million people who are just beginning to experience modern material life.[2] While Shanghai, Shenzhen, and China's other megacities are the country's economic engines, to truly feel the pull of its growth, I needed to visit Tuojia.

* * *

If one thing defines how China's rapid growth will reshape the physical world, it is climate change. But that was hard to see when I first arrived in the country in 1996. Global warming was just emerging as a widespread concern and, despite its massive population, China played a small role in global negotiations. It had been only four years since 154 nations—including China and the United States—had signed the UN Framework Convention on Climate Change, a treaty—often called the UNFCCC—that aimed for "the stabilization of greenhouse gas concentrations in the atmosphere at a level that would prevent dangerous anthropogenic interference with the climate system." Most important, China's emissions were less than half of what they are today and arriving in the country it was impossible to imagine that within a decade it would surpass the United States as the world's top emitter.[3]

Instead, my first impression was of darkness. As the plane carrying my Peace Corps group banked toward Beijing, I peered out my window at countryside punctuated by a handful of scattered single lights and thought for a moment that I was looking up at a clear night sky. After we collected our luggage from a creaky baggage carousel, we rode into the city on a highway lined with trees that faded into blackness. We checked into an upscale hotel a few minutes' walk from Tiananmen Square, but at eight or nine o'clock on a weekday night, only a few cars zipped along the roads outside.

The next day, I woke early and wandered through traditional lanes where locals hustled to shared public toilets and gathered for group exercises. Some bought fruits and vegetables from salesmen who displayed their goods on bicycle carts. A couple dressed in pajamas languidly hit a shuttlecock back and forth. Later that day an official at the U.S. embassy told our group that China's electrical capacity was only large enough to simultaneously provide each citizen with a steady stream of 150 watts. In the United States, the average capacity was twenty times greater. "In the United States, everybody could turn on their oven and their hair dryer," he said. In China, everyone could turn on a lightbulb.

That disparity left China a distant top contributor to global warming. In 1998, the Energy Information Administration (EIA), the information hub of the U.S. Department of Energy, estimated that China wouldn't surpass the United States as the world's top contributor until sometime between 2015 and 2020.[4] Other experts were more sanguine. In 2006, Elizabeth Kolbert, the author of *Field Notes from a Catastrophe*, wrote that China was "expected to overtake the United States as the world's largest carbon emitter around 2025."[5]

The sense that China's trajectory wouldn't put it atop the international emissions list for several decades left global warming a low priority among journalists in the country: despite its rapid growth, China seemed too rural and poor to change the physical planet. It also appeared to be a technological laggard: most of its factories were old and used outdated technologies, making it one of the world's least energy-efficient nations. (Even a decade later China would need two and a half times as much energy as the United States and nearly nine times as much as ultra-efficient Japan to earn the same number of dollars.)[6] If the world needed a high-tech Industrial Revolution to swap its fossil fuel–burning power plants, cars, and factories for wind turbines and solar panels, it seemed obvious that the technology would come from the world's rich, technologically advanced nations.

Since then, two things have radically shifted the picture: China proved the world's top energy analysts disastrously conservative and, despite its relative poverty, Western nations began to consider China a major competitor that should be forced to make similar commitments to cut greenhouse gas emissions, kick-starting an era of contentious politics about so far unanswered questions: When should China and other developing nations, which under the UNFCCC accepted only monitoring, cut back on fossil fuel use? And if the world accepts a fixed budget for carbon emissions, how should it be divided?

The first shift became obvious in 2007. The Netherlands Environmental Assessment Agency, a research group that advises the Dutch government, released a report helpfully titled "China Now No. 1 in CO_2 Emissions; USA in Second Position." Basing its computations on various sources—including that China produced almost half of the world's cement, which creates carbon dioxide in the production process—the group showed that Chinese emissions increased almost 9 percent in 2006 to overtake the United States, where emissions had declined slightly.[7]

The second shift started earlier but has grown into the most difficult issue facing climate change negotiations. In July 1997, five months before negotiators meeting in Kyoto, Japan, created the Kyoto Protocol—the treaty that put specific targets on the Framework Convention—the U.S. Senate unanimously passed the Byrd-Hagel resolution. Sponsored by Senator Robert Byrd (D-WV) and Senator Charles Hagel (R-NE), the resolution declared that the United States would not accept any global warming treaty that did "serious harm" to the American economy or exempted developing countries, which the senators feared would make life harder for American manufacturers. China was at the front of their minds. "We could see that China would eventually overtake the United States in greenhouse gases," Hagel would later say.[8]

In China, however, the calculus was radically different. Its leaders argued that a fair treaty should account for historical emissions, a method that would give them a much larger share of future emissions. (The United States and Europe are each responsible for almost 30 percent of total global carbon emissions between 1850 and 2000, while China accounted for only 7 percent; India and other poorer countries used a fraction of that.)[9] China also argued for per capita accounting, a standard by which their emissions are also small, before the recent U.S. recession roughly one quarter of the American average.[10]

Taken together, the negotiator argued, China should be able to emit much more than they had. "As for China's impact on surrounding countries, I'm first to admit the problem," Pan Yue, a former deputy minister of China's State Environmental Protection Agency, told the *Wall Street Journal* in 2004. "But let's talk about this in the context of international fairness. Whose development model are we emulating? Who has been shifting all of its pollution-heavy factories to China? . . . And who bears an even greater international responsibility than China—but has yet to shoulder it—on matters like greenhouse gas emissions?"[11]

The situation was further complicated in the United States because people began to talk about China's emissions not in terms of global warming but in the terms laid out by the Byrd-Hagel resolution: the American quality of life and American jobs. As it happened, Hagel attended the 1997 meeting that created the Kyoto Protocol and, on his way home, he stopped in Sichuan Province. He asked to meet a few Peace Corps volunteers, and four of us were shuffled into Chengdu, the provincial capital, for breakfast at a five-star hotel, a welcome escape from our unheated apartments an hour to the north.

As we ate, we talked about teaching in China, and Hagel talked about the Kyoto meeting. I had been busy studying Chinese when the Byrd-Hagel resolution passed and didn't have good questions, but my memory is that he supported global action. A few weeks later, however, I was back in Pengzhou, reading a *Newsweek* magazine on my fifth-floor balcony, brushing coal ash off each page as I turned it, and I came across an article that described the debate. One fact particularly caught my eye: U.S. opponents of the Kyoto Protocol had spent millions of dollars on negative advertising, arguing that cutting fossil fuel use "would send the economy into the toilet, push jobs overseas, force drivers out of their Range Rovers and basically condemn Americans to drinking warm beer in a cold house." Hagel was a chief spokesman: "We will kill this bill," he declared.[12]

The story provided a coming-of-age moment. Besides the fact that I had happily given up driving for two years and often enjoyed drinking warm beer in my cold apartment, I realized that Hagel had misrepresented himself to our small China-knowledgeable, climate-concerned group. The lesson was that at least some politicians would do whatever was to their political benefit. It seemed an ominous sign for the future.

Personal experience also began to color how I thought about global warming. By 2007, when the Netherlands Environmental Assessment Agency announced that China had become the world's top carbon emitter, I was working as a journalist. The news intrigued me, and I reported a series of stories about Asia's vulnerabilities to a warming planet. Partly I wanted to study the physics of climate change: like many Americans, I had thought of global warming as a potential problem for future generations, but the speed of China's emissions growth worried me. I also wanted to understand how climate change was affecting average people, and as I traveled to Australia, Tuvalu, and India over the coming months, the problem became increasingly personal.

In Australia, I drove six hours from Sydney to Griffith, a small farm town reliant on irrigation water pumped from the Murray River. The local river basin was experiencing the worst drought in recorded history—with below-average rainfall for more than six years—and the national government had decided that a warming trend might mean that the drought was less an anomaly than a new state of normal. Since 1950, Australia's average temperature had risen by 1.6 degrees Fahrenheit and computer models predicted it would rise another 2 degrees by 2030. A study by scientists at the Commonwealth Scientific and Industrial Research Organization, the Australian government's chief think tank, found that parts of southern Australia would get 15 percent less rainfall by 2015, a decrease sharply magnified by the fact that only a small fraction of rainwater ever reaches rivers.[13] To deal with what they saw as a new, drier climate, officials had cut allocations of irrigation water and opened a market in water rights. In many communities, water had become more valuable than land.

The human dynamic, however, was harder. Families that have spent their lives farming don't give up easily, and many were barely hanging on, investing in seeds and fertilizer, praying for rain, and then watching their crops wither and die. Suicides had spiked as farmers went bankrupt. "There's no sign of rain, there's no hope, and some people think there's just no point in going on," Margaret Brown, a vice president at the New South Wales County Women's Association, told me.

I spent a morning with Joe and Alice Dalbroi, third-generation farmers who were slowly losing their life savings but refused to pull the plug. Joe's grandfather had moved from Italy to start the farm in 1925 and Joe had run it for twenty-five years. "I can't get out," he said. "This is everything I know."

Alice, a friendly woman who puttered around their kitchen making coffee and sandwiches, worried more about their daughters. Both had married dry-land farmers—farmers with no access to irrigation water—and neither had brought in crops for several years. "Climate change could mean there's just going to be a drought ongoing," she said. "We can retire soon, but what will they do?"

A week later, I flew to Tuvalu, the world's fourth-smallest nation, to talk with residents about the possibility—some say inevitability—that their tiny South Pacific country will be swallowed by rising waters. Tuvalu is composed of nine coral atolls that could have been borrowed from Gauguin paintings. Five hundred miles north of Fiji, they're forested with palm trees and ringed by coral reefs. Altogether, its land covers less than ten square miles, but the atolls wrap around a huge lagoon and life there has the laid-back vibe of a Jimmy Buffet song: residents can sleep away their mornings and get lunch simply by climbing a coconut palm or dropping a net in the ocean. Hunger is unheard of.

Global warming, however, had given Tuvalu's nine thousand citizens a sense of foreboding. Excluding trees, the country's highest natural feature is a mound of coral and dirt nine feet above sea level. Most is significantly lower, just two or three feet above the ocean. As the world's average temperature climbed by 1.4 degrees Fahrenheit over the twentieth century, the average sea level rose by eight inches.[14] But the sea is not really level: tides, winds, and solar energy, which causes water to expand, mean parts of the world experience greater change than others, and between 1993 and 2007 a gauge installed on Tuvalu's largest atoll had shown a rise of three inches. Since 2000, seawater had bubbled through the ground in the capital during the year's highest tides, killing crops and flooding the airport. Rogue waves—large waves formed in calm weather—had washed across the city twice.

I rented a scooter and rode around Fongafale, Tuvalu's largest island, introducing myself to people and asking questions. Garry Clarke, a New Zealander who ran a meteorological outpost, said hurricanes in Tuvalu's South Pacific neighborhood had become more common and more intense as the ocean warmed. (Hurricanes draw their energy from warm water.) Perpetua Latasi, the government's chief climate change officer, worried about large areas of coral that had bleached and died.

I was interested in what is expected to be a growing surge of climate change refugees—people pushed off their land by floods, droughts, and rising seas—and visited Enele Sopoaga, Tuvalu's first UN ambassador.[15] But when I asked Sopoaga whether Tuvaluans would move, he said such thinking was dangerous. The nation's first priority was to get the world to reduce its greenhouse gas emissions. "The danger in talking about who might take us if we are forced to move is that it's too easy," he said. "They could put us in Nevada or Brisbane and that would be much cheaper than cutting back on emissions. But we don't want to move. This is our home."

Two months later, I flew to India's Bihar Province to visit a village named Basahi. The 2007 monsoon had set a record for most of the province, dumping three feet of water over twenty days, and in August the local Budhi Gandak River, a Ganges tributary, had breached a levee and sent a small tsunami crashing through the town, killing twenty-two people.

India had warmed by an average of 1.2 degrees Fahrenheit over the previous century, and because warmer air holds more water, scientists had predicted increased flooding. (For every increase of 18 degrees Fahrenheit, air holds twice as much water vapor.) A study by Indian researchers found that the number of "very heavy events"—defined as storms that dropped at least 5.9 inches of rain in a single day—had doubled since 1951. The Indian Red Cross had tripled the number of states where it stored emergency flood supplies, a shift that a spokesman likened to a "sea change" for the organization.

The United Nations had called the year's floods the worst in living memory; some 41 million people in India, Nepal, and Bangladesh had suffered losses.

Three months after the levee breached, Basahi looked apocalyptic: collapsed concrete buildings tilted at odd angles from a slowly evaporating lake; hundreds of villagers had built makeshift wood-and-plastic shelters atop a hill of sandbags; because their fields had been flooded, most had nothing to do. My guide introduced me to Ram Kumar Mahto, a thirty-two-year-old whose young daughter had died in the flood. Mahto had set up a small shrine to Vishnu, the Hindu god believed to offer protection, and as I was leaving, he tugged on my shirt. "Maybe you can pray for us," he said quietly.

———

Back in Beijing I began to study climate change and realized how hard it will be to reduce global greenhouse gas emissions. It is obvious to anyone living in a developed nation how completely we rely on fossil fuels: from the alarm clocks and coffee makers that wake us up to what we eat for breakfast—usually food grown with fossil fuel–based fertilizers—to how we get to and from jobs and how we entertain ourselves, almost all of it is powered by coal, oil, and natural gas. But it is still surprising just how reliant we are: globally, more than 80 percent of energy comes from burning fossil fuels, and despite the recent growth of alternative energy (primarily nuclear, hydro, wind, and solar), that ratio has remained largely unchanged over the past three decades, the very period when we have recognized the threat posed by climate change.[16]

At the same time, we have gotten much busier. A graph of the world's carbon dioxide emissions from burning fossil fuels starting near the beginning of the Industrial Revolution and ending in the modern era looks like the profile of a steep mountain: in 1870, the world burned almost no fossil fuels; today we burn enough to release more than 30 billion tons of CO_2 each year.

GLOBAL CO$_2$ EMISSIONS FROM FOSSIL FUEL COMBUSTION

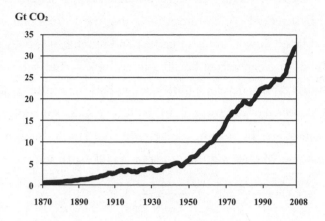

Gt CO$_2$

Source: IEA/OECD, "CO$_2$ Emissions from Fuel Combustion Highlights," 2011 ed., p. 19, fig. 14. Based on data from the Carbon Dioxide Information Analysis Center, Oak Ridge National Laboratory, U.S. Department of Energy.

At first glance, the most interesting thing about the diagram is that almost all of the rise happened after 1950, when the United States and other industrialized countries settled into their post–World War II growth spurts. (The world's population rose from 2.5 billion to 7 billion and its economy increased more than eightfold.)[17]

If we think about the future, however, shifts in *who* is driving that upward spike are more important. Between 1990 and 2009, the percentage of energy supplied by fossil fuels in the United States and European Union fell and few new coal-fired power plants were built.[18] Yet the developing world—driven primarily by China—added demand at a much faster rate. China's energy consumption nearly tripled between 1990 and 2009, and it met almost all of that increase by burning more fossil fuels. Today, fossil fuels—primarily coal, which is the most carbon-rich of the group—supply 87 percent of China's energy.[19] (The best black coal is almost pure carbon; if you burn a ton of it, you create four tons of carbon dioxide.)

If China maintains its current policies, its total demand is expected to almost double again by 2035, *adding* demand equivalent to what the United States now uses. According to the International Energy Agency, a think tank established by twenty-eight countries including the United States, most of Europe, and Japan, it would meet that demand roughly as it does today: 87 percent would be generated by burning fossil fuels.[20] And it has become a model for other rapidly developing nations: without significant policy shifts, the world is expected to add three times the current U.S. demand by 2035, 80 percent of it generated by burning coal, gas, and oil, a ratio almost perfectly in line with how the West grew during its era of rapid expansion.[21]

––––––––

If there is no change in course, the impact of that growth on the world's climate will be enormous. The International Energy Agency—which no one confuses with Greenpeace—finds that if governments maintain their current policies, the planet will warm by 6 degrees Celsius or more, enough to entirely rearrange life on Earth. A similar temperature spike some 250 million years ago is thought to have caused the extinction of 95 percent of species alive during the Permian period, an event some scientists have dubbed the "Great Dying." (The cause of the warming is contested, but geologists have shown that it corresponded with a rapid rise in atmospheric carbon levels.)[22]

Even if the world achieves all of the various promises governments have made to curb greenhouse gas emissions—such as largely unrealized commitments under the Kyoto Protocol and a vow by Barack Obama to reduce U.S. emissions by 17 percent over the next decade—the world's atmosphere would build up greenhouse gases "consistent with a long-term average temperature increase of more than 3.5 degrees" Celsius, enough that it might cause the world's seas to rise 6.5 feet.[23]

Both levels would likely trigger "climate feedbacks" where the natural world begins to release massive amounts of stored greenhouse gases on top of whatever communities emit. The Amazon rain forest, for example, may dry and burn, releasing 100 billion tons of carbon stored in its plant life. Permafrost—ground that has been permanently frozen, sometimes for hundreds of thousands of years—will thaw increasingly rapidly, releasing much more. (Estimates of how much carbon is stored in the world's permafrost run as high as 1.5 trillion tons, about two and a half times the amount currently held in the atmosphere.)[24]

There are countless other possible feedbacks, and one study found that at least some are likely to be triggered by a temperature rise of between 2 and 5 degrees Celsius.[25] If they are triggered, whatever governments do probably won't matter: we would become passive observers as the temperature spikes upward.

———

How China's rise is ratcheting up the threat of climate change was driven home to me by an environmental economist named Wang Tao. Wang worked for Britain's Tyndall Centre for Climate Change Research, one of the world's top institutes studying global warming, and he had written a report that struck me for its realism: given China's rapid growth, it accepted that the world will not be able to limit warming to 2 degrees Celsius.

In climate change research circles, that acceptance is almost heretical. The 2-degree Celsius goal was written into accords signed at UNFCCC meetings in Copenhagen and Cancun, and hundreds of researchers have found ways to massage China's growth so it fits within that planetary budget. If, for example, modelers anticipate China's economy slowing, they can significantly reduce its total emissions. Other researchers put China on a crash course away from fossil fuels: a report by scientists at the Lawrence Berkeley National Laboratory envisioned that over half of China's electricity might be generated by nuclear power in 2050.[26] Still other researchers have held down China's emissions by requiring its power plants to catch most of their carbon and bury it underground, a yet unproven engineering solution called carbon capture and storage that may pose serious health risks.

The reports showed that (for China and every other country) limiting greenhouse gas emissions is technically feasible. But they lost sight of political reality: each of the solutions would pose significant costs to the Chinese economy and, given China's focus on growth, they struck me as overly optimistic.

Wang's report, by contrast, seemed refreshingly honest. Wang had been born in a midsized city in Sichuan Province in 1980, and he understood the speed of Chinese change: the things that fascinate foreigners—buildings that seem to sprout from fields; empty highways that clog with traffic over a year or two—were normal to him and, looking across China, he didn't see things slowing down. He knew that hundreds of millions of rural Chinese will move to urban areas over the coming decades, a migration that will require China to build the equivalent of a Philadelphia-sized city every month until 2025.[27] He knew that those new urbanites would use almost twice as much energy as they had in rural areas.[28] And he knew that China's long-frugal urbanites were beginning to enjoy their new wealth. Families that had socked away money for decades were taking trips and buying cars. In 2009, years ahead of what experts predicted, China would surpass the United States as the world's largest automobile market. (Sales of passenger cars rose from 336,000 in 1995 to 8.7 million in 2009.)[29] Domestic air travel was rising exponentially, increasing seventeenfold between 1990 and 2010.[30] China's economy had grown 11 percent in 2007, the year before Wang wrote the report, and he and a colleague estimated that it would be between eight and thirteen times larger by 2050.[31]

Given that growth and China's political realities, Wang decided that limiting the world's temperature increase to 2 degrees was impractical to "a plausible global pathway." So he and a colleague decided to find ways that carbon dioxide could be stabilized in the atmosphere at around 450 parts per million, an amount that probably has not existed for 3 or 4 million years.[32]

This was not an ideal solution. According to the Intergovernmental Panel on Climate Change (IPCC), the thousands of scientists assembled by the United Nations to study global warming, an atmospheric concentration of 450 parts per million would likely cause the temperature to increase by 3 degrees Celsius above preindustrial levels.[33] Sitting in Beijing on a cold November night, an extra 3 degrees—5.4 degrees Fahrenheit—sounds good, but it would cause widespread havoc: more severe floods, droughts, and hurricanes and sea levels that would rise, on average, between two and six feet, enough to put much of Miami, London, and Shanghai underwater.[34]

But having grown up in China and realizing that the Chinese are unlikely to abandon their dreams of owning bigger houses and driving cars and taking international trips, Wang decided that it was important to be realistic. China has rich coal and natural gas deposits and—with the exception of hydroelectric dams—burning them provides the cheapest energy.[35] Unless the developed world transfers billions of dollars to subsidize clean energy, the Chinese are likely to use what they have. "A practical problem with using lower global budgets is that they make it more difficult to develop a plausible global emissions pathway," he finally wrote. "This is not to say that we agree to accept a higher risk of temperature rise, but to illustrate the challenging task we face."

———

When I met Wang in Beijing two years after the report was published, he was even more convinced that squeezing China into a small budget did not make sense. Since 2008, the world's carbon emissions had increased—in 2010 reaching a record 9.1 billion tons—and global negotiations seemed stuck.[36] "The world is treating climate change like an ostrich," Wang said. "We're just burying our heads in the sand and hoping the problem goes away."

When I asked if he thought negotiators might still find a way to limit the global temperature rise to 2 degrees Celsius, he replied that most experts had given up on that target. "Some scientists and officials still talk about it publicly, but privately they've made this decision," he said. "Almost none of the world's countries are making the needed reductions."

When I taught English in Sichuan Province, David quickly became one of my favorite students. During my first week, he called me over to his desk. "Mr. Simons, do you know that China looks like a rooster?" he asked.

He pulled out a map and showed me how the country's northeastern provinces look like a rooster's crowned head pushing into Russia and North Korea. Xinjiang and Tibet, its huge, lightly populated western provinces, form a billowing tail. Hainan, an island province that sits in the South China Sea, was an egg laid by a hen the rooster had befriended. Then he traced his finger west up the Yangtze River from Shanghai to Chongqing and, just south of the river, made a mark to show where he had grown up: Tuojia.

Over the intervening years I had visited David a half dozen times as his life progressed from being a student to being a married teacher and father. Each time, I learned a little more about Tuojia (pronounced tour-jah). On one trip, David told me that, in 1996, it had taken him three days to get from the village to Chengdu Teachers College. Even today no roads run to Tuojia and he had carried his suitcases two hours to where he caught a rickety bus to the Wu River, a Yangtze tributary. From there he had taken a two-day ferry trip to Chongqing, a twelve-hour train ride to Chengdu, and an hour-long bus journey to Pengzhou.

A few years later, he emailed me photographs of rice paddies surrounded by low, forested mountains. He followed up with a note:

Dear Mr. Simons:

I am glad to hear from you! And also I am very glad that you like the photos taken in my hometown. Yeah, the photos were taken in my hometown where I was born. The people are very traditional and friendly. Some of the people have never been to any other places out of my hometown. As you saw, the mountains are covered with trees and you can enjoy the green with pleasure, and people use the wood to set fire to cook dinner from the old to nowadays. Yeah, my hometown is a little different from the other places which you've ever visited. Do you know why? Because there are few big factories there. The air is so nice and fresh. We may even drink the water in the spring. Years ago, people carried the water every day, but now with the development of the world, people take water with the pipe more, but some people still do the traditional things in the morning every day, and there we can really enjoy the blue sky, it is quite different from that of Cheng Du. You also can enjoy the quiet and beautiful night. Some animals are sleeping in the daytime, but they come out for dinner at night, so you could hear them shout or fight at night. Of course, they live on people's crops like wild boars and so on. If you would like to go, I will show you around. I am sure you will love my beautiful hometown.

———

It took me over a year to take David up on his offer but, on a damp, gray January day, we set out together from Chengdu. David was thirty-five but after a decade and a half of teaching, he looked older. He had begun to bald and combed a wing of hair across the top of his head. He wore black slacks, a heavy gray jacket, and a pair of battered leather boots. In personality, he was like many teachers I knew: quick to laugh but also capable of becoming suddenly stern, a good skill for keeping teenagers in line. He saw his parents only once or twice a year and was carrying gifts. He had tied an electric hotplate up in string and would later buy a color television, the first his parents would own and one of the first in Tuojia.

At the beginning of our trip, we stood on a perfectly clean subway platform looking at a map with various colored lines. Many of the stations reflected Chengdu's ambitions: scattered among more traditional names were High-Tech Zone, Financial City, Century City, and Incubation Park. Near where we boarded, a mall was filled with luxury brands—Gucci, Louis Vuitton, Fendi, Dior—a reminder that China's interior is quickly catching up with Shanghai's consumerist ways.

Where we got off at Chengdu's North Train Station, the view was more reminiscent of my time as a Peace Corps volunteer. Tens of thousands of people crowded around the front of the building waiting for trains to take them home for New Year celebrations. A line to get through security disintegrated into a game of competitive Twister: everyone seized every inch of space to push forward.

We had tickets for one of China's new high-speed trains and fought our way through the crowds to board just before it pulled out of the station precisely on time. After the throng outside, entering the spotless cabin was like stepping back into the modern world, and I felt a kind of cultural whiplash: in China one moves repeatedly between outdated and futuristic environments, from backward to world-class technology.

We took our assigned seats—themselves a new concept on many Chinese trains—and watched a government propaganda video touting China's top tourist attractions. And then the train began to glide silently forward, rolling past a line of cranes and apartment buildings and glass-and-steel shopping malls. A screen displayed the indoor and outdoor temperatures and our speed. As it ticked up to 125 miles an hour, the city bled into the countryside: neat fields of winter wheat and rapeseed, bamboo groves, villages and towns cut by high-tension power lines, highways that stretched like ribbons across the flat land.

———

The train was a potent symbol of China's rise. The country had opened its first high-speed line—carrying trains capable of traveling at an average of at least 125 miles per hour—in 2007. Four years later, it had built the world's largest network. The United States, by contrast, has been talking about building a high-speed network for many years but, in 2012, had built only one commercial line considered "high speed"—the Amtrak Acela Express between Washington and Boston—and it would not count in China: the Acela reaches 150 miles per hour several times during its trip, but its average speed is half the Chinese standard.[37]

As I sat watching rural China blur by, I contemplated that disparity. China's ability to build world-class infrastructure rapidly is unmatched. But it reveals only part of the picture. Since the media (both Western and Chinese) tend to focus on China's most impressive growth—its most ambitious plans, fastest expansions, and greatest achievements—many Westerners have developed skewed views of the country. Few remember that for every high-speed train, there are dozens of slow, lumbering models left from the Deng Xiaoping era, packed with people unable to afford more expensive tickets. (David and I each paid the equivalent of $19 for our two-hour trip to Chongqing.) And because most foreigners who visit China spend their time in its biggest cities, it is easy for them to forget about the 650 million people— more than twice the population of the United States—still living in rural areas and moving between towns, cities, and rural homes: for months or years they take distant jobs, but when factories close or they've earned enough or become burnt out enough, they go home.

————

Most of China's "floating population" also goes home for Chinese New Year. Two hours after we left Chengdu, we were standing on a crowded concrete platform in northern Chongqing watching a police officer try to jam thirty people—including us—into a train car that seemed unable to fit anyone else. Inside the car, travelers had commandeered the entire aisle to sit on plastic stools and buckets. Others leaned against each other or walls. A few had shut themselves into a tiny bathroom that emptied directly onto the tracks. A man was propped against a huge sack of potatoes. Another had shoved a dozen four-foot-long bags of toilet paper into an overhead rack, caus-ing a slight commotion. ("That's a strange New Year's gift," a woman near me said. "Maybe he wants to sell them," someone offered.)

After the officer had forced a hole large enough that we could board, we engaged in another game of Twister, and I ended up wedged against the wall near the train's door. Over the next few hours, I got to know my neighbors well. A middle-aged construction worker told me about his job and how he had learned to live on 1,000 yuan (the equivalent of $160) a month and save the rest of his 4,000 yuan paycheck "in case anyone in my family needs it." A forty-year-old woman described the factory where she worked in southern China. She returned home to see her teenage daughter only once a year and was carrying a set of heat lamps the girl could use while she studied.

The train trundled slowly through a string of small towns and cities. In one, a twenty-five-year-old named Li Fang boarded and was quickly pushed against the wall with me. Li worked for a company that created architectural designs for foreign clients and earned the equivalent of $1,500 each month, a solid Chinese middle-class wage. When I told him I was working on a book about the environment, he said that China had adopted the model of "killing the chicken to get the egg."

"We're sacrificing the environment and our resources to get rich and we aren't going to be able to sustain it," he said. "The problem is, we can't slow down. We've got too many people and everyone wants more."

That was also the message of the train crammed with workers heading home from various corners of China for what is often their only annual holiday. "If we use only one word to describe our farmers, it's poor," Li said. "We're poor."

On its website the U.S. Environmental Protection Agency offers a tool they call a Household Emissions Calculator. Anyone can answer seventeen questions to calculate how many pounds of carbon dioxide they or their family emits each year. Then it offers suggestions to reduce the number.[38]

According to the site, the average two-person American household is responsible for 41,500 pounds—nineteen tons—of carbon dioxide annually. In homes, the largest share of energy—at 36 percent—goes to air conditioning. Lighting's share is 15 percent and refrigeration accounts for another 8 percent.[39]

One afternoon before we left for Tuojia, David and I sat down one afternoon and worked through the questions. To the first—"How many people live in your home?"—David answered two. He had divorced several years earlier and lived with his eight-year-old son, Zhang Yuge, who had taken the English name Edmund. For "What is your household's primary heating source?": natural gas, oil, electricity, propane, wood, or "I do not heat my house," he chose "I do not heat my house."

David worked as a middle-school English teacher, and he earned the equivalent of $630 a month, an amount that didn't allow many luxuries.[40] For "household vehicles," he listed a Lifan Flying Dragon motorcycle he had bought seven years earlier for $850. With a few calculations to convert kilometers to miles and liters to gallons, we determined that he used about a third of a gallon of gasoline each week. For "home energy," he entered that he and Edmund used just over one thousand cubic feet of natural gas and two hundred kilowatt-hours of electricity each month. They used no oil or propane. Another question asked if they "currently purchase green power," which the website defined as "electricity produced from solar, wind, geothermal, biogas and low-impact small hydroelectric sources." A dam a few dozen miles away produced electricity, but it couldn't be considered low-impact and David thought his electricity was produced as it is in most of China: by burning coal. So we checked the box marked no.

The next section, entitled "Waste," asked if David recycled cans, plastic, glass, newspapers, and magazines. Like most Chinese cities, his did not have an obvious municipal recycling program, but hundreds of people made their livings by picking through trash and sorting out anything with value.[41] We checked yes for all the boxes, cutting the amount of carbon David and Edmund's waste generated to almost half of the U.S. average. At the end of the process, a small box at the bottom of the screen showed that, together, they emitted 5,330 pounds of carbon dioxide each year, one-eighth of the American two-person-household average.[42]

The last section suggested ways David could reduce household emissions. If he performed regular maintenance on his motorcycle, he might cut twenty-three pounds of carbon dioxide. If he turned the thermostat from seventy-nine to eighty-two degrees Fahrenheit during the summer, he could save another ninety-one pounds. But he already did most of what it suggested: he turned off appliances he wasn't using, washed laundry in cold water and air-dried it, and used only compact fluorescent lightbulbs. The Household Emissions Calculator computed that if he and Edmund did everything suggested, they could save only 114 pounds of carbon dioxide each year, the equivalent of driving a Ford Explorer between New York City and Philadelphia.[43]

––––––––

After we finished with David and Edmund, we worked through the carbon emissions for David's parents. There were just the two of them: Zhang Dejun, David's father, who was sixty-four but strong enough to wrestle a two-hundred-pound pig, and Jiao Huichun, his mother. They didn't heat their house and collected wood for cooking. They owned a cow, a few chickens, and—for a few more days—a pig, but no vehicle. Electrical lines had reached Tuojia in 1980, but they began to use electricity only in 1982, when they installed their first lightbulb.

Almost thirty years later they had used—in total—less than a typical American house uses in a week or two. Other than a few more lights, their next purchase of anything that required electricity had been a telephone in 2002. In 2007, they bought an electric grain grinder for use during the harvest. In 2009, they added a cell phone. Between 2006 and 2011, they had used a total of 469.5 kilowatt-hours of electricity, and we figured their use at 10 kilowatt-hours a month, enough to run a single 100-watt bulb for just over three hours every day.

The Household Emissions Calculator told us that they produced 1,269 pounds of carbon dioxide each year, thirty-two times less than the average American two-person household, and when we looked for ways they could reduce their emissions, there were basically none. They had no vehicle to maintain, no thermostat to adjust, no electronics—save the cell phone they use to call their children—to turn off. To save money, David had already fitted the home's four lights with low-wattage bulbs.

More important, Zhang and Jiao were careful consumers. When I asked David's father about their annual budget a few days later, he broke it down to the last yuan. He had earned the equivalent of $800 in 2011 selling grain and vegetables—a fairly typical annual income for local farmers—and spent almost $200 on fertilizer.[44] He spent $5 each month on telephone bills and just over a dollar on electricity. Every two days, he smoked a 50-cent pack of cigarettes and drank a quarter's worth of *baijiu*, the Chinese grain alcohol. His wife had gotten sick that year, and they had spent $80 on medical bills. They bought a shirt and two pairs of pants and restocked their kitchen condiments (salt, soy sauce, vinegar, oil, chili peppers). "In the end, we can't save," he said.

But they were happy with what they had and looked forward to the small, incremental additions that David provided. Zhang particularly wanted to watch television, but he worried about their electricity bill. After David plugged in the electric hot plate he had brought from Chengdu, I found Zhang examining the spinning dials of a meter mounted on the side of his house.

"We used to use only two or three kilowatt-hours each month," he said. "Now with the hot plate and television, we'll probably use twenty."

To understand what China's rise means for the global climate, it helps to think about the Zhangs. Unlike in the United States, where families can cut their energy use simply by changing wasteful habits—turning down air conditioners, carpooling and biking more, turning off unused lights and electronics (which consume 45 percent of electricity used in American homes)—for most Chinese, reductions would come at steep costs: many people would literally have to switch off the lights they are currently using or give up access to things Westerners take for granted: telephones, computers, refrigerators, televisions.[45]

As China gets richer, we can instead expect its citizens to scale up. As they can afford more electricity, they will heat and cool more and will buy more of the electronic gadgets common in the West. When they have enough money, they will buy cars to take advantage of what will soon be the world's most extensive highway network.

They will also fly more. Like Fidelis in Papua New Guinea, David reminded me how much people new to travel yearn to see the world. He had flown for the first time the year before, and on our way to Tuojia, he showed me a few dozen photographs he had taken on the plane—of the flight attendants, the overhead bins, the in-flight meal, other passengers. "I wanted to know the difference between an airplane and a bus or train, so I took some photos," he said.

The flight had been to Malaysia and, from his window, David saw the ocean for the first time. When I asked how it felt to look down at that great blue expanse, his eyes widened: "It was great," he recalled. "So great."

———

Since half of China's 1.3 billion people live more or less like David's parents and another 400 or 500 million live like David and Edmund—they are installing air conditioning and heating for the first time, beginning to take their first flights, and considering buying their first cars—their experience is instructive.[46] As China becomes richer, those billion-plus people not yet in the middle and affluent classes will create the biggest wave of new personal consumption ever, and for people who worry about climate change, that built-in growth is often enough to spur a trip to the bar. This is partly because China's rise—and behind it the rise of the rest—will dwarf the various piecemeal improvements Western environmentalists have struggled for years to encourage, and sometimes force, governments to make. In the United States, for example, environmental groups have spent decades fighting for higher vehicle fuel-efficiency standards. A proposal by the Obama administration in late 2011 to almost double the average efficiency of new cars and light trucks was hailed as a major victory, not least because it set a positive example for the developing world.

But then one looks at China. In 2000, the country's vehicle fleet totaled about 15 million, roughly twelve for every thousand people. Eleven years later it had grown to 125 million, almost half the size of the U.S. fleet. By 2030, China's total—including motorcycles and tractors—is expected to number at least 600 million and could reach almost 1 billion.[47] "The sheer numbers of and future projections for China's vehicle fleet illuminate the energy and climate implications of China's on-road transportation, both at home and abroad," the authors of a 2011 report by the Carnegie Endowment for International Peace wrote. "Oil consumption, climate change, and air pollution will be pervasive concerns that China must reconcile as it motorizes."[48]

For me, however, the best encapsulation of the speed of China's growth came in a report by the McKinsey Global Institute, the economic research arm of the McKinsey consultancy. Called "Preparing for China's Urban Billion," the report noted that "if current trends hold" more than 350 million Chinese will move to cities by 2025, when China will have 221 cities with populations above 1 million.[49] Europe, by comparison, has 35 such cities.

The movement of a population greater than the entire United States to cities over sixteen years will require a construction frenzy unlike anything ever seen anywhere. The report's authors found that China will need to pave up to nineteen hundred square miles of roads, an area the size of Delaware, build enough subway lines that they could stretch between New York and San Francisco five times, and—by 2030—build almost 430 billion square feet of new floor space, an amount that will require the construction of "between 20,000 and 50,000 new skyscrapers (buildings of more than 30 floors)—the equivalent of up to ten New York cities."

Because "growth in private consumption has also largely been an urban affair," the shift will spark China's transformation to a consumption-driven society more in line with the West, and the additional buying power of urban Chinese will add a market the size of Germany. Their total demands will account for "around 20 percent of global energy consumption and up to one-quarter of growth in oil demand," the authors wrote. They added that by 2025 China will have to build enough new coal-fired power plants to produce between 700 and 900 gigawatts of electricity. Nine hundred gigawatts—900 billion watts—is equivalent to four-fifths of the current U.S. electrical capacity.

In Tuojia I could feel that future's pull. On my last afternoon I followed a dirt trail through rice paddies speckled with dry stalks left from the fall harvest. The day was cool and overcast, and I stopped to watch a man burn fake money to support his ancestors. Each bill was printed with the words "Heaven and Hell Bank Limited Corporation" and the number 6,800,000,000. Some bore pictures of consumer goods: a refrigerator, a washing machine, an air conditioner, a set of speakers, a Ferrari, a two-liter bottle of Coca-Cola.

Otherwise, Tuojia was quiet. I passed abandoned houses, their doors nailed shut and grass growing from their roofs. A few birds called from pine trees. The scene was idyllic but also anachronistic, and all I could think about was how quickly it was fading.

A Chinese friend had arrived in Tuojia from Chengdu the day before and that afternoon we headed south, spinning away from the village like time travelers, down the trails and then by car on a dirt road past an abandoned schoolhouse. Half an hour later, the driver turned onto a paved road and crossed the Wu River. A banner hanging outside a power plant read, "Development requires economic vigor."

Near strings of newly constructed pink, green, and yellow buildings—pastel colors common to expanding Chinese towns—we merged onto a highway that ran from Inner Mongolia to Guangzhou, the city of 12 million people just west of Hong Kong. The expressway was new and almost empty, but companies had anticipated a coming flood: billboards advertised luxury housing developments, *baijiu*, and—most frequently—cars.

The driver crossed into Guizhou Province at dusk and it was dark when we arrived at its capital. Where the highway dropped us on the outskirts of the city, a string of businesses sold heavy construction equipment: backhoes, front-end loaders, and steamrollers were lined up like toy soldiers. Downtown, the city was more modern: restaurants, bars, and department stores rubbed against apartment buildings decked in flashing neon.

11

HOPENHAGEN

We are participating in a slow-motion train wreck, yet all we can manage to discuss is the quality of the food in the dining car. Maybe this is because acknowledging the train wreck would require us to confront a slew of contradictions at the core of the entire modern industrial project.

—RICHARD HEINBERG, "CHINA'S COAL BUBBLE," POST CARBON INSTITUTE

Late on December 18, 2009, Barack Obama set out to find Wen Jiabao. It was evening on the final day of a conference hyped as "Hopenhagen"— held in the Danish capital, the meeting was billed as providing hope for a planet worried about global warming. The Kyoto Protocol's first commitment period would expire in three years, and a few weeks earlier it had seemed likely that the world's governments might extend and strengthen the treaty. In his first White House speech, Obama had proclaimed that "America will not be held hostage" to a warming climate and that the "days of Washington dragging its heels are over."[1] Beijing, the other key to any solution, had released its first national climate change plan and announced that it would reduce China's "carbon intensity"—a measure of how much carbon is emitted for every dollar the nation earns—by more than 40 percent over the coming decade. Activists had resisted the use of carbon intensity targets by other nations because total emissions can rise even as intensity falls. But

China was not beholden to any cuts under the Kyoto Protocol, and many experts viewed the commitment as a sign that Beijing might move further.[2]

By December 18, the last day of the gathering, however, hope had largely been pummeled out of the meeting. Despite his rhetoric, Obama had not been able to commit the United States to emissions reductions. In June, the U.S. House of Representatives had passed the Waxman-Markey bill—a cap-and-trade scheme for carbon emissions—but the White House had failed to build support in the Senate. (Passage in the Senate requires 60 percent approval, and unlike in the House, where populous coastal states have more votes, in the Senate each state has two votes, giving more weight to conservative, coal-reliant states.) One hundred and thirteen national leaders arrived for the meeting's final days, and when Obama addressed them that morning, all he could offer was another promise hemmed by conditions: "Almost all of the major economies have put forward legitimate targets, significant targets, ambitious targets, and I'm confident that America will fulfill the commitments that we have made, cutting our emissions in the range of 17 percent by 2020 and by more than 80 percent in 2050, in line with final legislation."

China had also failed to move further. The UN Framework Convention on Climate Change, the umbrella under which the Kyoto Protocol was created (its full title is the Kyoto Protocol to the UNFCCC), committed all signatories to the goal of avoiding "dangerous anthropogenic interference" with the climate—a statement of intent to limit greenhouse gas emissions to some to-be-determined level. But it also recognized that industrialized, richer nations, which it termed Annex I countries, had greater responsibilities than developing nations. Annex I governments had promised to "aim" to reduce emissions to their 1990 levels, while every other country had agreed only to "mitigate" climate change, a loosely worded statement that allowed them to continue with business more or less as usual. Within the Framework Convention, this difference was condensed into a principal of "common but differentiated responsibilities."

Since the Framework Convention was created in 1992, of course, China has grown dramatically. Its economy has sextupled and its carbon emissions have more than doubled; if negotiators had anticipated how rapidly China would rise, they almost certainly would have created a different treaty, perhaps requiring developing nations to reduce emissions after a fixed amount of growth.[3] As the protocol was written, however, China's emissions would not face binding reductions until some undetermined future date, and Beijing was entitled to technical and financial aid from richer nations.

Given how much had changed, many experts had hoped that China's leaders would make further concessions in Copenhagen. But by the final day of the gathering, it was clear that Beijing would not be moved. A few minutes before Obama spoke, Wen Jiabao, China's premier, climbed to the podium. Looking out at one of the largest-ever gatherings of world leaders, he began by reminding everyone that, overall, China was poor: its per capita gross domestic product "has only exceeded $3,000" and 150 million people lived below the poverty line of one dollar a day. He said that Beijing had "always regarded addressing climate change as an important strategic task" and reminded the gathering of steps China had taken, including its recently announced carbon-intensity target.

Then Wen laid out the core of Beijing's well-worn negotiating position: the world should stick with the Framework Convention's mandates (Wen said it should "maintain a consistency of outcomes"), account for historical and per capita emissions ("uphold the fairness rules"), focus on short-term reduction targets (and not, one read between the lines, set long-term binding goals that might commit China to fixed limits), and make sure developed nations actually reduce their emissions as required by the convention. (With the exception of the former members of the Soviet bloc, which had suffered an economic meltdown after the Soviet Union collapsed, few nations were on track to meet their goals.)

———

A few hours later, those battle lines put an end to hopes of reaching a new Kyoto treaty in Copenhagen. He Yafei, China's deputy foreign minister, had gathered with top leaders and diplomats from twenty-five of the world's richest nations. Negotiators had whittled down hundreds of pages of documents to a few key points aimed at limiting global carbon emissions in 2050 to half of what they were in 1990. An agreement had been drafted. But it left undecided how much of those reductions would come from industrialized—Annex I—nations and how much would come from everyone else.

More important, China and India opposed the inclusion of almost any hard targets. According to a recording of the meeting, an Indian negotiator said the group should not "prejudge options," a statement Western leaders took to mean they did not want to set targets that might lock them into reducing emissions, however small. (According to the German magazine *Der Spiegel*, the Indian statement prompted German chancellor Angela Merkel to burst out, "Then you don't want legally binding!")[4]

The Chinese negotiator thanked the group for its suggestions but added that China "must not accept the 50 percent [global] reductions," prompting French president Nicolas Sarkozy to call China's negotiating stance "utterly unacceptable." The West, Sarkozy said, was willing to reduce greenhouse gas emissions by 80 percent, but China, "which will soon be the biggest economic power in the world, says to the world, 'Commitments apply to you, but not to us.'"

Obama reminded He Yafei that passing climate change legislation in Western democracies is difficult, as he had learned during his first year in office: "From the perspective of the developed countries, in order for us to be able to mobilize the political will within each of our countries to not only engage in substantial mitigation efforts ourselves, which are very difficult, but to also then channel some of the resources from our countries into developing counties, is a very heavy lift," Obama said, adding that, "If there is no sense of mutuality in this process, it is going to be difficult for us to ever move forward in a significant way."

The logjam led to the Copenhagen Accord, a document that was more holding action than progress. Later that night, Obama—who was in a hurry to beat a storm to Washington—tracked down Premier Wen, bursting in on him and a small group of other leaders. Working together, they sketched out an agreement that committed governments to the goal of keeping the planet's temperature from rising by more than 2 degrees Celsius.

The accord, however, had no teeth: there was no way to enforce compliance. When it was presented to the entire conference late that night, many delegates were furious. The Sudanese chair of the Group of 77, a coalition of the world's poorest nations, equated the document to "a suicide pact, an incineration pact, in order to maintain the economic dominance of a few countries." A Venezuelan delegate cut her hand and asked if she had to bleed to be heard. "You are witnessing a coup d'état against the UN," she said. (As the delegates were about to formally reject the document, a last-minute technical maneuver created a motion to regard it as "noted.")

As news broke, analysts began to dissect what had happened. Mark Lynas, a climate change adviser to the Maldives who attended the meeting with China, the United States, and two dozen other nations, reported that China had insisted that most of the numbers—which would have created a workable framework for cuts—be taken out: a commitment to a global emissions peak in 2020 was replaced by a suggestion that emissions should peak "as soon as possible"; the long-term target of cutting emissions to half of the 1990 amount was excised; the Chinese delegate even insisted on removing an aspirational target of keeping the global average temperature rise below 1.5 degrees Celsius but was shamed into allowing it to remain.[5]

"All this raises the question: what is China's game?" Lynas asked in an editorial. He pointed out that China had shown growing concern about global warming and was "strong in both the wind and solar industries." But "China's growth, and growing global political and economic dominance, is based largely on cheap coal," he added. "China knows it is becoming an uncontested superpower; indeed its newfound muscular confidence was on striking display in Copenhagen. Its coal-based economy doubles every decade, and its power increases commensurately. Its leadership will not alter this magic formula unless they absolutely have to."

Ed Miliband, Britain's climate and energy secretary, wrote that "despite the support of a coalition of developed and the vast majority of developing countries," China had vetoed key numbers sought by the West. But he was more diplomatic about the significance of Beijing's actions: China's muscular approach was "one of the straws in the wind for the future," he wrote, adding that "the old order of developed versus developing has been replaced by more interesting alliances."

Miliband seemed to suggest something that other experts have said directly: the United Nations had proven too large and fractious to create a strong climate change treaty; any effective legislation would have to begin with talks within a much smaller pool of nations controlling the largest share of emissions. In all likelihood, they will revolve around only two: the United States and China, the nations now jointly responsible for 40 percent of annual global carbon emissions, the superpowers carefully eyeing each other across the Pacific.

———

As I continued reporting after the Copenhagen meeting, I heard that argument again and again: any significant global warming treaty will have to be hashed out between Beijing and Washington. Jerry Fletcher, a West Virginia University economist who ran part of the U.S.-China Clean Energy Research Center, the most significant (but still poorly funded) bilateral effort to develop renewable energy, told me that if the United States and China can create a working agreement to control greenhouse gas emissions, the rest of the world will follow. "The U.S. and China are big enough that once they go, everyone goes," he said.[6]

Xu Jintao, an expert on global warming at China's Peking University, said that in light of Copenhagen's failure, global efforts should focus entirely on getting China and the United States to act. "When we think about emissions reductions . . . the rest of the world doesn't matter much," he said. "If China doesn't take a more positive position, we may as well do nothing."

Stapleton Roy, who had served as the U.S. ambassador to China when the UNFCCC was created, argued that if Beijing and Washington "aren't prepared to get serious about global warming issues, since we contribute the most, other countries aren't going to be able to discipline themselves to do anything serious.

"In terms of dealing with China, the most important thing is that if we're going to advocate policies that will have costs for the Chinese economy, we have to be in a position to show that we're willing to pose the same costs on our own society, and I'm not sure we have a strong position on that," Roy said.

For their part, the Chinese seemed satisfied by the outcome in Copenhagen. A rare leaked internal document commissioned by the Ministry of Environmental Protection and circulated to top Chinese officials shortly after the gathering argued that the West had conspired to undermine the Kyoto Protocol's distinction between developed and developing nations but that "the overall interests of developing countries have been defended."[7]

"It was unprecedented for a conference negotiating process to be so complicated, for the arguments to be so intense, for the disputes to be so wide and for progress to be so slow," the report stated. "There was criticism and praise from all sides, but future negotiations will be more difficult."

I had flown from Boston to Copenhagen at the beginning of the second week of the UNFCCC meeting and arrived to a cold, windswept chaos. The United Nations hadn't anticipated how many people would show up in Denmark and had accredited thousands more than could fit in the conference center; I spent my first half day waiting outside the building in freezing temperatures as a long line snaked slowly toward its doors.

When I realized I wouldn't get in, I abandoned the conference to wander the city. Tens of thousands of activists, protesters, and pundits had arrived and many had set up tents in its downtown, which, with street after street of pastel ornamental buildings, resembled a collection of giant wedding cakes. I walked for hours between various stalls and encampments. In a cobblestone square, WWF had erected a life-size ice polar bear that was slowly melting. A group of artists had strung sinister-looking red lights at a height of twenty-three feet, the level the oceans will reach if Greenland's glaciers melt. Other groups held press conferences to announce new data about retreating sea ice and increased Amazon clearing and worrying shifts in animal migrations.

When I finally got inside the conference center a day later, I found a different kind of jockeying: a drumroll of accusations, threats, grandstanding, denialism, and leaked documents that highlighted the political theater of international climate change negotiations, a drama that should be played as tragedy but frequently descends to farce. Over my first few days at the conference, various delegations traded barbs over the obvious impasse, a strategy that seemed aimed more at passing the buck than at solving problems. U.S. delegates said they could not offer greater commitment until China accepted international monitoring of the country's emissions. The Chinese delegation said it would not accept monitoring as "a matter of principle."[8] Politicians and celebrities took advantage of the media frenzy to push their agendas. Al Gore called on President Obama and the Senate to pass climate legislation by the coming Earth Day. Representatives of the world's poorest nations staged a walkout to protest inaction by richer countries. A group of Republican lawmakers held a press conference attacking the science of climate change: Joe Barton, a congressman from Texas, said he did not believe "that the theory of anthropogenic climate change has been proven"; John Sullivan of Oklahoma argued that "when there's so much fraudulent data out there and there's this culture of corruption in the scientific community, I don't think anyone can come to a conclusion whether it's real or not." At night many of us—politicians, negotiators, scientists, protestors, journalists—retired to overpriced restaurants to dine on pickled herring and drink mulled wine.

I also found the discussions, and the media's echo chamber, confusing. What, for example, did it mean that China had pledged to reduce its carbon intensity by at least 40 percent by 2020? Some experts argued that the pledge would produce a significant carbon savings. Others called it greenwashing: because China's economy was growing rapidly and, over time, would require less heavy industry, which was migrating to nations with cheaper labor, its carbon intensity would drop anyway. Or, what did the Obama administration's promise to reduce U.S. emissions "in the range of 17 percent by 2020 and by more than 80 percent in 2050, *in line with final legislation*" mean given that the Senate had not passed the Waxman-Markey bill and seemed unlikely to pass significant climate legislation anytime soon? (After the Republican Party won control of the House of Representatives in 2010, quick passage of a bill became even less likely.)

Most important, all of the politics were overlaid by the fact that despite understanding the risks of climate change for decades, the planet's emissions have increased dramatically. Three months before the Copenhagen meeting, UNEP released a report summing up recent science. Among its findings was that global growth in carbon dioxide emissions from energy and industry had exceeded even the most fossil fuel–intensive scenario envisioned by the IPCC at the end of the 1990s: between 1990 and 1999, emissions grew an average 1.1 percent each year; from 2000 to 2007, they grew an average 3.5 percent; emissions in 2010 would be the largest in human history.[9]

With the exception of a few countries, it was unclear how much governments actually wanted to deal with the problem: from a planetary perspective, we were poking holes in the bottom of a sinking ship even as we debated how to plug them.

———

The confusion has been compounded by contrasting views of China. In recent years, two main narratives have emerged. In one, China is portrayed as the world's destroyer: its growth is so large and rapid that it alone could sink efforts to curb climate change; Beijing's commitment to development is so strong that its leaders are unwilling to bargain if a treaty would slow its economy. (This is the argument Mark Lynas made when he said China's economic rise is "based largely on cheap coal" and Beijing "will not alter this magic formula unless they absolutely have to.")

In the second narrative, China plays a green-tech savior. Even as China has become the world's top source of carbon emissions, it has also become its largest producer and consumer of renewable energy technologies. In 2009 it surpassed the United States as the world leader in clean energy finance and investment. More recently it has become both the world's largest market for wind turbines and its largest manufacturer and exporter of solar cells. (In 2007, only two of the world's top ten producers of solar photovoltaic modules were Chinese; by late 2011, seven were.)[10]

Equally important, China's manufacturing strengths—together with government subsidies and easy access to low-interest loans—have driven down the cost of both technologies: in late 2011, the price of a wind turbine was roughly one-third what it had been four years earlier; the cost of solar panels had fallen by 40 percent in a single year. In some parts of the world solar electricity had become competitive with coal- and gas-fired power plants, the *Financial Times* reported.[11]

And China is likely to push the cost of renewable energy even lower. Worried about energy security, transportation bottlenecks (caused by China's overloaded roads and railways, which are needed to move fossil fuels), and growing pressure to reduce greenhouse gas emissions, Beijing mandated in 2005 that renewable sources (including hydroelectric dams) will meet 15 percent of its total energy demand by 2020, a policy that will require the nation to build large new wind and solar farms and to quintuple its nuclear capacity. The International Energy Agency envisions that over the next twenty-five years, China could add wind and solar power almost equal to everything installed globally in 2011.[12] In a 2010 report titled "Who's Winning the Clean Energy Race?" the Pew Charitable Trusts stated that China "is emerging as the world's clean energy powerhouse."[13]

———

China is thus pushing the world into a future powered increasingly by renewable energy even as it helps push the world over the climate change cliff. At first, this seems like a paradox. But it is precisely because China is so large and is growing so fast—and because it hit its economic stride when the world's atmosphere was already dangerously full of greenhouse gases—that Beijing is investing in renewable technologies.

What is clear is that China is a game changer—some say *the* game changer—both for climate change and how we deal with it: its greenhouse gas emissions will surge, perhaps almost doubling before they peak, but when the world finally acts, it is likely to emerge as a leader in the new-energy economy.[14]

The big questions are when that will happen and what the world will look like when greenhouse gases finally stabilize, and I spent much of my week in Copenhagen talking with scientists about how various pledges might move the planetary thermostat. By the end of the conference, the UNEP had found that the world had locked in less than half of the reductions needed to provide a 50 percent chance of preventing the temperature from rising by more than 2 degrees Celsius. A study by Germany's Potsdam Institute found that even if every proposal made in Copenhagen were fully implemented, average planetary temperatures would rise by 3.2 degrees. A study by the Massachusetts Institute of Technology, Ventana Systems, and the U.S.-based Sustainability Institute calculated that the proposals would leave the world almost 4 degrees warmer by 2100.[15]

The results highlighted why climate change is the perfect "tragedy of the commons": since we share a single atmosphere, growth by one nation can offset emissions reductions by others. Globalization makes that seesaw effect more likely: if one nation phases out fossil fuels—if, say, the United States puts a heavy tax on carbon—its action would cause global oil, coal, and natural gas prices to drop as supply and demand reset, spurring consumption somewhere else.[16]

The dilemma is the opposite of the cold war's concept of mutually assured destruction: instead of a situation where a nuclear strike by one nation means death for all, the *refusal* of one nation—at least one the size of China or the United States—to join emissions reductions can doom a treaty since, in a competitive global economy, nations must work to reduce costs. A few cents added to the price of a manufactured good can be the difference between success and failure, and few politicians can afford to require more expensive energy.

Without a technological breakthrough that makes clean energy cheaper than fossil fuels, there is little benefit and significant risk to taking the first step, and the more I studied, the more I realized that to truly address climate change, China and the United States will have to act in unison: it seems likely that we will move together or we won't move at all.

Two years after the Copenhagen meeting I caught a taxi north from my Beijing apartment to Tsinghua University, China's answer to MIT, to listen to Nicholas Stern address a room full of China's present and future energy leaders. Stern was one of Britain's top climate analysts under former prime minister Tony Blair, and he became famous when the British government released a document that overlaid climate change models with economic theory. Among other things, the study—which became known as the Stern Report—found that failing to curb global warming could reduce the world's economic output over the twenty-first century by as much as one-fifth.

Since then, Stern had taken an academic job, but he continued to lecture about global warming and China had become a frequent stop. When I arrived at the university's lecture hall twenty minutes early, it was filled with several hundred students, professors, and officials.

The gathering felt somber and serious. But Stern has been successful at raising awareness partly because he communicates in an accessible way. Often he frames climate change in terms of stories, and near the beginning of his lecture, he sketched the broad strokes of how *Homo sapiens* have changed the physical planet: how we evolved some two hundred thousand years ago but only began cultivating large areas of land after the last Ice Age; how engineers have created technologies—in the late 1700s tapping the enormous power of fossil fuels—and communities have used them to increase their populations and material wealth; how those changes have dramatically impacted the land, seas, and—for almost all of that period without our understanding—atmosphere. "The story starts with people and it ends with people," Stern told the audience.

Climate change became a significant part of the story in the early 1990s, but until recently—Stern estimated roughly 2005—governments hadn't done much to change course. Given the improving clarity of scientific modeling, however, global warming had become humanity's most important challenge: while scientists "cannot predict with great precision the effects of greenhouse gases on global warming . . . [the risks] really call into question the whole relationship between human beings and the planet," Stern said. "The planet will survive. The question is what will the relationship between human beings and the planet look like if we fail to manage climate change?"

Stern then sketched out some probable impacts of unmanaged warming— much of southern Europe will become a desert, cities and nations ("Cairo, Bangladesh, and so on") will be flooded, hundreds of millions of people will be forced off their land—and laid out what he called "extremely simple" arithmetic showing how the world might avoid that future. To have a 50 percent chance of keeping the world's temperature from rising by more than 2 degrees Celsius, he calculated that the entire human population should emit no more than 32 billion tons of greenhouse gases in 2030, significantly less than the 47 billion tons emitted globally in 2011.[17]

China now claims well over a quarter of that 32-billion-ton budget and, assuming a business-as-usual trajectory, could be responsible for almost half of it in 2030. The obvious point is that if China does not become more ambitious in cutting emissions, "the overall target would be almost impossible to achieve," Stern said.

———

As stories go, the rest of Stern's lecture was more of a fairy tale, if fairy tales occasionally come true. He acknowledged that for the world to avoid "dangerous anthropogenic interference," China—and presumably India, Brazil, Russia, and the rest of the world's large developing nations—will have to accept slower growth, at least temporarily. "The story I'm telling is not a story of equity," he told the audience. "It's a story of inequity. It's a story driven by basic arithmetic."

But he postulated that China might do it anyway. In his fairy tale—which at this point began to lose touch with reality—"high-carbon growth killed itself. It created an environment so hostile that development stopped." China would play a hero by launching a new clean-energy industrial revolution. "I've argued that the world needs a new industrial revolution but I also want to argue that that revolution is a very exciting time," Stern told the crowd. "This is a story of innovation, creativity, and change. We shouldn't be frightened of the change. We should be excited about the change as an opportunity for really strong innovation and growth."

I had returned from Tuojia village two months earlier, however, and it was hard to accept Stern's optimism. Like David and his parents, most Chinese are focused on building comfortable material lives. China's leaders know this and—because stability is their chief concern—believe they need to develop the economy while minimizing inflation. Given China's size, this is difficult, and Beijing has spent billions of dollars subsidizing fossil fuels: as the global price of oil spiked to $145 a barrel in 2008, for example, the Communist Party capped the price of gasoline and diesel fuel; in 2010, it spent $21 billion, most of it to reduce the price of electricity.[18] It seemed unlikely that the leadership would agree to a treaty that significantly slowed growth or raised prices.[19]

It also seemed unlikely that China's leaders would move before the United States makes serious commitments. Partly this is because of the Chinese concept of "face": China's leaders have argued publicly that Western nations need to cut emissions before they act. To change their position now would cause them, in direct translation, "to lose face." Xu Jintao, the Peking University professor, stressed the importance of this problem: "The Chinese government has money," he told me. "It can do anything it wants. But it can't act if the action is perceived as costing China or belittling China."[20]

The predicament reminded me of an Escher drawing: a person moves in a logical direction but ends up back where he started. Hemmed in by energy lobbyists, concerns about manufacturing jobs, and fear about China's rise, Washington seems unable to commit until China acts.[21] Concerned about domestic stability and nationalism, Beijing is trapped until the United States moves. The rest of the world is stuck in limbo.

To deal with climate change, that cycle must be broken, and it seems likely that Washington and Beijing will have to move together. Eventually, as the costs of global warming become more obvious, this will almost certainly happen. But Americans might also become more proactive if they recognize how the rise of China—and behind China, the rise of the rest of the developing world—has shifted the calculus of national interests. Whatever economic benefit the country gets from burning fossil fuels will almost certainly be offset by the costs of dealing with a heating planet caused—in the future—largely by other nations.

———

With his fairy-tale ending, Stern was more upbeat. But at the end of the lecture a young man stood up to ask if he thought the world would make the changes he envisioned.

"Am I optimistic or pessimistic?" Stern echoed, as if he was weighing the question for the first time.

"What I try to do and others try to do is to show what can be done and to show why what can be done looks not only a sensible thing to do but an attractive thing to do. If you tell the story that way, you increase the probability of it happening. If you say we have to do huge amounts of things, indeed it's so huge that it's impossible, then nobody's going to do anything. So our job is to show what can be done and to show why it looks good."

"Will people actually do it?" he asked, looking out at the audience. "There, I don't know."

EPILOGUE

The troubles of the world
Cannot be solved except
Before they grow too hard.
The business of the world
Cannot be done except
While relatively small.

—Laozi, sixth-century bc Daoist philosopher

Almost a year after I visited Trinidad, Colorado, I watched the world's last Siberian cranes begin their annual journey home. I was standing beside a sloping marshland in eastern China's Jiangxi Province, and they lifted off from the edge of a shallow lake, rode thermal updrafts into a clear sky, and, high overhead, formed wide Vs. Relying on million-year-old instincts and knowledge passed between countless generations, they then turned north across China's battered plains.

The lake was named Poyang, and I'd traveled there to remember what's at stake in our rapidly changing world, to be reminded that even at the heart of China—a country that has carried the planet's largest population for centuries and epitomizes today's environmental crisis—pockets of resiliency remain. Cranes had also struck me as potent ambassadors for the besieged wilderness. The crane family (Gruidae) evolved at least 9 million years ago, and its members are among the largest and best-traveled of today's birds: adult Siberian cranes sometimes stand taller than five feet; Eurasian and demoiselle cranes cross the Himalayas—flying to heights of more than three miles—during migrations between Russia and India.

Those traits—their size, longevity, strength, and beauty—have sparked admiration among every culture cranes have touched. Officials in imperial China considered them the second most important bird, after the mythical phoenix, and used them as symbols of both longevity and the empress, perhaps a reason they were to a degree protected. (Statues of cranes stood on either side of the emperor's throne in the Forbidden City's Hall of Supreme Harmony.) In his eponymous fables, Aesop extolled their ability to "rise above the clouds into endless space, and survey the wonders of the heavens, as well as of the earth beneath, with its seas, lakes, and rivers, as far as the eye can reach." Because cranes often mate for life, some communities have revered them as symbols of commitment. In *The Birds of Heaven*, Peter Matthiessen, the great chronicler of the natural world, writes that "every land where they appear has tales and myths about the cranes, which since ancient times have represented longevity and good fortune, harmony and fidelity."[1]

Cranes, however, are also reminders of how we have reshaped the planet. Eleven of the fifteen crane species are threatened or endangered by human activity—hunting, trapping, and, most important, draining and flooding marshes. Among them, Siberians are considered most at risk. In the early twentieth century, Siberian cranes existed in three distinct populations and probably numbered some ten thousand. Besides wintering at Poyang Lake, a group settled into a small man-made marsh not far from India's Taj Mahal. Another found refuge on the Iranian shore of the Caspian Sea.

With the exception of a lonely male that returns most autumns to Iran, however, today's entire Siberian crane population—some four thousand birds—now winters at Poyang Lake, and China's rapid growth has imperiled their future: in 2000, the International Union for the Conservation of Nature classified the species as critically endangered, "owing to fears that its global population will decline extremely rapidly over the next three generations following the development of the Three Gorges Dam . . . which threatens the wintering grounds used by the vast majority of individuals."[2]

I had traveled to Poyang Lake with James Burnham, a thirty-five-year-old doctoral student who had logged seven long, cold winters researching the lake's birds for the International Crane Foundation, a small nonprofit group based in Baraboo, Wisconsin, and as we drove north from the provincial capital that morning, he ticked off threats facing what he called the "Sibes": as China's economy took off, fishing increased; recently, locals had begun clearing aquatic vegetation from inlets to raise crabs, depriving the birds of feeding grounds; hunting and poisoning—sometimes intentionally for food, sometimes through industrial runoff and pesticides—had become persistent concerns.

The biggest problems, however, were physical changes to the lake itself. Poyang is composed mostly of shallow marshes, and as land became more valuable, farmers had drained roughly half its area.[3] Sand dredging had further changed its ecology by deepening sections, drying out neighboring wetlands. And the provincial government had recently proposed what may serve as the birds' tombstone: a large dam that would keep the lake's winter water level high, allowing fishing and crab farming throughout the year. Officials had promised to protect crane habitat, but many scientists doubted their efforts would be enough. James Harris, the International Crane Foundation's vice president, argued that the dam would destroy almost all of Poyang's migratory bird habitat.[4] Other scientists had gone further, stating that if the dam is built, Siberian cranes faced almost certain extinction.

As we drove out of Jiangxi's capital, past the familiar oddities of China's growth (including a near-full-size replica of Berlin's Brandenburg Gate), I asked James if he thought the Siberian cranes would survive the changes. He had already struck me as a cross between Thomas Edison and John Muir. In the field he spent much of his time peering through binoculars and taking careful notes. But he was also a passionate advocate for the natural world:

during our first meeting, he spent ten minutes critiquing a newspaper that had reported, wrongly, that the dam might help Poyang's birds by preventing the lake from drying out during droughts, an argument frequently made by the project's backers. "I'm frustrated by all the pro-dam propaganda out there," James said. "I want to just swing for the fences."

When I asked his opinion about the Sibes' future, James paused. Then he said, "I'm kind of in a bad spot because of the latest news with the dam. I wish I could be cautiously optimistic, but I'm pretty worried. I guess I'm cautiously pessimistic. If they build the dam, I don't know how the birds will respond.

"I mean, they've been around for a long time and they've proven adaptable. But Poyang Lake is the last real bastion for them. If it's ruined, I have a hard time seeing that they'll be able to find an alternative."

————

Still, the birds are there. A few hours later, James began to survey a flock of Siberian cranes that, half a mile distant, looked like a dusting of snow. Occasionally a few launched themselves into the sky and circled upward in looping spirals. (That afternoon, he would count 2,550 Sibes; the day before he had counted 3,400 in the same spot.)

The day had warmed and I took the opportunity to stretch my legs. Finless porpoises—a species sometimes mistaken for *baiji*, the recently extinct Yangtze River dolphin—occasionally swim into the nearby Xiu River, and I wandered along its bank for twenty minutes. But other than a few empty beer bottles that bobbed along its edge, nothing broke the water's surface.

A group of Chinese photographers proved more interesting. On a day-to-day level, photographers have become the Siberian cranes' biggest nuisance: almost without fail one gets too close and spooks the flock, often intentionally, and, at about two in the afternoon, that happened. The birds began to lift off by the hundreds, a cloud of white wings and bodies silhouetted against tan grass and tea-green water.

The sight was a majestic reminder of how much—and how little—

remains: almost all of the world's remaining Siberian cranes, a species that predates *Homo sapiens* by millions of years, rising into the March sky, banking and then flying north, perhaps setting out on their long trip home. At the beginning of their journey and—for this book—the end of mine, they struck me as a powerful metaphor for the retreating wilderness and our own swift passage on this precious, troubled Earth. Even more than tigers or birds of paradise, they seemed to capture the delicate line between existence and extinction, the rapidly fading horizon of clean air, water, and land upon which all life ultimately depends.

As the birds rose higher into the warm afternoon sky, one group caught my eye. A few hundred feet above the marsh, five birds turned and flew directly toward me. Like all cranes, they moved in almost perfect unison. Yet each bird also provided its own template for beauty, its legs stretched straight behind it, its neck curved forward, the black feathers at the end of each wing reaching like fingers.

As the flock passed overhead, I leaned back and then turned to watch until they crested the top of a small hill. Only after they disappeared behind a stand of bamboo did I turn and begin to make my way back to where James was taking notes.

But then I realized that I might never see a Siberian crane again. If the dam is built, most of the wetlands surrounding Poyang Lake will be destroyed. The cranes might find no alternative. In a generation or two, they might be gone for good. So I scrambled up the steep hillside to look again at the now-distant birds. Staring into the infinite hard-blue sky, I watched until they were completely gone.

For journalists, the most important question is, So what? When we understand that the rate of global warming is rising sharply, that the world's last untouched forests are shrinking rapidly, that biodiversity is declining at an accelerating pace, and that global consumer demands are spiking upward, we should take time to ask ourselves, "So what? What should we do about it?"

As I approached the end of my reporting, I began to ask those and similar questions with growing urgency. What have I learned? What should communities and nations do? What should I do? Even if we should do those things, will we? What would we lose?

Thinking back over my trips, I began to formulate answers. The most important message is also the simplest: unless we live more sustainably, the speed of environmental change will accelerate as the demands of China and the rest of the developing world rise. Midrange UN estimates put our global population at more than 10 billion by 2100, four times the 1950 population, and more of those people will be able to afford the material comforts now available only to the world's richest citizens. By 2040, five emerging nations— China, India, Brazil, Russia, and Mexico—are expected to have a larger combined economic output than the G7 nations, the seven countries that have dominated the world's economy for two centuries.[5] Behind them, dozens more will be developing rapidly.

In itself, that spread of material wealth is good. But we must realize that if we continue to use natural resources as we currently do, the growth will reshape the physical planet: unless we find ways to produce and consume more sustainably, our growing demands will degrade our shared environment at an ever-faster rate.

A second truth—as clear as the physics of gravity—is that the planet will eventually regain balance. This could happen because we—as a global society—protect what remains. Or it could happen because the world becomes so stressed, our natural systems so taxed and overused, that our population begins to shrink or is forced to live more frugally. It seems likely that both will happen: we will clear more of the final frontier forests, pull more wildlife from the lands and out of the oceans, and pump more greenhouse gases into the atmosphere; as the environmental costs become increasingly obvious, we will address the problems with stepped-up urgency. For me, the real questions are, *when* will that happen and *what* will be left? And to those questions we can offer only guesses.

*   *   *

At the end of my research, it seems clear that our greatest threat is global warming. Humans have confronted many crises over recent centuries—plagues, wars, nuclear standoff, terrorism—but we have never faced one as complicated (both by the number of actors and by the economic costs) as climate change. If we cannot find the will to act, we will cause the planet to warm enough to trip ecological feedbacks that will remind us that, despite our Confucian conceits of mastering nature, we are not in control: if the permafrost melts or the Amazon burns or ocean currents shift, we will be taken for whatever ride nature dictates. One thousand years from now, whoever is alive may talk of a second Great Dying, but unlike during the Permian period, the creatures killed off will include most of those unlucky enough to live through the decades or centuries when everything changes.

The world's other environmental problems could have greater significance over this century. We have only one chance to save the last great tracts of pristine rain forest and the millions of complex, unique creatures that share the planet. To some people, it may not seem important that New Guinea preserves jungles that have never heard a chainsaw or that tigers hunt muntjacs in Indian grasslands. But if those jungles fall or the last wild tiger is killed, we will all be diminished.

Partly, there is the practical fact that wildlife and forests are critical to healthy ecosystems we rely on for food and water. But at the end of my journey, the emotional and spiritual role of wilderness seems more important: Can we imagine a world where the only wilderness is fenced in and crowded with day-trippers? Or telling children that an animal called a tiger *once* existed? We live in an often cynical age, and if we destroy our shared natural heritage, it seems possible that we will lose the most powerful reminder that we all came from the same place and form a single family.

What, then, should we do? Here I have a few conclusions. First, we need to think differently. When I was growing up in the 1980s, the environmental mantra was "Think globally, act locally": we could feel good if we recycled, installed low-flow showerheads, and participated in Earth Day events.

Now—given the world's increasing planetary metabolism, given the rise of China and the rest—we should flip the terms: we should think locally and act globally. If we think locally, we will remember our responsibility to our children and grandchildren. That will spur us to *act* globally: to cut our national greenhouse gas emissions and work with other nations to build a viable global treaty; to invest in preserving the greatest remaining wilderness areas and the biodiversity they protect, no matter where they are.

To do this, we should move toward an ethic of shared responsibility. The radical division of wealth around the world is less a result of Western genius than the product of geography and chance. In 1800, China was the world's most advanced and wealthiest nation. Then the wheel turned: its people— smart, industrious, ambitious, just like people everywhere—suffered more than a century of war and upheaval. Today it is returning to prominence.

Likewise, that New Guinea, Brazil, and Russia protect many of the world's final untouched forests and India and many African nations are home to much of our remaining wildlife is a product of the past: wealthy nations plundered their natural estate in the process of getting rich. Because of globalization, those developing nations can now sell their resources, and their people are as smitten as everyone else by the gleam of cars and suburban houses, computers and televisions. If we cannot help them achieve what they want, many will sell what they have.

Fortunately, the planet is rich enough that if we decide to save what's left, we can. The world's timber companies could meet global demand by sustainably managing 20 percent of our remaining forests. With well-managed operations that reduce and recycle waste, farms and livestock companies could sustainably produce enough food for everyone. Engineers could use already available technologies to transition to energy systems that preserve our quality of life without releasing greenhouse gases.[6] Lawyers, politicians, and diplomats could create regulations that help us consume natural resources wisely. If we could do those things, we could stop the destruction.

A key to making that happen, however, is that wealthy nations will have to get better at sharing. If, for example, we do not share the income from sustainable logging, poorer countries will see little reason to protect their old-growth forests. Instead they would join the clearing, adding supply, driving down cost, driving up demand. Likewise, if we fail to provide opportunities for poor communities within our most pristine wilderness areas, many will continue to hunt wildlife.

We have begun to address the problems. Governments and nongovernment organizations increasingly employ people living in and around national parks. A key concept of the UN Framework Convention on Climate Change is that wealthy nations will help poorer nations transition to renewable forms of energy. In 2009, U.S. Secretary of State Hillary Clinton announced that Washington was willing to coordinate a $100 billion annual fund to help developing nations reduce greenhouse gas emissions and cope with the impacts of global warming.[7]

Perhaps Edward O. Wilson put it most clearly. In *The Future of Life*, he wrote: "The juggernaut of technology-based capitalism will not be stopped. Its momentum is reinforced by the billions of poor people in developing countries anxious to participate in order to share the material wealth of the industrialized nations. But its direction can be changed by mandate of a generally shared long-term environmental ethic. The choice is clear: the juggernaut will very soon either chew up what remains of the living world, or it will be redirected to save it."[8]

Just as I was finishing this book, my wife gave birth to our first child. We had chosen a hospital in eastern Beijing, and, two days later, I went home to prepare for their arrival. I hailed a taxi and headed west past rows of crowded restaurants and bars then turned south into a district that housed the emperor's ministers during the Qing dynasty but now bustles with banks and malls. In my neighborhood, I walked by shops selling Chicago Bulls jerseys and rap CDs, hand-painted scrolls and embroidered silks.

I had lived in Beijing for almost a decade and had seen it all countless times. But suddenly everything seemed new. Only hours earlier, I'd watched my daughter's face light up as she took her first bath. I'd held her to our hospital window to see the sky for the first time. In her, I remembered that— however one looks at it—life is miraculous.

As I thought about her, I felt a wave of joy but also, because of what I'd been writing, sadness. I wanted her to see what I had seen and was unsure she ever would. By the time she's old enough to travel, will wild tigers and cranes remain? Will any forests be as healthy as the ones I visited in New Guinea? It happened to be an unusually clear day and, looking at the sky, I was both thrilled by its depth and frightened by the gases I knew were accumulating there, molecule by molecule, changing her future.

────────

It is common to say that the planet belongs to today's youth. In one sense, of course, the statement is true: they will remain after we're gone. In another, however, it is badly misleading: the youth are mostly passive travelers carried along by older generations that control money and power. Those of us with the ability to create change must ask ourselves what kind of world we want to leave to future generations. We need to accept that the West—with a current population of just over 1 billion—rearranged the planet's biodiversity, atmosphere, and land in little more than a century. Then we need to ask ourselves what will happen as 4 or 5 billion more people approach our standard of living. Even though we may have disagreements about how quickly the environment will degrade and the ability of technology to solve problems, the trends are so clear and the stakes so high that a shift in how we manage the world seems not only prudent but obviously necessary.

What, then, can we do? Here the answers are harder but, at their root, also simple. In short, we need to do what we were taught in kindergarten: share, take care of what we have, work together, play fair.

We can begin by taking personal action. We can change our incandescent lightbulbs for compact fluorescents (which are twenty times more energy-efficient). We can carpool. We can reduce our consumption of meat and fish. We can recycle more and buy less.

It is much more important, however, that we demand government action. Given that growth in the developing world will far outpace our individual conservation efforts, we will spin our wheels without a global approach. For Americans, the importance of national action is particularly stark. For at least another decade the United States will be the world's largest economy, and even if China eclipses us in dollar terms, Washington will remain the world's most influential government for much longer. It seems clear that if the United States can generate the political will to act, China can be convinced to join.

I am optimistic that if we act, China will stand with us because this is their century and the Chinese people do not want it marred by environmental collapse. Like the West in the twentieth century, China's environmental ideals are evolving rapidly. Citizens see their problems and want solutions. The changes required will be difficult, but the country's domestic environmental crisis will hasten their arrival. If the West moves further to address climate change and other environmental problems, Beijing's leaders are likely to compromise.

I am also optimistic because we can solve our worst environmental problems at a relatively low cost. Jeffrey Sachs, an economist at Columbia University, argues that if the world invested only 2 to 3 percent of its annual income, we could create a sustainable trajectory that addresses the intertwined challenges of the environment, population growth, and poverty.[9] Nicholas Stern has said that the world can avoid the worst impacts of global warming by redirecting 2 percent of our earnings.[10] Other experts have come to similar conclusions.

Finally, I am optimistic because I choose to be so. Throughout history humans have overcome countless challenges. Today's are more complex, but we have the tools we need to address them: we have incredible knowledge and enough resources that we all can live sustainably and well.

In the end, our environmental challenges are the sharpest reminder that the world belongs to all of us: Chinese, Americans, Indians, Europeans, Tuvaluans, Papua New Guineans—everyone. We need to decide what matters. And then we need to act.

NOTES

PROLOGUE

1. The 1976 figure is listed on page 11 of Wuyuan Peng's "The Evolution of China's Coal Institutions," published by Freeman Spogli Institute for International Studies in 2009. The 1997 and 2009 figures are available on the U.S. Energy Information Administration website: http://www.eia.gov/countries/country-data .cfm?fips=CH. The U.S. data is also from the EIA. All of these figures are given in short tons, the commonly used measurement in the United States.

2. According to World Bank data, China's GDP in constant yuan grew from 4.6 trillion in 1992 to 26.9 trillion in 2010. Data is available through the World Bank data bank: www.databank.worldbank.org.

3. Cline Mining's plan to increase production is quoted in Lee Buchsbaum's article, "Cline Revives New Elk in Colorado," which was published in *Coal Age* on August 26, 2010. The company announced plans to ship coal through Corpus Christi, Texas, in a February 8, 2011, press release.

4. According to Dan Jaffe, Asia is now responsible for about 40 percent of the world's industrial mercury emissions. Other researchers have found that China's mercury emissions are growing at more than 5 percent annually.

5. The doubling of Chinese CO_2 emissions is noted on page 47 of the International Energy Agency's 2011 edition of "CO_2 Emissions from Fuel Combustion Highlights."

6. According to Jim Butler, new greenhouse gas emissions between 1990 and 2010 meant that the global average temperature would rise by an additional 0.7 degrees

Fahrenheit. His larger point was that the speed of emissions has increased in step with China's economic growth.

7. According to the World Bank's World Development Indicators, China was the world's tenth largest economy in nominal GDP terms in 1979.

8. Pete Engardio and Dexter Roberts, "The China Price," *Businessweek*, December 6, 2004.

9. Author interview with Sun Xiufang, a Beijing-based analyst for Forest Trends, a Washington, D.C.–based nonprofit group that studies forest conservation issues, spring 2011.

10. Author interview with James Hewitt, a London-based business consultant specializing in wood-based products, spring 2011. Using trade data, Hewitt concluded that in 2009 China imported roughly 25 million cubic meters of tropical logs out of a global total of roughly 55 million cubic meters. China imported 60 million tons of wood pulp from tropical nations out of a total of roughly 150 million tons. Trade data for tropical timber exports are notoriously difficult to calculate because of reporting inconsistencies across countries. But it is clear that China's impact on the world's tropical forests is growing rapidly. According to Forest Trends, the volume of wood imported by China has roughly doubled since 2000 and China's share of global trade in logs and wood pulp used to make paper has surged as it became the world's largest paper and paperboard producer; see Sun Xiufang and Kerstin Canby, "China: Overview of Forest Governance, Markets and Trade," Forest Trends for FLEGT Asia Regional Programme, November 2010, 7, 29. These issues are more fully explored in Part III of this book.

11. Sun and Canby, "China: Overview of Forest Governance, Markets and Trade," 9.

12. UN Office on Drugs and Crime, "The Globalization of Crime: A Transnational Organized Crime Threat Assessment," 149–159, provides a good overview of the trade and states that "the primary destination of wildlife products sourced in Africa and South-East Asia is China." Because of the illegality of the trade, definitive assessments of national sales are impossible, but most experts agree that China is the top destination. In 2008, the environmental group Traffic declared that China was "the most important country globally as a destination for illicit ivory." Experts I talked with stated that China is the top destination

for tiger parts and rhino horn, as well as products made from dozens of other species. This topic is explored in Part II of this book.

13. Between 1996 and 1998, the exchange rate was 8.4 yuan to the dollar. In January 2012, the exchange rate was 6.3 yuan to the dollar.

14. Jianjun Tu, "Industrial Organization of the Chinese Coal Industry," Stanford Program on Energy and Sustainable Development, working paper presented in Beijing in March 2011, 20.

15. These facts come from the following sources: Joseph Kahn and Jim Yardley, "As China Roars, Pollution Reaches Deadly Extremes," *New York Times*, August 26, 2007; Katherine Morton, "China and the Global Environment: Learning from the Past, Anticipating the Future," Lowry Institute for International Policy, 2009; "China's Environmental Crisis," Council on Foreign Relations, http://www.cfr .org/china/chinas-environmental-crisis/p12608, accessed August 24, 2011.

16. Morton, "China and the Global Environment," 3.

17. Khalid Malik, the UN resident coordinator and UNDP resident representative in China, made these remarks in Beijing on December 18, 2006.

18. C. Nellemann, L. Miles, B. P. Kaltenborn, M. Viture, and H. Ahlenius, eds., "Last Stand of the Orangutan," United Nations Environment Program, 2007. The report found that 98 percent of Indonesia's natural rain forest might be destroyed by 2022, with lowland forest falling much sooner. Determining how many Indonesian logs are exported to China is more difficult because many of the logs are shipped through other countries, but China is considered the major market for Indonesian timber exports. These issues are explored more fully in Part III of this book.

19. Robert L. Pitman, "A Fellow Mammal Leaves the Planet," *New York Times*, December 26, 2006.

20. Thomas Malthus, *An Essay on the Principle of Population,* 1798 (New York: Oxford University Press, 2008).

21. Garrett Hardin, "The Tragedy of the Commons," *Science* 162 (1968):1243–1248.

22. The Millennium Ecosystem Assessment is available for free download at www .maweb.org/en/index.aspx. UNEP and other organizations provided broad

updates to the assessment ahead of the Rio+20 environmental conference in mid-2012. See, for example, UNEP, "Keeping Track of Our Changing Environment: From Rio to Rio+20 (1992–2012)" (Nairobi: Division of Early Warning and Assessment, United Nations Environment Program, 2011).

23. "Living Planet Report 2010," WWF in association with the Zoological Society of London and the Global Footprint Network, October 13, 2010.

24. Press release, "Human Demand Outstripping Nature's Regenerative Capacity at an Alarming Rate: 2010 Living Planet Report," Global Footprint Network, October 13, 2010.

25. The details of this paragraph are explained in the relevant sections of this book. The 2007 UN Intergovernmental Panel on Climate Change report, the work of thousands of scientists from around the world, argued that a global mean temperature rise of 1.3 degrees Fahrenheit over the preceding century was—with at least a 90 percent certainty—due to human activity, particularly the burning of fossil fuels and changes in land cover.

26. Edward O. Wilson, *The Future of Life* (New York: Vintage, 2003), xxiii.

27. Ibid.

28. CIA World Factbook, https://www.cia.gov/library/publications/the-world-fact book, accessed June 2011. In 2011, China's per capita annual earnings were $4,400 in nominal GDP. China's per capita GDP in purchasing power parity terms, a measurement that seeks to capture the relative value of what people can buy with their earnings, was $7,600. The U.S. average per capita earnings in June 2011 were $47,200.

29. The facts in this paragraph come from various sources. U.S. electrical consumption is listed in the International Energy Agency's "2010 Key World Energy Statistics," 50–57 (dividing the total electrical consumption in the United States—in 2008, 4,155.92 terawatt-hours—by the then-population of just over 304 million people). Use of crude oil and natural gas data are derived from the CIA World Factbook and the BP *Statistical Review of World Energy*. According to the Factbook, the United States consumed 18.69 million barrels of oil every day in 2009; dividing by the 2009, U.S. population of 307 million people, each American was responsible for 22.22 barrels of oil; each barrel of crude oil holds

42 gallons. According to BP, the United States consumed 589 million tons oil equivalent of natural gas in 2009, or a per capita average of 1.9 tons; one ton oil equivalent of natural gas is a measure of the energy released when the gas is burned and is equal to 41.8 billion joules; one cubic meter of natural gas is equal to 37.2 million joules. Thus, on average, each American was responsible for 2,156 cubic meters of natural gas. Tons of carbon dioxide emissions per capita is listed on page 57 of the International Energy Agency's "2010 Key World Energy Statistics." American meat consumption in 2002 is listed in the UN Food and Agriculture Organization FAOSTAT online statistical service (FAO, Rome, 2004), http://faostat.fao.org, accessed June 2011. U.S. motor vehicle ownership is listed in the Department of Energy's "Changes in Vehicles per Capita Around the World," http://www1.eere.energy.gov/vehiclesandfuels/facts/2010_fotw617.html, accessed September 3, 2011. According to the DOE, every 1,000 Americans owned 842 motor vehicles in 2008. The trash figure is listed in the U.S. Environmental Protection Agency's "Municipal Solid Waste Generation, Recycling, and Disposal in the United States: Facts and Figures for 2008," http://www.epa.gov/osw/nonhaz/municipal/pubs/msw2008rpt.pdf, accessed September 3, 2011.

30. The sources for China's per capita consumption come from the same sources as for the United States (listed above), with the exception of China's motor vehicle ownership. That number was reported in Li Fangfang, "Chinese Auto Market Takes Over US as World's Largest," *China Daily*, January 9, 2010.

31. Author interview with Fatih Birol, chief economist of the International Energy Agency, December 2009.

1. THE YANGTZE

1. "Three Gorges Project Sets 10 World Records," *People's Daily*, June 9, 2006. The best overall history of the Three Gorges Dam and reservoir is Deirdre Chetham's *Before the Deluge: The Vanishing World of the Yangtze's Three Gorges* (New York: Palgrave Macmillan, 2002), which I consulted throughout this chapter. More up-to-date information about the dam can be found on websites. One source is "China's Three Gorges: Power to the People or Environmental Catastrophe?" CBC/Radio Canada, http://www.cbc.ca/news/background/china/threegorges.html, accessed September 27, 2011.

2. The quotes and facts in this section primarily come from two books: Richard

Adams Carey, *The Philosopher Fish: Sturgeon, Caviar, and the Geography of Desire* (New York: Counterpoint, 2005), and Inga Saffron, *Caviar: The Strange History and Uncertain Future of the World's Most Coveted Delicacy* (New York: Broadway, 2002). Chinese sturgeon were a relative latecomer to the larger sturgeon family.

3. Carey, *The Philosopher Fish.*

4. Ibid.

5. "Water Schools Shed Light on Degenerating Yangtze," *People's Daily*, April 11, 2009; C. M. Wong et al., "World's Top 10 Rivers at Risk," WWF International, March 2007.

6. Wong et al., "World's Top 10 Rivers at Risk," 42.

7. B. Muller et al., "How Polluted Is the Yangtze River? Water Quality Downstream from the Three Gorges Dam," *Science of the Total Environment* 402, no. 2–3 (2008): 232–247.

8. Peter H. Gleick, *The World's Water 2008–2009: The Biennial Report on Freshwater Resources* (Washington, D.C.: Island Press, 2008), 79–97.

9. Shi Jiangtao, "Pollution Makes Yangtze 'Cancerous,'" *South China Morning Post*, May 31, 2006. By the summer of 2010, the first year that the Three Gorges Reservoir reached its maximum capacity, the costs were visible: in early August, Chinese state media reported that dam operators were clearing 6 million pounds of garbage from behind the dam every day. A layer of trash nearly two feet deep covered an area the size of twelve football fields. In some places it was so dense that people could walk on it; see Tini Tran, "Trash Threatens to Block Three Gorges Gates in China," Associated Press, August 2, 2010.

10. In one county along the river, shifting land forced the relocation of more than 13,000 people; see Jim Yardley, "Chinese Dam Projects Criticized for Their Human Costs," *New York Times*, November 14, 2007.

11. Jianguo Liu and Jared Diamond, "China's Environment in a Globalizing World," *Nature*, June 2005.

12. The effort to find Yangtze River dolphins is chronicled in Samuel Turvey's *Witness*

to Extinction: How We Failed to Save the Yangtze River Dolphin (Oxford: Oxford University Press, 2008).

13. Greg T. O. LeBreton, F. William H. Beamish, and R. Scott McKinley, eds., *Sturgeons and Paddlefish of North America* (Dordrecht, Netherlands: Kluwer Academic Publishers, 2004).

14. Ibid., vi.

2. BASELINES

1. Daniel Pauly, "Anecdotes and the Shifting Baseline Syndrome of Fisheries," *Trends in Ecology and Evolution* 10, no. 10 (October 1995): 430.

2. Colin McEvedy and Richard Jones, *Atlas of World Population History* (New York: Facts on File, 1978), 167. According to R. Cameron and L. Neal, the global population in 1800 was roughly 906 million; see *A Concise Economic History of the World: From Paleolithic Times to the Present* (New York: Oxford University Press, 2002), 189.

3. Mark Elvin, *The Retreat of the Elephants* (London: Yale University Press, 2004), 312.

4. Ibid., 321.

5. Ibid., 11.

6. Ibid., 464.

7. In ibid., 43, Elvin quotes a poem written during the Zhou dynasty (1045–256 BC) that lauded the clearing of forests as a symbol of the emperor's divine right to rule:

> We uprooted the trees then! Lugged trunks aside
> —Those that, dead, still stood upright, and those that had toppled.
> We pruned back the branches, or flattened entirely
> The stands in their long lines and the thick-tangled coppices.
> We cut clearings among them. We widened the openings
> Through tamarisk forests and knob-jointed cane-trees.
> We tore from the soil, or else lopped back, groves
> Of wild mulberry bushes and spiny Cudranias . . .
> When our Lord God Above had examined these hillsides,

We ripped out oaks whose leaves fall, and those green the year round,
Clearing spacious expanses amid pine and cypress.
Here God made our state, and our sovereign, His counterpart.

8. Ibid., 15.

9. *Stanford Encyclopedia of Philosophy*, http://plato.stanford.edu/entries/zhuangzi, accessed September 27, 2011.

10. Jonathan Watts, *When a Billion Chinese Jump: How China Will Save Mankind—or Destroy It* (London: Faber and Faber, 2010), 20. Watts's book is one of the best general overviews of China's domestic environmental crisis and offers a thorough exploration of the philosophical roots of today's problems.

11. The impact of China's Confucian traditions on its environment, particularly under the Chinese Communist Party, is deeply explored in Judith Shapiro's *Mao's War Against Nature: Politics and the Environment in Revolutionary China* (New York: Cambridge University Press, 2001).

12. Elvin, *The Retreat of the Elephants*, 62. Italics are Elvin's.

13. Quoted in Shapiro, *Mao's War Against Nature*, 62.

14. James Kynge, *China Shakes the World: A Titan's Rise and Troubled Future—and the Challenge for America* (New York: Houghton Mifflin, 2006), 134.

15. Quoted in Shapiro, *Mao's War Against Nature*, 31.

16. Quoted in ibid., 107.

17. Ibid., 107. Shapiro writes that about half of more than 1,065 lakes were filled and that the total lake surface area was reduced by three-fourths.

18. Shapiro blames those three factors for China's current crisis: "Although many rapidly developing societies engage in environmentally damaging behavior, the destructive influence of the Mao years on traditional values has facilitated China's plunge into the current phase of materialistic exploitation of nature," she writes. "This story is not, therefore, merely a cautionary tale of historical significance, but also an exploration of the social and historical roots of behavior patterns that affect environmental health today, not only of China but of the world." See *Mao's War Against Nature*, 11.

3. THE THREE GORGES DAM

1. Liangwu Yin, *The Long Quest for Greatness*, quoted in Deirdre Chetham, *Before the Deluge: The Vanishing World of the Yangtze's Three Gorges* (New York: Palgrave Macmillan, 2002), 162. It should be noted that imperial China developed deep experience in dam building. By the twentieth century, however, its engineers had fallen behind the West.

2. According to International Rivers, a nonprofit organization based in Berkeley, California, Chinese companies and banks are the world's top builders and financiers of new dams. In 2012, they were involved in constructing 289 dams in seventy countries. The Gezhouba Dam Group, where Wu worked, had projects in sixty nations and employed more than 20,000 foreign workers. In 2010, it signed almost $4 billion worth of contracts for new projects. (More information about Chinese dam builders working internationally can be found on the International Rivers website: http://www.internationalrivers.org/en/china, accessed January 10, 2012.)

3. The Three Gorges Dam was built to withstand a 7.0-Richter-scale quake. An earthquake that struck 580 miles to the west in Sichuan Province in 2008 measured 7.9.

4. Chetham, *Before the Deluge*, 155.

5. The stories of both Li Rui and Dai Qing are told in *Before the Deluge*.

6. Elizabeth C. Economy, *The River Runs Black: The Environmental Challenge to China's Future* (Ithaca, NY: Cornell University Press, 2004), 4.

7. Ibid., 5.

8. By one count, as little as 10 percent of China's environmental laws are enforced; see Samuel Turvey, *Witness to Extinction: How We Failed to Save the Yangtze River Dolphin* (Oxford: Oxford University Press, 2008), 42.

9. Ibid., 201.

10. John Platt, "China's Yangtze Finless Porpoise Faces 80 Percent Decrease in 30 Years," *Scientific American*, June 8, 2011.

4. TIGER, TIGER, BURNING BRIGHT

1. Peter Matthiessen quotes biologist Ullas Karanth saying that seeing a tiger is "always like a dream" in *Tigers in the Snow* (New York: North Point Press, 2000), viii.

2. The Environmental Investigation Agency and the Wildlife Protection Society of India, "Skinning the Cat: Crime and Politics of the Big Cat Skin Trade," September 2006. The report is available at http://www.eia-international.org/skinning-the-cat.

3. The seizures are detailed in "Skinning the Cat." According to Richard Ellis, the average tiger yields 55 pounds of bones. Richard Ellis, *Tiger Bone & Rhino Horn: The Destruction of Wildlife for Traditional Chinese Medicine* (Washington, D.C.: Island Press/Shearwater Books, 2005), 90.

4. Ben Davies, *Black Market: Inside the Endangered Species Trade in Asia* (San Rafael, CA: Earth Aware Editions, 2005), 60–61. Davies records that King George V killed several tigers and eighteen rhinoceros in Nepal in 1911, just one of many hunting trips by Britain's royal family.

5. This is according to the Born Free Foundation, an England-based nonprofit; http://www.bornfree.org.uk.

6. See IUCN Red List of Threatened Species, http://www.iucnredlist.org/apps/redlist/details/15955/0, accessed July 2011.

7. "Tigers—an Iconic Species in Danger of Extinction," Traffic, http://www.traffic.org/tigers, accessed August 16, 2011.

8. Hou Jinglun, *Medicated Diet of Traditional Chinese Medicine* (Beijing: Beijing Science and Technology Press, 1994).

9. Ibid., 31.

10. Jonathan Watts, "Chinese Zoo Closed amid Tiger Starvation Investigation," *The Guardian*, March 17, 2010.

11. According to Traffic, the average retail price of raw tiger bone offered in shops across China in 2005 and 2006 was $6.42 per gram, or $160,000 for the 25 kilograms of bones in an adult tiger; see Kristin Nowell and Xu Ling, "Taming the Tiger Trade: China's Markets for Wild and Captive Tiger Products Since

the 1993 Domestic Trade Ban," *Traffic East Asia*, 2007. In *When a Billion Chinese Jump: How China Will Save Mankind—or Destroy It* (London: Faber and Faber, 2010), Jonathan Watts offers details on the value of other tiger parts.

12. The sale of tiger parts was banned under China's 1988 Wildlife Protection Law, which prohibited the killing of some 1,300 endangered species, encouraged the establishment of nature reserves, and made wild animals the property of the state. In 1993, Beijing strengthened that law in regard to tigers by explicitly banning the sale of any product that contained any tiger part or derivative—including wines in which tiger bones had been soaked. Yet farms have continued to operate openly. Until recently, the Xiongsen Bear and Tiger Mountain Village in China's southern Guangxi Province offered tiger-shaped bottles filled with what it advertised as "bone-strengthening wine." Shop assistants claimed the brew was distilled in vats containing tiger paws. The company's website advertised wines containing "the bones of captive-bred animals which have died at the breeding center"; see Nowell and Xu, "Taming the Tiger Trade," 30. Until 2008, tourists could also buy tiger steaks advertised as "big king meat"; see Andrew Jacobs, "Tiger Farms in China Feed Thirst for Parts," *New York Times*, February 13, 2010. A steady stream of visitors—many of whom arrive only long enough to buy a few bottles of wine—underscores the superficiality of China's environmental laws.

13. UN Office on Drugs and Crime, "The Globalization of Crime: A Transnational Organized Crime Threat Assessment," 2010.

14. Ibid., 156.

15. Neil MacFarquhar, "Talks to Address Trade in Tuna and Ivory," *New York Times*, March 11, 2010.

16. Samuel Wasser et al., "Elephants, Ivory, and Trade," *Science*, March 12, 2010, 1331.

17. UN Office on Drugs and Crime, "The Globalization of Crime," 159. The value of rhino horn is given in Sarah Lyall's, "Rhino Horns Put Europe's Museums on Thieves' Must-Visit List," *New York Times*, August 26, 2011.

18. According to Save the Rhino International, there were fewer than 29,000 wild rhinos alive in 2012.

19. Juliet Elipern, *Demon Fish: Travels Through the Hidden World of Sharks* (New York: Pantheon Books, 2011), Kindle edition, location 1162. The number of sharks killed annually is contested. Some scientists suggest as few as 23 million, others as many as 100 million. Quantifying the trade is difficult both because many countries do not report their shark catch (or report it together with related species) and because many fishermen do not report their total catch to avoid taxes or limits or because of poor recordkeeping. Elipern's figure of 73 million sharks killed each year references the work of Shelley Clarke, a biology professor at Imperial College, London, who studied specific shark fin markets and then used mathematical modeling to estimate global sales.

20. Wild Aid and Oceana, "The End of the Line? Global Threats to Sharks," 2007, 38–39, http://oceana.org/en/news-media/publications/reports/end-of-the-line-global-threats-to-sharks.

21. Jane Flanagan, "Rhino Poaching on the Rise in South Africa," *The Telegraph*, July 18, 2010.

22. Watts, *When a Billion Chinese Jump*, 87.

23. Traffic, "The State of Wildlife Trade in China: Information on the Trade in Wild Animals and Plants in China in 2007," 3, http://www.traffic.org/general-topics.

24. Jane Goodall, introduction to Davies, *Black Market*, 11. Goodall quotes a wildlife conservationist in Cambodia comparing the Chinese market to "a giant vacuum cleaner sucking out all the animals" in his and neighboring countries. Goodall calls the "size of the Chinese demand for wild animals and their body parts, and its cultural influence throughout the region . . . frightening" but notes that "the blame cannot be laid only on China. The smuggling of exotic birds and other animals, including fish and reptiles, into Europe and America for the pet trade is a highly profitable business for dealers in many Asian countries" and the "commercial hunting of wild animals for food, has also grown out of all proportion worldwide."

25. Watts, *When a Billion Chinese Jump*, 91.

26. Ibid., 91.

27. These and other examples of the importance of top predators to ecosystems are described in William Stolzenburg, *Where the Wild Things Were* (New York: Bloomsbury, 2008).

28. Such early fascinations leave deep marks and it is no coincidence that a wide range of companies and governments associate themselves with the tiger's image. ExxonMobil, in 2012 the world's most profitable company, uses a tiger as its symbol; see "The World's Biggest Public Companies," Forbes Global 2000 Leading Companies, http://www.forbes.com/global2000/list, accessed April 21, 2012. Six nations—Bangladesh, Nepal, India, Malaysia, North Korea, and South Korea—have adopted tigers as their national animal.

29. India protects some 60 percent of Asia's remaining elephants, which number around 50,000.

30. According to the 2001 Indian census, 80 percent of Indians described themselves as Hindus. Vincent Sheean gives the dates of Buddhist domination of India in "The Buddhism That Was India," published in *Foreign Affairs* 29, no. 2 (1951): 287.

31. According to the most recent census data, India's population is 1.21 billion, 17 percent of the world's 6.95 billion people.

32. The Tibetan desire to own tiger skins also has a long cultural context. For generations, rich Tibetans laid down tiger skins for their brides during wedding ceremonies. Between the second and ninth centuries, a group of Tibetan kings presented their military commanders with animal skins to wear on their robes. Tiger skins were given to the greatest leaders, perhaps setting a precedent for the more recent demand; see Environmental Investigation Agency and the Wildlife Protection Society of India, "Skinning the Cat: Crime and Politics of the Big Cat Skin Trade," 13.

5. THE SIXTH GREAT EXTINCTION

1. David Quammen, *The Song of the Dodo* (New York: Scribner, 1997), 263.

2. Richard Ellis, *No Turning Back: The Life and Death of Animal Species* (New York: Harper Perennial, 2004), 160.

3. According to the website The Sixth Extinction (http://www.petermaas.nl/extinct/index.html), there were twenty confirmed extinctions in the 1960s.

4. The UN Millennium Ecosystem Assessment notes that the rate of known extinctions in the past century is roughly 50 to 500 times greater than the extinction

rate calculated from the fossil record of 0.1 to 1 extinctions per 1,000 species per 1,000 years. The rate jumps to as much as 1,000 times higher than the background extinction rates if possibly extinct species such as the Yangtze River dolphin are included. Millennium Ecosystem Assessment, *Ecosystems and Human Well-being: Synthesis Report* (Washington, D.C.: Island Press, 2005), 5.

5. Ibid.

6. Ibid. Stuart Pimm, an expert on extinction rates at Duke University's Nicholas School of the Environment (and who did much of the science used in the Millennium Ecosystem Assessment), explains the shift from the baseline number of extinctions to what we're seeing today by relating it to the world's birds. Since about 10,000 species of birds currently exist globally, one species would have become extinct every hundred years at the baseline extinction rate. That means that assuming a person lived to one hundred, only one species of bird would have become extinct over his or her life. Today, however, bird species are going extinct almost every year, "and there would be several going extinct per year if it weren't for conservation efforts," Pimm wrote in an email to the author. "Moreover, a thousand species of birds are at imminent risk of extinction at present, showing that the extinction rate could increase rapidly. Similar arguments apply to mammals." Pimm was the lead author of a July 1995 study titled "The Future of Biodiversity," published in *Science*, that first explained the science behind the baseline extinction numbers.

7. "Wildlife Crisis Worse than Economic Crisis," IUCN, press release, July 2, 2009.

8. Ibid. To determine which species are threatened, IUCN-affiliated scientists analyze population sizes, geographic distributions, and rates of decline, among other factors.

9. Ibid.

10. Ibid.

11. Richard P. Tucker, *Insatiable Appetite: The United States and the Ecological Degradation of the Tropical World* (Lanham, MD: Rowman & Littlefield, 2007), 1. Tucker recounts how American demand for sugar cane, bananas, coffee, rubber, beef, and timber has led to the clearing of huge swaths of tropical forests, often with little or no effort to protect or even to understand local wildlife. "Americans

were largely unaware of the ecological consequences of their prosperity," Tucker writes. "The great distance between corporate policymaking and consumers on the one hand, and the social and environmental impacts in production locations on the other, meant that the impacts of investment and consumption were (and remain today) mostly beyond the horizon of consumers' awareness. In the vacuum of information, the advertising industry romanticized the tropical producers as Chiquita Banana and Juan Valdez and gave no hint of the environmental price paid for our satisfactions" (p. 218). Today's complicated global supply chains make assessing responsibility for environmental damage even more difficult. Furniture is a good example: According to the International Trade Administration, more than half of the furniture sold in the United States in 2010 was made in China. Since China relies heavily on imported timber—much of it illegally felled in some of the world's most beautiful, biodiverse forests—it is fair to say that much of the furniture sold in the United States had direct negative impacts on wildlife. But tracing those supply chains to their sources is difficult. This is covered more fully in Part III of this book.

12. Beijing announced its nuclear expansion plans on March 5, 2011, as part of its twelfth five-year economic development plan. See Deborah Seligsohn and Angel Hsu, "How Does China's 12th Five-Year Plan Address Energy and the Environment?" World Resources Institute, March 7, 2011, http://www.wri.org/stories/2011/03/how-does-chinas-12th-five-year-plan-address-energy-and-envi ronment. For background about China's nuclear power expansion, see David Biello, "China Syndrome: Going Nuclear to Cut Down on Coal Burning," *Scientific American,* March 28, 2011.

13. Traffic, "The State of Wildlife Trade in China: Information on the Trade in Wild Animals and Plants in China in 2007," 12.

14. Rachel M. Wasser and Priscilla Bei Jiao, eds., "Understanding the Motivations: The First Step Toward Influencing China's Unsustainable Wildlife Consumption," *Traffic East Asia,* 2010.

15. Ibid., 9.

16. Fred Pearce, "Rhino Rescue Plan Decimates Asian Antelopes," *New Scientist,* February 12, 2003. The story notes that research commissioned by WWF at the Chinese University of Hong Kong found saiga horn to be as effective as rhino

horn in fighting fevers, and in 1991 WWF began a campaign to publicize it as an alternative. The following year, the UN Environment Program appointed a WWF ecologist to persuade pharmacists across Asia to adopt saiga horn. After the decimation of the wild saiga antelope population, the campaign was abandoned.

17. Richard Ellis, *Tiger Bone & Rhino Horn: The Destruction of Wildlife for Traditional Chinese Medicine* (Washington, D.C.: Island Press/Shearwater Books, 2005), 39.

18. Ibid., 40.

19. Ibid., 191.

20. Ibid., 193.

21. Ibid., 238.

22. For more information on this topic, see Kristen Nowell and Xu Ling, "Taming the Tiger Trade: China's Markets for Wild and Captive Tiger Products Since the 1993 Domestic Trade Ban," *Traffic East Asia,* 2007.

23. Center for Biological Diversity et al., "Emergency Rulemaking Request to Repeal Arkansas' Turtle Collection Law," March 11, 2009, http://www.biological diversity.org/campaigns/southern_and_midwestern_freshwater_turtles/pdfs/ EMERGENCY-PETITION-ARKANSAS-WEB.pdf.

24. Ibid., 12. The study results assume an equal distribution of male and female turtles. A second study found that removing 10 percent of adult snapping turtles could cut their population by half in fifteen years.

25. According to the IUCN's Tortoise and Freshwater Turtle Specialist Group, "anywhere from 48 to 54% of all 328 of their species [are] considered threatened." This is listed in a report by the Turtle Conservation Coalition entitled "Turtles in Trouble: The World's 25+ Most Endangered Tortoises and Freshwater Turtles: 2011," February 2011, available at http://www.iucn-tftsg.org/ trouble/. The report notes that "turtles and tortoises are at a much higher risk of extinction than many other vertebrates: birds (ca. 13%), mammals (ca. 21–25%), sharks and rays (ca. 17–31%), or amphibians (ca. 30–41%) . . . and paralleled among the larger groups only by the primates (ca. 48%)" (p. 9).

26. "Turtles in Trouble," 21.

6. CORBETT NATIONAL PARK

1. The World Bank–led program is called the Global Tiger Initiative.

2. Eric Dinerstein et al., "The Fate of Wild Tigers," *BioScience* 57, no. 6 (June 2007): 508–514.

3. Jim Corbett, *Man-Eaters of Kumaon* (New Delhi: Oxford University Press, 1944), and David Quammen, *Monster of God: The Man-Eating Predator in the Jungles of History and the Mind* (New York: W.W. Norton, 2003), 4.

4. Quammen, *Monster of God*, 431.

5. Philip Shabecoff's *A Fierce Green Fire* (Washington, D.C.: Island Press, 2003) offers a clearly written history of the impact of early North American development on wilderness and wildlife.

6. This study and the two studies described in the next paragraphs are detailed in the very readable book *Where the Wild Things Were: Life, Death, and Ecological Wreckage in a Land of Vanishing Predators* by William Stolzenburg (New York: Bloomsbury, 2008).

7. Thomas Lovejoy, introduction to Michael Soule and Bruce Wilcox, eds., *Conservation Biology: An Evolutionary-Ecological Perspective* (Sunderland, MA: Sinauer Associates Press, 1980).

8. Secretariat of the Convention on Biological Diversity, *Global Biodiversity Outlook 3*, Montreal, 2010. See particularly pages 24–31. The report states, "Preliminary assessments suggest that 23% of plant species are threatened."

7. A FOREST LAID FLAT

1. Alfred Russel Wallace, *The Malay Archipelago: The Land of the Orang-Utan and the Bird of Paradise, a Narrative of Travel with Studies of Man and Nature*, vol. 2 (Public Domain Books, 2006), Kindle edition, location 4104.

2. Vojtech Novotny, *Notebooks from New Guinea: Fieldnotes of a Tropical Biologist* (Oxford: Oxford University Press, 2009), Kindle edition, location 219.

3. Unless otherwise noted, all of the quotes from Wallace are from *The Malay Archipelago*.

4. It is impossible to exactly quantify the share of global biodiversity found in

New Guinea, but scientists generally offer a figure between 5 percent and 7 percent. The Wildlife Conservation Society states that Papua New Guinea alone protects "almost 7 percent of the world's biodiversity" including "more than 200 species of mammals and 700 species of birds, as well as 21,000 species of plants"; see the Wildlife Conservation Society Papua New Guinea page, http://www.wcs.org/where-we-work/asia/papua-new-guinea.aspx, accessed February 24, 2012.

5. Edward O. Wilson, *The Future of Life* (New York: Vintage, 2003), 144.

6. Norman Myers et al., "Biodiversity Hotspots and Major Tropical Wilderness Areas: Approaches to Setting Conservation Priorities," *Conservation Biology* 12, no. 3 (June 1998): 516–520. Myers, an adjunct professor at Duke University, specializes in biodiversity. Some of his work, particularly related to climate change, has been criticized by some experts as lacking empirical data.

7. Sze Pang Cheung, Tiy Chung, and Tamara Stark, "Merbau's Last Stand: How Industrial Logging Is Driving the Destruction of the Paradise Forests of Asia Pacific," Greenpeace International, April 17, 2007.

8. The Greenpeace report cites a study of one logging concession in Papua New Guinea where forty-five trees were felled for every tree selected for commercial removal. Much of the destruction comes because loggers must cut roads into concessions and to trees of high commercial worth. Often they leave less valuable parts of trees, including roots and branches.

9. Cheung, Chung, and Stark, "Merbau's Last Stand," 26.

10. Author interview with Sun Xiufang, a China analyst for Forest Trends. While data on total forest products consumption is complicated by factors including how well data is kept and how much wood is taken for personal use in cooking and heating, Sun said China's consumption had risen from about 120 million cubic meters in 1998 to more than 350 million cubic meters in 2010.

11. Sun Xiufang and Kerstin Canby, "China: Overview of Forest Governance, Markets and Trade," Forest Trends for FLEGT Asia Regional Programme, November 2010. According to the report, imports rose from 40 million cubic meters to 113 million cubic meters; exports, measured by dollar value, grew from roughly $3 billion to $27 billion. The United States became China's top export

market for forest products in 2000; in 2005 the United States took 35 percent of that segment's export value, according to Forest Trends. China's efficiencies have also pushed down the price of wood products: the International Tropical Timber Organization, a UN-backed intergovernmental group, listed China's "highly competitive prices" as a "significant factor helping to boost wood's overall market share in the global flooring market"; see International Tropical Timber Association, "Annual Review and Assessment of the World Timber Situation 2009," November 2009, http://www.itto.int.

12. Sun and Canby, "China: Overview of Forest Governance, Markets and Trade," 9. The 94 percent figure comes from an author interview with Bob Flynn, RISI's director of international timber.

13. Sun and Canby, "China: Overview of Forest Governance, Markets and Trade," 15. The report notes, "For new housing units alone, China's Sino-Forest company has estimated roughly 1 billion cubic meters of wood fiber will be required over the next 3 to 5 years for construction, furniture, and decoration (compared to the estimated 160 million cubic meters of domestic consumption in 2008)." In 2010, China's total consumption of wood products was slightly more than 350 million cubic meters, including timber and pulp used in products that were exported.

14. Andy White et al., "China and the Global Market for Forest Products; Transforming Trade to Benefit Forests and Livelihoods," Forest Trends, 2006.

15. Ibid., 13. During that nine-year period, more than 14 percent of Russia's forests were damaged by fire or logging, much of it illegal. This is also noted in Anonymous, "Seeing the Wood," *The Economist*, September 25, 2010.

16. Tamara Stark and Sze Pang Cheung, "Sharing the Blame: Global Consumption and China's Role in Ancient Forest Destruction," Greenpeace International and Greenpeace China, March 28, 2006. The Greenpeace accounting relied primarily on Chinese customs data and data provided by China to the UN Food and Agriculture Organization. Data on global timber and wood pulp exports and imports is notoriously difficult to track because much of it is not recorded and nations use different accounting practices.

17. The calculation that more than half of the forest losses came after the beginning of the Industrial Revolution comes from Richard Houghton, a senior scientist at the Woods Hole Research Center (author interview). In a manuscript titled

"Historic Changes in Terrestrial Carbon Storage," Houghton states that carbon lost from human clearing of land, largely from the conversion of forests to agricultural areas, was greater over "the past century or so" than "for all of time before 1850." In *Collapse*, Jared Diamond writes that "more than half of the world's original forests have been cleared or heavily damaged in the last 8,000 years and more than half of those losses happened in the past 50 years as global population and consumption have risen." Jared Diamond, *Collapse: How Societies Choose to Fail or Succeed* (New York: Viking Press, 2005).

18. World Commission on Forests and Sustainable Development, "Our Forests, Our Future: Summary Report," 1999, http://www.iisd.org/publications/pub .aspx?id=333. See also Anonymous, "Seeing the Wood."

19. Dirk Bryant, Daniel Nielsen, and Laura Tangley, "The Last Frontier Forests: Ecosystems and Economies on the Edge," World Resources Institute, 1997.

20. Leao Serva, "An Assault on the Amazon," *New York Times*, November 16, 2011. See also "Global Forest and Trade Network," WWF, http://gftn.panda.org/gftn_ worldwide/north_america/, accessed November 15, 2011.

21. Stark and Cheung, "Sharing the Blame," 13.

22. The import price of merbau in China more than doubled between 2004 and 2006 to $660 per cubic meter, partly explaining how traders have profited. Large, old-growth tropical hardwoods tend to hold between 4 and 6 usable cubic meters of wood.

8. NEW GUINEA

1. The U.S. embassy in Beijing began posting hourly Twitter updates on the level of PM 2.5 in 2009, and on that November afternoon the level went above 500, the EPA's top reading, for the first time. The embassy's tweet described the city's pollution level as "crazy bad," an undiplomatic description that was apparently programmed by a computer specialist with a sense of humor. The embassy quickly changed the terminology to "beyond index." Partly because of pressure created by the U.S. measurements, the Beijing government began publicly reporting PM 2.5 levels in early 2012, but from only one station in the city.

2. UNEP, "The Great Apes: The Road Ahead," 2002, http://www.globio.info. This

and other reports prompted Indonesia's government to introduce a series of export bans between 2001 and 2004. Since the crackdown, "illegal logging in the country and the flow of illegal timber smuggled out have declined," the Environmental Investigation Agency reported in 2011. However, "threats to forests remain in the form of unbridled expansion of plantations and mining. A recent report found that 40–61 percent of all logging in Indonesia still involves illegalities"; see "The Bali Declaration Ten Years On," EIA, 2011. For another early warning about rapid deforestation in Indonesia, see D. Holmes, "Deforestation in Indonesia: A View of the Situation in 1999," World Bank, Jakarta, 2000.

3. Mark Broich et al., "Remotely Sensed Forest Cover Loss Shows High Spatial and Temporal Variation Across Sumatera and Kalimantan, Indonesia 2000–2008," *Environmental Research Letters* 6, 014010. The Greenpeace report "Sharing the Blame," published in 2006, states that Indonesia had "already lost 72 percent of its large intact ancient forests."

4. Phil Shearman et al., *The State of the Forests of Papua New Guinea: Mapping the Extent and Condition of Forest Cover and Measuring the Drivers of Forest Change in the Period 1972–2002* (Port Moresby: University of Papua New Guinea, 2008), 17.

5. According to estimates in the *IPCC Fourth Assessment Report: Climate Change 2007,* global forest vegetation contains 283 billion tons of carbon in biomass, 38 billion tons in dead wood, and 317 billion tons in soils (in the top 30 centimeters) and litter. The total carbon content of forest ecosystems, 638 billion tons, exceeds the amount of carbon in the atmosphere; UN Food and Agricultural Organization, "State of the World's Forests 2011" (Rome: FAO, 2011), 59.

6. Stephan Faris, *Forecast: The Consequences of Climate Change, from the Amazon to the Arctic, from Darfur to Napa Valley* (New York: Henry Holt, 2009), 114. Faris reports that, in 2006, the amount of carbon released into the atmosphere by Brazilian deforestation amounted to three times the amount released by all of the country's cars and industries.

7. FAO, "Global Forest Resources Assessment 2010," Rome, 2010. The report states that forests cover 31 percent of the world's total land area and that 36 percent of those forests are "primary," which the FAO defines as "forest of native species where there are no clearly visible indications of human activities and the ecological

processes have not been significantly disturbed." Numerous sources state that roughly 80 percent of terrestrial biodiversity is housed in forests. One source is Anonymous, "The World's Lungs," *The Economist*, September 25, 2010.

8. Bruce Beehler, *Lost Worlds: Adventures in the Tropical Rainforest* (New Haven, CT: Yale University Press, 2008), Kindle edition, location 36.

9. U.S. Fish and Wildlife Service Endangered Species Program, "Why Saving Endangered Species Matters," USFWS, February 2002. The document notes that scientists have "only partially investigated about 2 percent of the more than 250,000 known plant species for possible medicinal values."

10. The World Health Organization estimates that in many developing nations more than 80 percent of people rely on natural cures; see FAO, "State of the World's Forests 2011," 79. Drug companies are reluctant to test the wild pharmacopeia at least partly because it is difficult to patent natural cures.

11. Novotny explained that the center scientists would likely identify the familes of all of the insects they collect but may be unable to identify their genera and species. Since they haven't been classified, no one can say with any precision how many insects will be found, if they are ever fully researched. Novotny estimated the number at 250,000 because he (conservatively) estimated that New Guinea protects 5 percent of global species diversity, and many scientists currently estimate the total number of insect species globally at 5 million. Because of poor information sharing, it is also impossible to say how many insect species in New Guinea have so far been identified. Novotny believes the number is somewhere between 10,000 and 20,000. Whatever it is, "we know only a tiny fraction of the total," he said.

12. Vojtech Novotny, "Rain Forest Conservation in a Tribal World: Why Forest Dwellers Prefer Loggers to Conservationists," *Biotropica* 1–4 (2010): special section 1–4.

13. Goodwill Amos, a Papua New Guinea National Forest Service expert, said that the country had between 12 million and 13 million hectares of intact rain forest in 2010.

14. Phil Shearman et al., *The State of the Forests of Papua New Guinea*, 25.

15. Ibid.

16. According to a Papua New Guinea Forest Authority report, Papua New Guinea exported 2,835,402 cubic meters of logs in 2007. The comparison of how much usable wood can be taken from a full-grown New England maple (roughly 1 cubic meter) or Pacific coast Douglas fir (roughly 2 cubic meters) comes from Bob Flynn, the director of international timber for the timber consultancy RISI.

17. Very few Chinese are even aware that the furniture or floorboards they buy may come from illegally felled trees or from trees felled in some of the world's last old-growth forests. William Laurance, a biologist at Australia's James Cook University, recently wrote that when he served as the president of the Association for Tropical Biology and Conservation, he talked with Chinese journalists about the problem of illegal logging and the risks it posed for Chinese companies. "To my knowledge, not a single story about my concerns was reported in China, even though I emailed the journalists a summary of my comments translated into Mandarin Chinese," Laurance wrote. "When it comes to illegal or predatory logging, it has not been easy to get Chinese attention"; see William Laurance, "China's Appetite for Wood Takes a Heavy Toll on Forests," *Yale Environment 360*, November 17, 2011. The Greenpeace campaign is reported in Geoff Mohan's "Mattel Drops Paper Company Linked to Indonesia Deforestation," *Los Angeles Times*, October 5, 2011.

18. *The State of the Forests of Papua New Guinea* estimates that Papua New Guinea's primary and secondary forests together stored at least 4.7 billion tons of carbon in 2002. The estimate did not include carbon stored in the soil, which could also be lost to the atmosphere if the forest is cleared and the soil dries (p. 19). According to the U.S. Energy Information Administration, the world emitted just over 31 billion tons of carbon dioxide from burning fossil fuels in 2010, an amount equal to 8.5 billion metric tons of carbon. (To convert carbon dioxide to carbon, divide by 3.67.)

19. Quoted in Bill McKibben, *The End of Nature* (New York: Anchor Books, 1999), 74.

20. Ibid., 72.

9. OUR FUTURE FORESTS

1. The World Commission on Forests and Sustainable Development, "Our Forests, Our Future: Summary Report," 6.

2. According to Houghton, the "amount of carbon lost from terrestrial ecosystems" since roughly 1850, near the beginning of the Industrial Revolution, is one to three times greater than all of the losses that came before that date.

3. Because mature forests are carbon neutral—neither taking in nor releasing carbon outside of their annual winter-summer cycle—their regrowth would only buy us a century or so, but that might give people time to figure out alternatives to a heavily fossil fuel–based economy.

4. WWF, "China's Role in Global Trade: Opportunities and Risks in the Forestry and Mining Sector," May 2011.

5. As the price of soybeans spiked, the rate jumped almost sixfold between the spring of 2010 and the spring of 2011. The losses were centered on Brazil's Mato Grosso state, the heart of the country's soy farming region; see BBC, "Brazil: Amazon Rainforest Destruction Rises Sharply," May 19, 2011.

6. The former editor in chief of *Diário de São Paulo* wrote that "according to the World Wildlife Fund, at current rates of deforestation, 55 percent of the Amazon rain forest could be gone by 2030"; see Leao Serva, "An Assault on the Amazon," *New York Times*, November 16, 2011.

7. Environmental Investigation Agency, "Putting the Brakes on Drivers of Forest Destruction: A Shared Responsibility," December 2009, http://www.eia-global.org/PDF/Report–Copenhagen–Dec09.pdf.

8. According to the Food and Agriculture Organization ("Global Forest Resources Assessment 2010," Rome, 2010), the world used roughly 1.7 billion cubic meters of wood in all of its various industrial industries (paper, lumber, cardboard, furniture, etc.) in 2005. It used another 1.7 billion cubic meters of wood as fuel. The Forest Trends and CIFOR report, "China and the Global Market for Forest Products," states that China's forest products imports grew at an average rate of 16 percent between 1997 and 2005, when it imported 134 million cubic meters (pp. 6–7). Continued 16 percent growth would have put China's 2015 imports at 591 million cubic meters. That prognosis now looks too dire since estimates of China's total forest products imports in 2005 were revised down in later reports. The average rate at which China's imports have grown, however, has remained at roughly 16 percent through 2011, according to Bob Flynn at RISI.

9. Cathy Harper, "Resource Grab Endangering Asia Forests," *Australia Network News*, October 6, 2011.

10. China's growing demand for tropical imports—including trees, sugarcane, fruit, coffee, meat, palm oil, and soy—mirrors the growth of Western demand in the nineteenth and twentieth centuries. To look more closely at the developed world's impact on tropical forests, it helps to examine demand for particular products. For example, Americans had their first taste of bananas when a ship captain bought 160 bunches of the fruit at a Jamaican wharf and sold it in New York in 1870. A century later, the United States was hooked on the fruit: in the 1970s, the average American ate nearly 25 pounds of bananas a year.

    Coffee offers another case study. In 1900, Americans imported 750 million pounds of coffee beans from the Caribbean, 13 pounds a year for every citizen. By 1961, demand had reached 3 billion pounds, almost all of it supplied by plantations in Latin America. A 1963 survey reported that the average American over the age of ten drank 3 cups of coffee each day for a total of 441 million cups, half of the world's total trade.

    Given that bananas, coffee, and many other products sought by Americans grew only in the tropics, it is not surprising that between 1950 and 1985, roughly half of the Eastern Hemisphere's rain forests were cleared. The environmental historian Richard Tucker has called these ecological impacts an "almost totally ignored . . . dimension" of the American empire: "The twentieth-century American empire . . . has surpassed all others in its grasp of Nature's global resources and thus in its worldwide ecological impacts," Tucker wrote in his 2007 book *Insatiable Appetite*, which provides the details of trade in bananas and coffee.

11. Jared Diamond, *Collapse*, 473.

12. FAO, "Global Forest Resources Assessment 2010."

13. UN Office on Drugs and Crime, "The Globalization of Crime: A Transnational Organized Crime Threat Assessment," UNODC, 2010.

14. These figures come from various sources. China's illegal shipments from Myanmar and Indonesia are listed in the UNODC report "The Globalization of Crime" (p. 167). Elizabeth Economy, the director for Asia Studies at the Council on Foreign Relations, gave the figures for Brazil and Gabon during a talk at the University of Southern California in 2007. The Tanzania figure is given in

WWF's "China's Role in Global Trade: Opportunities and Risks in the Forestry and Mining Sector." The Papua New Guinea figure came from a World Bank study. The European Union parliament recently estimated that illegal sources, in sum, could account for as much as 40 percent of global industrial wood production; see European Parliament press release, "MEPs Adopt Rules to Keep Illegal Timber off the EU Market," April 2009.

15. Tim Radford, "Huge Rise in Siberian Forest Fires Puts Planet at Risk, Scientists Warn," *The Guardian*, May 31, 2005.

16. *U.S. Federal Register* 76, no. 39, February 28, 2011, http://www.illegal-logging .info/uploads/228FR.pdf.

17. Chen Yong was a deputy director at the State Forestry Administration's Center for International Forest Products Trade. Chen said that while China was not planning to enact a law similar to the Lacey Act amendment or the EU's Timber Action Plan regulation, Beijing had been helping countries from which it imports timber to improve their forest management. Among other things, the State Forestry Administration invites "several hundred" forestry officials to China each year to study forest management practices. "We can only enforce our domestic regulations but we hope other countries will also do a good job of enforcing their own laws," Chen said. China has recently taken other steps that could lead to better enforcement of other nations' forestry laws: in 2011, Chinese officials commissioned an analysis of China's role in importing illegal timber and drafted guidelines to improve the sustainability of its timber-importing companies. Chinese officials also point out that even as imports have grown, China has reforested vast areas domestically. According to the FAO, forest cover in China increased from 157 million hectares in 1990 to 197 million hectares in 2005.

18. Diamond, *Collapse*, 473.

19. "PNG Constitutional Planning Committee Report," 1974, Chapter 2: National Goals and Directive Principles, http://www.paclii.org/pg/CPCReport/Cap2 .htm, accessed November 18, 2011.

20. Forest Trends, *Logging, Legality, and Livelihoods in Papua New Guinea: Synthesis of Official Assessments of the Large-Scale Logging Industry*, vol. 1 (Washington, D.C., 2006), 47, http://www.forest-trends.org/documents/files/doc_105.pdf.

21. Villagers in Papua New Guinea generally do not want to disclose the financial

arrangements they make with logging companies, perhaps out of fear that the government will try to take some of the money, perhaps because they worry that other villages received more. The national government had set a minimum payment of 30 kina per cubic meter of kwilla extracted.

22. This and other quotes in this section are taken from Jane R. Camerini, ed., "Collecting Birds of Paradise," *The Alfred Russel Wallace Reader* (Baltimore, MD: Johns Hopkins University Press, 2002).

23. Italics are Wallace's own.

10. TIME TRAVEL

1. The data about Shanghai's level of ownership and disposable income comes from the *China Statistical Yearbook*, 2011 edition (Beijing: China Statistical Press, 2011). Jonathan Watts's book *When a Billion Chinese Jump: How China Will Save Mankind—or Destroy It* (London: Faber and Faber, 2010) offers a clear portrayal of Shanghai's rising consumer ethic and includes the fact that Shanghainese surpassed the per capita UK carbon footprint (p. 166).

2. According to BP's *2011 Statistical Review of World Energy*, energy use in China created 8.33 billion tons of carbon dioxide in 2010. The global total for 2010 was 33.16 billion tons, giving China a 25 percent share; see Nina Chestney, "China's CO_2 Emissions Rose 10 Percent in 2010: BP Data," *Reuters*, June 8, 2011. Other organizations have slightly different figures.

3. According to the International Energy Agency, China emitted 2.9 billion tons of carbon dioxide in 1995 and 6.9 billion tons in 2009. The IEA calculates carbon emissions using both a "reference approach"—which looks at the emissions from total energy demand—and a "sectoral approach"—which attempts to quantify how various fuels are used. I am using the IEA's reference case numbers throughout this book. Unless otherwise noted, IEA data is listed in *World Energy Outlook 2011*.

4. Energy Information Administration, *International Energy Outlook 1998*, p. 142.

5. There was considerable debate about when China would overtake the United States as the top emitter. In his 2005 best-selling book *Collapse*, Jared Diamond wrote "If current trends continue—emissions rising in China, steady in the

U.S., declining elsewhere—China will become the world's leader in carbon emissions, accounting for 40 percent of the world's total, by the year 2050." Other recent estimates also turned out to be off by many years.

6. Elizabeth Kolbert, *Field Notes from a Catastrophe: Man, Nature, and Climate Change* (New York: Bloomsbury, 2006), 181.

7. Netherlands Environmental Assessment Agency, "China Now No. 1 in CO_2 Emissions; USA in Second Position," press release, June 19, 2007. The cement figure is given in John Vidal and David Adam, "China Overtakes US as World's Biggest CO_2 Emitter," *The Guardian*, June 19, 2007. The International Energy Agency also later calculated, using different figures, that China overtook the United States as the world's top emitter of carbon dioxide in 2007.

8. Daniel Yergin, *The Quest: Energy, Security, and the Remaking of the Modern World* (New York: Penguin Press, 2011), Kindle edition, locations 8119–8128.

9. This figure is quoted in Wang Tao and Jim Watson, "China's Energy Transition: Pathways for Low Carbon Development," Sussex Energy Group SPRU, University of Sussex, UK, and Tyndall Centre for Climate Change Research, 2009, 12.

10. Elizabeth Rosenthal, "China Increases Lead as Biggest Carbon Dioxide Emitter," *New York Times*, June 14, 2008. Rosenthal noted that India's per capita carbon emissions were less than one-tenth of the American average.

11. Matt Pottinger, "Invisible Export—A Hidden Cost of China's Growth: Mercury Migration," *Wall Street Journal*, December 20, 2004.

12. Sharon Begley, "Wake Up Call," *Newsweek*, December 21, 1997.

13. Craig Simons, "A 'Sunburnt' Country Battles Drought," Cox News Service, November 4, 2007. Most rainwater is caught by plants, aquifers, and an increasing number of channels and ponds dug by people who want to store as much runoff as possible.

14. "4th Assessment Report, Working Group I, Summary for Policy Makers," IPCC, 2007. The report notes that the "total temperature increase from 1850–1899 to 2001–2005 is 0.76°C," which is equal to 1.37°F.

15. Shortly before my trip, the UN High Commissioner for Refugees estimated that roughly twice as many people are forced to move because of environmental

factors as because of war or persecution, a ratio many experts expect to rise as global warming becomes more severe.

16. International Energy Agency, "CO_2 Emissions from Fuel Combustion Highlights," IEA, 2011, 18. In 2009, fossil sources accounted for 81 percent of total global energy supply, a share that had remained relatively unchanged for the previous thirty-five years.

17. Global economic growth is difficult to calculate but according to Jeffrey Sachs, an economist at Columbia University, a "rough estimate suggests that the gross world product, the sum of the gross domestic products of every nation in the world, has risen by a remarkable eight times" between 1950 and 2008. Jeffrey Sachs, *Common Wealth: Economics for a Crowded Planet* (New York: Penguin Books, 2008), 19.

18. Most of the coal-fired power plants in the United States are more than thirty years old and are nearing retirement. According to the Edison Electric Institute, utilities will take roughly 14 percent of total coal-fired electricity generation in the United States offline by 2022. Much of that capacity will be replaced by alternative fuel sources. In 2010, Credit Suisse predicted that coal demand in the United States could drop by 15 to 30 percent over the coming decade; see Jonathan Thompson, "As Coal Use Declines in US, Coal Companies Focus on China," *Yale Environment 360*, December 8, 2011.

19. The rest of China's energy is provided by the following sources: "biomass and waste"—plants and fuels derived from plants, together with recyclable waste—contributes nine percent; hydroelectricity contributes 2 percent; and nuclear power supplies 1 percent. Power generated by wind turbines is growing rapidly, but its contribution is minimal, and while China is the world's top manufacturer of solar panels, it exports almost all of them: in 2010, solar accounted for only a fraction of 1 percent of its generated electricity; see *World Energy Outlook 2011*, 592.

20. IEA, *World Energy Outlook 2011*, 593. In a "current policies scenario," China's total energy demand—about half of which would be accounted for by generating electricity—would grow by just over 2 billion tons of oil equivalent by 2035. In 2009, the total primary energy demand in the United States was 2.2 billion tons of oil equivalent, an amount that is likely to remain relatively stable through 2035 even without new policies (p. 556).

21. IEA, *World Energy Outlook 2011*, Tables for Scenario Projections, 543–615.

22. For more about the die-off, see Jennifer C. McElwain and Surangi W. Punyasena, "Mass Extinction Events and the Plant Fossil Record," *Trends in Ecology and Evolution* 22, no. 10, October 4, 2007.

23. Obama made the promise before the 2009 Copenhagen climate change conference. As with most national pledges to reduce emissions, the commitment was complicated by various numbers: the U.S. pledge was to reduce its emissions by 17 percent from its 2005 levels by 2020. The IEA scenarios for future carbon emissions are detailed in their *World Energy Outlook 2011*, chapter 6.

24. Justin Gillis, "As Permafrost Thaws, Scientists Study the Risks," *New York Times*, December 16, 2011.

25. IEA, *World Energy Outlook 2011*, 207.

26. Nan Zhou et al., "Peak CO_2? China's Emissions Trajectories to 2050," Lawrence Berkeley National Laboratory, June 2011.

27. According to the McKinsey Global Institute, 350 million rural Chinese will move to cities between 2005 and 2025, an average of 1.8 million each month. Philadelphia has a population of 1.5 million; Barcelona has a population of 1.6 million.

28. The average Chinese urban resident used 71 percent more energy than the average rural resident in 2009, according to China's National Bureau of Statistics. The ratio has been falling rapidly as rural Chinese get richer, however. In 2006, urban residents used twice as much energy as rural residents. In 2000, they used almost three times as much. *China Energy Statistical Yearbook 2011* (Beijing: China Statistical Press, 2011).

29. Jenny Barchfield, "China Surpasses U.S. as World's Top Energy Consumer," Associated Press, July 20, 2010.

30. *Minhang Jingji Yu Jishu*, China's Civil Aviation Economy and Technology magazine, reports that 30 million passengers flew in China in 1990. According to China's Civil Aviation Administration, Chinese domestic airlines carried 519 million passengers in 2010.

31. Wang and Watson, "China's Energy Transition," 3.

32. According to Paul Pearson of Cardiff University, there is evidence that atmospheric carbon dioxide levels reached 450 parts per million during the Pliocene
period. During the mid-Pliocene, evidence suggests that the average global
temperature was between 2 and 3 degrees Celsius warmer than today and that
seas were eighty feet higher. For more information, see M. M. Robinson, H. J.
Dowsett, and M. A. Chandler, "Pliocene Role in Assessing Future Climate
Impacts," *EOS* 89, no. 49 (December 2008): 500–502, and Gary S. Dwyer and
M. A. Chandler, "Mid-Pliocene Sea Level and Continental Ice Volume Based on
Coupled Benthic Mg/Ca Palaeotemperatures and Oxygen Isotopes," *Philosophical
Transactions of the Royal Society A* 367 (2009): 157–168.

33. Wang and Watson, "China's Energy Transition," 21. The report states that a concentration of 450 parts per million would cause the global temperature to rise
by between 1.9 and 4.4 degrees Celsius, with the most likely result being an
overall warming of three degrees. To convert Celsius to Fahrenheit, multiply by
nine-fifths and add 32.

34. Because the climate is complex and can feed back upon itself in unexpected
ways, the IPCC has generally been careful not to overstep what can be proven,
making it difficult for them to say with certainty that such climatic shifts would
happen. However, they have said that as the world warms, the frequency of
"heavy precipitation events" is "very likely" to increase, the area of land affected
by drought is likely to increase, and "intense tropical cyclone activity" is likely
to increase. The rise in sea level that would result from warmer global temperatures is less controversial; see IPCC, "Climate Change 2007: Synthesis Report,"
November 2007, 13.

35. Costs vary by location and accounting method. For example, wind power is
cheaper in places where it is windy; hydroelectric dams require a large amount
of capital up front but because the energy they tap is essentially free, pay off over
time. Wang Tao offered the following rough breakdown for the costs of producing a kilowatt-hour of electricity in China in 2011: from hydro, less than one-
fifth of a yuan; from coal, less than one-third of a yuan; from wind, less than
0.8 yuan; from solar, slightly above 1.4 yuan. A simple way to think about this
is that, in 2011, solar power cost roughly twice as much as wind power, which
cost twice as much as coal-generated power, which cost twice as much as hydropower. China is by far the world's top producer of hydroelectricity and it plans

to grow its hydropower production significantly over coming decades, but hydrogeneration is obviously limited by the number of rivers in the country and the cost of transporting the energy produced by the stations.

36. This and other figures on 2010 energy use and carbon emissions are taken from IEA, *World Energy Outlook 2011*. The Global Carbon Project, an international collaboration of scientists who track carbon data, announced that emissions from fossil fuels rose by 5.9 percent in 2010, the largest percentage increase since 2003, creating the largest total increase on record. The total global emissions in 2010 were 49 percent higher than global emissions in 1990, the reference year used by the Kyoto Protocol. Information about the study is available at www.globalcarbonproject.org/carbonbudget/10/hl-com pact.htm.

37. According to media reports, the Acela's average speed is roughly 70 mph. The Obama administration proposed spending $53 billion on high-speed rail lines, but congressional Republicans eliminated the project from the budget.

38. The EPA's Household Emissions Calculator website is http://www.epa.gov/ climatechange/emissions/ind_calculator.html.

39. For the country as a whole, the largest source of carbon emissions is electricity generation, at 39 percent, followed by transportation at 31 percent and industrial uses of fossil fuels, such as making plastic, at 13 percent. The breakdown of U.S. emissions sources is listed in the EPA's *Inventory of U.S. Greenhouse Gas Emissions and Sinks: 1990–2009*, available at http://www.epa.gov/climate change/emissions/usinventory.html.

40. The government had raised David's salary from $315 a month after an earthquake in Sichuan Province killed some 70,000 people in early 2008. Many schools collapsed during the earthquake—by one account killing more than 5,600 students—and officials faced intense criticism that the schools were poorly built. The government raised the salaries at least partly to placate teachers, many of whom had lost students, friends, and colleagues. In other parts of China, teacher salaries remain lower.

41. The Economist Intelligence Unit, a research group affiliated with the *Economist* magazine, found that in 2011, 95 percent of "waste" in Beijing was "collected and adequately disposed of." The city had six official recycling plants but likely

had tens of thousands of freelance operations that made some use of discarded materials; see "Asian Green City Index," Economist Intelligence Unit, sponsored by Siemens AG, 2011.

42. This ratio is a little smaller than the per capita emissions ratio for the United States and China if Chinese are not required to account for energy used in export-related manufacturing, which consumes roughly one-third of the country's total energy demand. According to the International Energy Agency, per capita carbon dioxide emissions in the United States in 2008 were 18.3 tons. In China, they were 4.9 tons. Subtracting a third from the Chinese figure to account for energy used in export manufacturing brings per capita emissions to 3.2 tons, a bit under one-sixth of the American number. These numbers, however, are only partly helpful as they hide many things, such as how people are using the energy. In China much of it goes to building roads and making steel, not to heating and cooling homes. It is more helpful to look at how individuals—like David and his parents—use energy. The IEA reports national carbon emissions in their annual publication "CO_2 Emissions from Fuel Combustion."

43. Every gallon of gasoline that is burned produces roughly 19 pounds of carbon dioxide, so a Ford Explorer, which gets about 20 miles to the gallon, would release 114 pounds of carbon dioxide over a 120-mile ride.

44. The national average rural income in 2011 was 5,919 yuan, according to Chinese government data.

45. In the 1970s, 91 percent of American household electricity was consumed by seven things: stoves, indoor lights, refrigerators, freezers, water heaters, air conditioners, and space heating; 9 percent was classified as "other." Today, 45 percent is classified as "other," a category that includes computers, DVD players, televisions, smart phones, and all the other electronics that dominate modern American life; see Yergin, *The Quest*, Kindle location 10570. That explosion of home electronics partly explains why 43 percent of energy in the United States is used by the residential, commercial, and agriculture sectors, compared with a 19 percent share for those sectors in China. Fully 71 percent of China's energy is used by industry, compared with 25 percent in the United States; see "Common Challenge, Collaborative Response: A Roadmap for U.S.-China Cooperation on Energy and Climate Change," Asia Society and the Pew Center on Global Climate Change, January 2009.

46. That leaves 200 to 300 million Chinese whose lives might be more recognizable to Westerners as middle class, and only a tiny fraction of that group earns enough to compete with America's or Europe's middle class: only 2 percent of urban Chinese households have joint incomes above $34,000 a year. By comparison, more than half of all Americans earned at least $34,000 in 2010; see Yuval Atsmon and Max Magni, "Meet the Chinese Consumer of 2020," *McKinsey Quarterly*, March 2012.

47. China's motor vehicle numbers are complicated by what one includes. Growth projections are clouded by possible future policy shifts. But the trends are clear and China's rapid adoption of cars and trucks is perhaps the most pointed example of how quickly Chinese emissions will grow. Even in 2006, experts estimated that China's car fleet would increase *only* sixfold over the first decade of the twenty-first century. Instead it grew by a factor of twenty. These numbers are given in Deborah Gordon and Yuhan Zhang's report "Driving Force: Energy and Climate Strategies for China's Motorization," Carnegie Endowment for International Peace, April 14, 2011. Another good source is Daniel Sperling and Deborah Gordon's book *Two Billion Cars: Driving Toward Sustainability* (New York: Oxford University Press, 2009).

48. Even with high fuel-efficiency standards, Chinese demand for energy to run its vehicle fleet will be tremendous. According to the International Energy Agency, China is expected to surpass the United States as the world's top oil consumer by 2035, an estimate that might prove conservative.

49. Jonathan Woetzel et al., "Preparing for China's Urban Billion," McKinsey Global Institute, March 2009.

11. HOPENHAGEN

1. Daniel Yergin, *The Quest: Energy, Security, and the Remaking of the Modern World* (New York: Penguin Press, 2011), Kindle edition, location 8458.

2. To understand carbon intensity, imagine that a nation produces $100 worth of goods in a year and emits 100 pounds of carbon. Its carbon intensity would be one pound of carbon for every dollar. If in the next year the same country produced $200 worth of goods and emitted 150 pounds of carbon, its carbon intensity would have fallen to three-quarters of a pound of carbon for every dollar while its total emissions would have increased. Under the administration of George W. Bush, the United States adopted a "greenhouse gas intensity" strategy

that Bush said was preferable to joining the Kyoto Protocol because it recognized that "a nation that grows its economy is a nation that can afford investments and new technology." Many environmental groups called the strategy a political shield for business as usual.

3. China's carbon emissions in 1992 were just over half of U.S. emissions; in 2009, according to IEA data, China's emissions were 30 percent greater than U.S. emissions. A good source for historical emissions data is the Oak Ridge National Laboratory's Carbon Dioxide Information Analysis Center. To determine China's economic growth, I used real per capita GDP figures.

4. *Der Spiegel* obtained audio recordings of the meeting, which it summarized in a story and video. The quotes used here are from Tobias Rapp, Christian Schwagerl, and Gerald Traufetter, "The Copenhagen Protocol: How China and India Sabotaged the UN Climate Summit," *Spiegel Online*, March 5, 2010.

5. Mark Lynas, "How Do I Know China Wrecked the Copenhagen Deal? I Was in the Room," *The Guardian*, December 22, 2009. In his editorial, Lynas states that the Chinese negotiator insisted that the 1.5 degree Celsius target be removed but ceded after the president of the Maldives asked how he could "ask my country to go extinct." The number, however, is "surrounded by language which makes it all but meaningless," Lynas wrote.

6. The U.S.-China Clean Energy Research Center was founded in 2009 and is the most significant bilateral initiative to develop renewable technologies and share expertise. By government standards, however, it is a tiny project. It spent its first year largely unfunded. In April 2010, the U.S. Department of Energy announced that it would provide $7.5 million each year for five years but added that the money could only be used by American scientists and that anyone who wanted access needed to find matching funds. Given the potential costs of Chinese emissions to the United States and to the world, the investment seems a pittance. According to Jerry Fletcher, "There really is no collaboration on renewables right now." He attributed this dearth partly to fear in the United States about China's rise and growing manufacturing competitiveness and partly to the belief that the United States should not help China become stronger. He argued that there should be closer collaboration, particularly in the area of developing carbon capture and storage technology. Because China is building so many new factories and power plants there is an opportunity for researchers to

study CCS on the ground, a key to advancing the technology. "[China] can do things we can't do because they've already got the carbon sitting there waiting for them to capture and store it," he said.

7. Jonathan Watts, Damian Carrington, and Suzanne Goldenberg, "China's Fears of Rich Nation 'Climate Conspiracy' at Copenhagen Revealed," *The Guardian*, February 11, 2010.

8. John M. Broder and James Kanter, "China and U.S. Hit Strident Impasse at Climate Talks," *New York Times*, December 14, 2009.

9. Global emissions in 2010 were 49 percent higher than in 1990, the Kyoto Protocol reference year. According to the Global Carbon Project, a nonprofit supported by governments and scientific organizations, the 2010 increase brought the atmospheric concentration of CO_2 to 389.6 parts per million, 39 percent above the concentration at the beginning of the Industrial Revolution and the highest level in at least 800,000 years. The UNEP figures come from "Impacts of Climate Change Coming Faster and Sooner: New Science Report Underlines Urgency for Governments to Seal the Deal in Copenhagen," press release, September 24, 2009.

10. Leslie Hook and Ed Crooks, "China's Rush into Renewables," *Financial Times*, November 28, 2011.

11. Ibid.

12. "Emission Reduction Efforts in China Recognized," *Xinhua News Agency*, December 9, 2011.

13. Pew Charitable Trusts, "Who's Winning the Clean Energy Race? Growth, Competition and Opportunity in the World's Largest Economies," March 2010, 7.

14. Predicting future national emissions growth—not to mention when it will peak—is difficult because it hinges on so many variables: future economic growth, energy prices, technologies, and policies, among other factors. Many governments, scientists, and nonprofit groups have, however, tried to make such predictions. Perhaps the best overview of various recent predictions for how Chinese emissions will grow was done by scientists at the Lawrence Berkeley National Laboratory. The comparison of predictions by five prominent organi-

zations shows a wide divergence of results, from an emissions peak at just over 8 billion tons of carbon dioxide a year—an amount already surpassed in 2010, when China emitted 8.3 billion tons—to a peak at almost 13 billion tons. Where China actually ends up on the spectrum is, of course, extremely important. But we should not forget that China is the head of a much larger second wave of nations that are following its lead. If China peaks at 10 billion tons but Indian emissions grow to 12 billion tons, we may be no better off. Because the problem is one of the global commons, it requires a global accounting; see Nina Zheng, Nan Zhou, and David Fridley, "Comparative Analysis of Modeling Studies on China's Future Energy and Emissions Outlook," Lawrence Berkeley National Laboratory, September 2010.

15. The three groups have continued to update their models. The UNEP (http://www.unep.org/climatepledges) tracks global emissions pledges and how much more is needed to achieve a 50 percent chance of keeping the temperature rise under 2 degrees Celsius. The Climate Action Tracker (http://www.climate actiontracker.org), an effort by three groups including the Potsdam Institute, and the Climate Scoreboard (http://climateinteractive.org/scoreboard), which uses a climate model developed at MIT, both calculate likely global temperature increases given current government commitments to curbing greenhouse gas emissions.

16. Environmental groups have used this reasoning to argue that the United States should not export coal. Their decades-long struggle to reduce coal dependence would be undermined if coal not burned domestically enters the global marketplace, pushing down its price and driving up consumption.

17. Nicholas Stern lecture at Tsinghua University. Stern made his calculations using the total carbon dioxide equivalent of all the various greenhouse gases.

18. International Energy Agency, *World Energy Outlook 2011*.

19. The Communist Party is particularly worried about inflation, which has been a key driver of unrest over recent decades. (The 1989 protests centered around Tiananmen Square, for example, were preceded by 25 percent inflation.) In 2010, China reportedly experienced some 180,000 protests, more than four times the protests in 2000 and ranging in size from a few dozen people to many thousands. Most were sparked by local concerns, but rapid inflation could bring

enough people onto the streets that they might unite to challenge the government; see Tom Orlick, "Unrest on Rise as China Booms," *Wall Street Journal*, September 26, 2011.

20. Another reason that China might be slower to sign on to a strong climate change treaty is that, like the United States in the early twentieth century, it is governed by technocrats who seem to believe they can engineer solutions to problems—a philosophy built on the Confucian ideal of mastering the natural world. Hu Jintao trained at Tsinghua as a hydraulic engineer. Wen Jiabao earned a postgraduate degree in geology. Jiang Zemin, the president before Hu, began his career as an electrical engineer. Xi Jinping will become the president and party secretary in late 2013 and studied chemical engineering at Tsinghua. There has been a tendency over recent decades for Chinese leaders to seek to engineer solutions to environmental problems.

21. Ever since the Byrd-Hagel resolution passed the Senate in 1997, the argument that Washington needs to wait for China to move has been well defended. The Clinton administration's ambassador to the UN signed the Kyoto Protocol, but, because it would have failed passage, Clinton never submitted it to Congress. The Bush administration stated directly that the failure to commit China to reductions made it hard or impossible for the United States to join: "The Kyoto Protocol was fatally flawed in fundamental ways," George W. Bush said in 2001; a primary flaw was that China, by then the world's second-largest emitter, "was entirely exempted from the requirements" of the treaty; see President Bush's Speech on Global Climate Change, June 11, 2001, http://georgewbush-whitehouse.archives.gov/news/releases/2001/06/20010611-2.html. The Obama administration has also suggested that China will have to agree to limits before the United States can commit. Todd Stern, Obama's chief climate negotiator, has said that no climate change deal "will be possible if we don't find a way forward with China"; see Todd Stern's remarks at the Center for American Progress on June 3, 2009, http://www.americanprogress.org/wpcontent/uploads/events/2009/06/av/stern_remarks.pdf.

EPILOGUE

1. Peter Matthiessen, *The Birds of Heaven* (New York: North Point Press, 2001), 4.

2. IUCN Red List of Threatened Species, http://www.iucnredlist.org/apps/redlist/details/106002786/0, accessed March 30, 2012.

3. According to Burnham, satellite images show that the lake originally covered 6,000 square kilometers. During the 1980s and 1990s, between 2,000 and 3,000 square kilometers were reclaimed.

4. Li Jiao, "Scientists Line Up Against Dam That Would Alter Protected Wetlands," *Science*, October 23, 2009, 508–509.

5. Fareed Zakaria, *The Post-American World* (New York: Norton, 2008). The G7 nations are the United States, Germany, Japan, France, the United Kingdom, Italy, and Canada.

6. The shift to renewable energy is likely to be less costly to Western lifestyles than many people anticipate. A 2011 report by WWF and Ecofys, a clean energy consultancy based in the Netherlands, suggested that the world could meet its energy needs almost entirely with renewable sources by 2050 at a cost that "does not demand radical changes to the way we live" and would never surpass 2 percent of the global GDP; see "The Energy Report: 100% Renewable by 2050," WWF, Ecofys, and OMA, 2011. Other scientists have made similar estimates. And as money flowed into expanding wind, solar, nuclear, and other energy sources, it would create tens of millions of jobs, helping to redistribute what has become an increasingly skewed income disparity in the West (itself largely a product of the low-cost manufacturing in China and other developing countries).

7. Clinton's announcement, made at the UNFCCC Copenhagen meeting, was somewhat vague. Clinton said that "in the context of a strong accord in which all major economies stand behind meaningful mitigation actions and provide full transparency as to their implementation, the United States is prepared to work with other countries toward a goal of jointly mobilizing $100 billion a year by 2020 to address the climate change needs of developing countries." Since China did not accept binding targets at the meeting, the U.S. offer was moot, but the figure was included in the Copenhagen Accord (where funding was made contingent on "meaningful mitigation actions and transparency," wording obviously aimed at China).

8. Edward O. Wilson, *The Future of Life* (New York: Vintage Books, 2003), 156.

9. Jeffrey Sachs, *Common Wealth: Economics for a Crowded Planet* (New York: Penguin Books, 2008), 311. Sachs notes that the transition to sustainable energy

"will likely require no more than 1 percent of rich-world income and less than that in low-income countries. The enhanced conservation of biodiversity will require perhaps \$35 billion per year, or 0.1 percent of rich-world income. Science for sustainable development . . . might be targeted at \$70 billion per year, roughly 0.2 percent of rich-world GNP. Extreme poverty . . . can be ended within the envelope of 0.7 percent of rich-world GNP, an amount long promised but not delivered." Sachs adds that the total cost of 2 to 3 percent of world earnings would be a political challenge but not an economic one. In 2010, for example, the world spent \$1.6 trillion on its militaries, according to the Stockholm International Peace Research Institute. That amount is equal to 2.3 percent of the world's total economic output.

10. Juliette Jowit and Patrick Wintour, "Cost of Tackling Global Climate Change Has Doubled, Warns Stern," *The Guardian*, June 26, 2008.

ACKNOWLEDGMENTS

No book is an island, but here that is particularly true. I researched and wrote it over a year and a half, but it grew from more than a decade of experiences in China and Asia and benefited from hundreds of people who have offered insights, friendship, and hospitality.

First there was my time as a Peace Corps volunteer in Sichuan province, when my students and colleagues, as well as the other American volunteers, provided an unforgettable introduction to China. Many of the students I taught at Chengdu Teachers College have become friends and I am grateful for their kindness. David (Zhang Chao) embodies the friendship shown by many.

Then there were my years as a magazine and newspaper journalist. I am grateful to Melinda Liu, *Newsweek*'s longtime China bureau chief, for helping me find my feet, and to Andy Alexander and Chuck Holmes at Cox Newspapers for giving me a beat big enough that I couldn't possibly get bored: the things I saw as I reported across Asia revealed the fragility of our planet and inspired this project. A few people deserve particular recognition: Lone Droscher-Nielsen, the director of the Nyaru Menteng Orangutan Rescue Center in Borneo, impressed me with her passion for wildlife; Janos Bogardi, the director of the Institute for Environment and Human Security at United Nations University, started me thinking about the importance of precautionary planning, particularly in regard to climate change; and Sze

Pan Cheung, a Greenpeace expert, helped me recognize the impact of China's timber demand on the world's forests. As a Knight Science Journalism Fellow at MIT, I was lucky enough to learn from some of the world's top researchers. Thanks especially to Penny Chisholm, Elfatih Eltahir, Gilbert Metcalf, Michael Vandenbergh, fellowship director Phil Hilts, and the Knight Foundation.

For the book itself, I am indebted to the scientists and experts who took time from their busy schedules to help and to friends who offered everything from places to stay to instructions on how to remove leeches. Some are mentioned in the preceding pages, but I want to offer special thanks to the following people: *in China*, Jesse Atkinson, Carter Brandon, Chang Shiyan, Leo Chen, Chen Yong, Sze Pang Cheung, Dai Xiaojie, Feng Yongfeng, Jiang Kejun, Lei Hongpeng, Li Hua of Everglory International Co., Evan Osnos, the Schmitz-Chu family, Sun Xiufang, Wang Canfa, Wang Chengyou, Wang Song, Wang Tao, Wang Yongchen, Wei Qiwei, Wu Bo, Xu Jintao, Yang Fuqiang, Zhang Dejun and Jiao Huichun, Zhang Jingjing, Shane Zhao, and Zhu Gongqian; *in India*, Deep Contractor, Tykee Malhotra, Jehangir Pocha, Valmik Thapar, and Belinda Wright; *in Papua New Guinea*, the staff of the Binatang Research Center, Benny Francis, Goodwill Amos, Fidelis Kimbeng and his family, Vojtech Novotny, Semcars and Junior, Phil Shearman, and Bob Tate; *in the United States*, Bruce Beehler, Jim Butler, Kerstin Canby and Forest Trends, Bill Chandler, Jerry Fletcher, Bob Flynn, Leslie Glustrom, Peter Hessler, Bruce Hope, the International Crane Foundation (particularly James Burnham and Jim Harris), Dan Jaffe, Johanna Lewis, Thomas Lovejoy, Susan Moran and Tom McKinnon, Kirk Olson, Fred Palmer, Juan and Courtney Pena, Stuart Pimm, Stapleton Roy, Roger Singer, David Smith, Bill Speidel, Ed Steinfeld, Richard Stone, Pieter Tans, Steve Trent, Peter Paul van Dijk, Alex Wang, Adam Weiss, the Woods Hole Research Center (particularly Richard Houghton and George Woodwell), Zhou Nan, and my in-laws—YR, Sen, and Jay; *elsewhere*, Hanna and Carsten Donau, James Hewett, Julian Newman, Paul Pearson, Louis Putzel, and Sam Turvey. This book is built largely on what they shared, and while I take responsibility for my opinions (and any errors), I acknowledge my debt: they are, and will remain, my friends and teachers.

Likewise, I have benefited from writers who tilled similar ground before me. While researching, I read dozens of books, scores of reports, and hundreds of newspaper and magazine stories. A few writers deserve particular credit. Jonathan Watts, a longtime Asia environment correspondent for the *Guardian* newspaper (now their Latin America correspondent) and friend, went far out of his way to offer advice, contacts, and corrections. His book, *When a Billion Chinese Jump: How China Will Save Mankind—Or Destroy It*, is a superb account of China's environmental crisis and proved an invaluable source to which I'm particularly indebted. Judith Shapiro's *Mao's War Against Nature: Politics and the Environment in Revolutionary China* provides a clear—and fascinating—framework to understand the roots of China's environmental meltdown; she, too, offered invaluable advice and friendship. Samuel Turvey's *Witness to Extinction: How We Failed to Save the Yangtze River Dolphin* offers a heartrending account of the loss of the *baiji*, and, in the bigger picture, of the Yangtze itself. Jennifer Turner, the director of the China Environment Forum at the Woodrow Wilson International Center for Scholars in Washington, D.C., was an incredible font of information and context, as were the CEF's publications.

Jennifer and the Woodrow Wilson Center also generously provided me with a quiet place to write and the assistance of Sukran Moon, a very capable researcher. Back in Beijing, Qiu Xiaolei, my longtime assistant at Cox Newspapers, once again proved skillful at finding obscure data and correcting my errors. The D.C.-based Alicia Patterson Foundation provided funding that allowed me to travel to Southeast Asia, China, and within the United States. I am grateful to its board of directors and to Margaret Engel.

In the publishing process, thanks go first to Janet Silver, my agent, for believing in the idea and finding it a good home. At St. Martin's Press, Michael Flamini offered encouragement, good judgment, and patience.

I am also fortunate to have a group of smart, knowledgeable, and verbally dexterous friends in China who kept me on my toes even as they helped me relax. Farther afield, Vijay Venkatesh kick-started the project by never forgetting to ask when I'd get around to writing that book I'd mentioned. Juan Pena set off my globe-trotting one chilly winter night by suggesting we visit Colombia.

Further back, my family deserves credit for helping me trust myself and then giving me space to do so. Without their example, I would not have taken the leaps that led me to China and into journalism. My brother, Ken, and sister, Donna Maribel, instilled a healthy fear of statistics and offered continual support. Thanks also to my parents for commenting on an early draft.

My wife, Jen, deserves a lion's share of my gratitude. She—somehow—found ways to calm me down when my work seemed stalled and maintained her wonderful sense of humor and optimism even as we moved to Boston, Beijing, and Washington, D.C.: I never would have written this without her support.

Last but—except in size—not least, my daughter deserves recognition. We learned of the pregnancy as I was beginning to write and, through it all, I thought of her. Someday, she and her generation will inherit whatever we leave behind. May we prove courageous and generous.

INDEX

Aesop, 220
Africa
    Chinese investment in, 159–60
    logging in, 9
    Western exploitation of, 226
air pollution
    in Beijing, 137–38
    in China, 12
    from China, reaching America, 4–5
    measurement of, 4–5
Alaska, 109
albedo, 7
alpha predators, 107
alternative energy, 186
Amazon region
    carbon stored in trees, 141, 188
    deforestation, 130, 132, 160
    mahogany logging, 126–27
Americans
    consumption of, environmental cost
        of, 87–88
    per capita income and individual
        wealth, 18
    See also United States
Amos, Goodwill, 146–48
Amtrak Acela Express, 194
Arkansas, turtle collection and
    export, 97

Armageddon, predicted by E. O.
    Wilson, 17
Asia, environmental crisis in, reaching
    across borders, 13
Atitlán grebe (*Podilymbus gigas*),
    84–85
atmosphere, carbon dioxide in, 3,
    140–41, 156–58
Audubon Society of Central Arkansas,
    97
Australia
    global warming's effects in, 183–84
    relations with Papua New Guinea,
        166
Avatar (film by James Cameron),
    152–53

balance of nature, 169–70
Barton, Joe, 210
Basahi, India, 185–86
baselines, 41–42
beef and veal, exports, 161
Beijing, China, 137–38, 227–28
    recent rapid changes in, 11
Bihar Province, India, 185–86
Binatang Research Center, 139, 144,
    150, 153, 165
biological deserts, 141–42

biological diversity
  loss of, 86–87, 111–12
  and medical discoveries, 141
  recent and continuing loss of, 115–18
birds of paradise (*avis paradiseus*),
    121–23, 169
bison, near extermination of, 107
Blohm, Bendix, 37
blue antelope (*Hippotragus leucophaeus*),
    85
Borneo, 13
box turtles, 97, 99
Brazil
  agribusiness in, 160
  economic growth, and resource
    consumption, 224
  exploitation of, 226
  logging and deforestation, 160,
    161, 163
  See also Amazon region
Brazilian rosewood, 130
Britain, and China, 178
Brown, Lester, 89, 119
Brown, Margaret, 183
Buddhism
  Chinese, 45
  Indian, 77
Burma, 99
Burnham, James, 221–22
Butler, Jim, 5–8
bycatch, 41
Byrd, Robert, 181
Byrd-Hagel resolution, 181–82

cadmium, 32
Cambodia, 13, 130
cap-and-trade, 204
Cape Cod, Massachusetts, 155
capitalism
  and pressure on living world, 227
  in today's China, 177

carbon capture and storage, 158, 189
carbon dioxide
  in atmosphere, 3, 140–41, 156–58
  rise of concentration in atmosphere
    since Industrial Revolution, 6–7,
    186–87
  stabilizing in the atmosphere, at 450
    ppm, 190
carbon emissions
  agreement to cut, 180
  China, 178, 179, 180–82, 183
  current figures, 211
  deforestation and, 140–41, 157
  Europe, 181
  historical, and fairness, 181–82
  monitoring of, 210
  U.S., 181
carbon intensity targets, 203–4,
    210–11
carbon monoxide, 5
Caribbean monk seal (*Monachus
    tropicalis*), 84
Carnegie Endowment for International
    Peace, 201
Carson, Rachel, 150
caviar, 37–38
Center for International Forestry
    Research (CIFOR), 130, 148, 161
Central Park, New York, 144
Chengdu, China, 69, 90–92, 193, 202
Chen Yong, 164
Chiang Kai-shek, 50
children, as drivers of environmental
    change in families, 88
China
  advanced society of, in 1800, 42–43,
    226
  author's experiences in, 10–14
  central management, top-down
    approach of, 57–59
  in climate talks, 203–11

coexistence with animals not
desired in, 76
as combustive agent, 19–21
economic growth, and climate
change, 7, 179
economic growth, and resource
consumption, 129–32, 224
economic growth, rate of, 2, 8, 204–5
economy, environmental costs of,
9, 17–21, 88–89, 159
energy consumption, 187–88,
196–201
environmental exploitation by,
historically, 43–48
impact on planet Earth, 8–10,
116–18
liberation of economy, 100
lifestyle improvement, environmental
threat from, 117–18, 160–62, 164,
199–201, 216
log imports, 147, 160, 161, 162–64
population, 8
seen from air, 138
slower growth of, urged, 215–16
social problems in, 12–13
speed of change in, 11, 190
as superpower, 207–8
technological prowess, 194
and tropical tree destruction
worldwide, 127, 143
viewed as destroyer of the
environment, 211
viewed as green-tech savior, 211–13
wildlife destruction in, 91
and wildlife destruction worldwide,
99–102
See also Chinese people; rural China;
urban China
China (Beijing) International Building
Materials and Interior Decoration
Exposition, 162

China Wildlife Conservation
Association, 89
Chinese Academy of Fisheries Sciences,
29–30
Chinese New Year, 195
Chinese paddlefish, 27
Chinese people
consumerism and materialism of,
54, 178
per capita income and individual
wealth, 18
selfish mentality of, claimed, 74
Chinese sturgeon (*Acipenser sinensis*),
27–31
Chinese water deer, 63
Chongqing, China, 25, 33–34, 39
chromium, 32
Clarke, Garry, 185
climate change, 183–86
attack on science of, 210
China's contribution to, 179
history and projection of, 6–7
international accords on, 10
land use and, 156–59
See also global warming
climate feedbacks, 188–89
Cline Mining, 4
Clinton, Hillary, 227
Club of Rome, 15
coal consumption
China, 2, 207
U.S., 2
coal dust, particulate matter with
diameters smaller than 2.5
millionths of a meter (PM 2.5),
4–5
coal exports, U.S. to China, 3–4
coal mines, U.S., 2
colonialism, European, 169
Colorado Bureau of Land
Management, 3

Commonwealth Scientific and
    Industrial Research Organization
    (Australia), 183
Communist Party, Chinese, 57–59
*Compendium of Materia Medica,
    The (Bencao Gangmu),* 93
Confucianism, 46, 48, 93
Conrad, Joseph, 140
Conservation International, 98
consumer ethic, Chinese, 178
Contractor, Deep, 104–6, 108–10,
    112–15
Convention on International Trade in
    Endangered Species of Wild Flora
    and Fauna (CITES), 68, 71,
    73–74, 130
Copenhagen Accord, 206–7
    firm numbers lacking in, 207
Copenhagen climate change conference
    of 2009, 148, 203–11
coral reefs, 42, 185
Corbett, Jim, *Man-Eaters of Kumaon,*
    105
Corbett National Park, India,
    76, 103–15
    established early and superior to
        most Western reserves, 108–9
cranes, 219–21
cuisine, Chinese, 95–96
    cost to wildlife, 96
Cultural Revolution, 57

Dai Qing, 57
Dalai Lama, 80
Dalbroi, Joe and Alice, 184
dam-building
    China's expertise in, 54–55
    environmental threat of, 221–23
Daoism, 45, 219
Darwin, Charles, 122
Davidson, Eric, 159

Dean, Cathy, 72
deforestation
    Amazon, 130, 160
    and carbon emissions, 140–41,
        157
    China, 129
    increasing pace of, 131–32
    Indonesia, 138
    New Guinea, 143–49, 165–68
    worldwide, due to Chinese demand,
        130–32
Delaware Bay, 28–29
Democratic Republic of the Congo,
    159–60
Deng Weiming, 59–60
Deng Xiaoping, 50, 99, 129, 177
desertification, 12
"deserts"
    biological, 141–42
    green, 108
developing nations
    carbon emissions and fossil fuel use,
        180
    emissions reduction by, 204–7,
        227
    energy consumption, 187–88
    help from wealthy nations for
        emissions reduction, 227
    interests of, vis-à-vis industrialized
        nations, 209
    lifestyle improvement, environmental
        threat from, 117–18, 161
    slower growth of, urged, 215
Diamond, Jared, 124
disposable income, Chinese, 178
dodo bird (*Raphus cucullatus*), 84
dolphin. *See* Yangtze River dolphin
    (*baiji*)
drinking water, 12
drought, 184
dust events originating in Asia, 5

earnings, per capita, China vs.
    U.S., 18
Earth. *See* planet Earth
Earth Policy Institute, 89
Earth System Research Laboratory,
    Global Monitoring Division
    (of NOAA), 6
economic growth
    China, 2, 8, 129–32, 204–5
    and environmental change, 224
    worldwide, 87, 224
Economy, Elizabeth, 58
ecosystems, healthy, 74, 110–12,
    228–30
ecosystem services of nature,
    16, 140–41, 148
electrical capacity
    Chinese, 179
    U.S., 179
elephant bird (*Aepyornis maximus*),
    83–84
elephants, 44, 75
    world population of, 71
Elizabeth Kolbert, *Field Notes from a
    Catastrophe*, 180
Ellis, Richard, 94, 96
Elvin, Mark, 43, 46
emperor, Chinese, 220
endangered species, international
    trade in, 89–92
energy consumption
    China, 187–88, 196–201
    reducing, 196–99
Energy Department, U.S., 180
Energy Information Administration
    (US), 179
Entwistle, Abigail, 91
environment
    balanced, 110
    five threats to (HIPPO), 44
    global, UN study of, 86

environmental crisis
    centuries-old warnings of, 14–17
    China's contribution to, 19
Environmental Investigation Agency,
    68, 161
environmentalism, "think globally, act
    locally" mantra, 225–26
environmental organizations
    efforts against global warming,
        2–3
    piecemeal improvement programs of,
        200
    and sustainable economies, 88
Environmental Protection Agency
    (U.S.), 196
environmental writers, 149–50
Europe
    carbon emissions, 181
    environmental destruction in, 101
    trees, health of, 156
    wilderness cleared in, 107
Europeans
    colonization by, 169
    consumption of, environmental cost
        of, 87–88
European Union, import laws, 163
European Union—China Biodiversity
    Program, 72
evolution, 169–70
exports, Chinese, and greenhouse gas
    production, 19
extinctions
    mass, prehistoric, 83–86
    See also species extinctions

"face," Chinese concept of, not to lose,
    216
farming, global warming's effect on,
    183–84
farmland, carbon released to
    atmosphere from, 157

farms for breeding of wild animals,
    70–71, 73
Fauna & Flora International, 91
Fengdu. China, 52
fertilizers, 159
Finisterre Mountains, New Guinea,
    170
finless porpoise (*Neophocaena
    phocaenoides asiaeorientali*),
    62, 222
fish, restocking of, 30, 35–37
Fish Commission, U.S., 38
fishing fleets, 41
fish stocks, monitoring of, 41–42
Flannery, Tim, 173
Fletcher, Jerry, 208
"floating population" of China, 195
flooding, 9, 126, 146, 185–86
Flynn, Bob, 132, 161–65
food, Chinese demand for, and world
    trade, 130
Food and Agriculture Organization
    (UN), 17, 41, 162
*Foolish Old Man Who Moved the
    Mountains, The* (fable), 47
forests
    biological diversity of, 141
    clear-cutting of, 142
    clearing of, for farmland, 44, 47
    cutting of, and carbon dioxide added
        to atmosphere, 157–58
    eco-services of, 140–41, 148
    fires in, deliberately set to ease
        logging, 163
    global decline of, 155–56, 162–63,
        225
    last trees from, made into furniture,
        128
    managed, 109
    old-growth, clearing of, 162
    protection of, through funding, 148
    reasons for saving, 140–43
    selective cutting of, damage of,
        142–43
    spiritual values of, 149–50, 172
    sustainable logging in, 162
    See also deforestation
Forest Trends, 130, 148, 161
fossil fuel consumption
    and economic progress, historically,
        214
    and global warming, 158, 186
fossil fuel power plants
    building of, in developing world,
        187–88
    China, projected, 201
Francis, Benny, 166–68
furniture, made in China, for export
    and domestic use, 129–30
future generations, responsibility to, 228

Gabon, 163
Gaia hypothesis, 45
Gezhouba Dam, 53–55
glaciers, melting of, 7
Global Biodiversity Outlook 3 (UNEP),
    117
Global Footprint Network, 16
globalization
    and lifestyle improvement, 226
    and tragedy of the commons, 213
    and wildlife destruction worldwide,
        101–2
global warming
    attempts to limit or slow, 3, 10,
        189–91
    China's contribution to, 179
    effects of, in Australia, Tuvalu, and
        India, 183–85
    fossil fuel consumption and, 158,
        186
    as humanity's greatest threat, 225

predictions of, 188–89, 215
  See also climate change
global warming treaties
  need for U.S.-China accord, 208–9,
    214, 217, 229
  U.S. refusal to accept, 181
Global Witness, 163
Goetz, Scott, 159
Golden Port, near Shanghai, China,
  127–28, 132–35
Goodall, Jane, 73
Gore, Al, 210
government action for environmental
  health, 229
Goya, Francisco, 33–34
grasslands, desertification of, 47
great auk (*Alca impennis*), 84
Great Leap Forward, 47, 57
"green deserts," national parks of the
  West, called, 108
greenhouse gas emissions
  China, 2–3
  political problems connected with,
    189
  reducing, 186, 189
  stabilizing of, and future global
    temperature, 213
greenhouse gases, 19, 159
Greenpeace, 126, 131, 132, 147
green power, 197
greenwashing, 210
grizzly bears, near extermination of,
  107
Group of 77, 207
G7 nations, 224
Guangdong Province, China, 138
Guatemala, 85
Guizhou Province, 202

Hagel, Charles, 181–82
Han Chinese, 68, 80

Hardin, Garrett, 14–15
Harris, James, 221
harvesting
  sustainable, 87
  unsustainable, 71
Hawaii, 84
Ha Yafei, 205–6
health problems in China, 13
Hehauchi warehouse, Chengdu,
  China, 90–92
Heinberg, Richard, 203
herbivores, uncontrolled by predators,
  harm to plant life from, 110
Hinduism, 77
HIPPO (Wilson's term), 44
Hoffmann—La Roche, 94
honeyeater, Hawaiian, extinct, 85
Houghton, Richard, 156–59
Household Emissions Calculator (of
  U.S. EPA), 196–98
housing, and wood demand, 130
Huai River, 58
human population
  effect on Earth's metabolism, 7
  growth since World War II, 187
  predictions, 224
  warnings about growth, 14–17,
    46–47
human species
  change to the planet by, historically,
    214–15
  successful exploitation by, 1
hunters, 69

imperial China, 220
imports
  environmental cost of, 87
  illegal, laws on, 133, 163
India, 74–81
  bureaucracy of, failure to protect
    wildlife, 80–81

India (*continued*)
  in climate talks, 206
  coexistence with animals in, 76–78
  diversity of, 67–69
  economic growth, and resource
    consumption, 224
  exploitation by colonial powers,
    226
  global warming's effects in, 185–86
  land use in, and disappearance of
    wildlife habitats, 77
  lifestyle improvement, environmental
    threat from, 164
  population of, 76
  trade with China, 79
Indian philosophy, and animals, 76–78
Indian Red Cross, 185
Indonesia, 13, 99, 130, 138
  logging and deforestation, 134, 138,
    161, 163
industrialized countries
  economic growth of, 187
  emissions reduction by (Annex I
    nations), 204–7
  shared responsibility of, for planetary
    health, 226–29
Industrial Revolution
  carbon dioxide emissions since
    beginning of, 186–87
  resource depletion since start of, 6–7,
    16–17
insects, species of, 142
Intergovernmental Panel on Climate
    Change (IPCC), 190
international conservation, 62
International Crane Foundation, 221
International Energy Agency, 188, 212
International Union for the
    Conservation of Nature (IUCN),
    29, 69, 86, 96, 126, 220. *See also*
    Red List

itai-itai disease, 32
ivory, 10
  illegal, 71

Jaffe, Dan, 4–5
Japan, log imports, 146
Jiao Huichun, 198–99
journalists, "So what?" question of,
    14, 222
jungles, 121–26
Junior (guide), 170–71

Kalimantan (Borneo), Indonesia,
    134, 138
Kaua'i 'ō'ō (*Moho braccatus*), 84
Keeling, Charles David, 156
Keeling curve, 156–57
Kellndorfer, Josef, 130, 160
keystone species, 74, 111
Kimbeng, Fidelis, 121, 125–26, 150–54
king bird of paradise (*Cicinnurus
    regius*), 169
Kipling, Rudyard, *The Jungle Book*, 75
kwilla (*Intsia bijuga*), 126–27, 134–35,
    165, 167–68
Kyoto Protocol, 181, 209
  creation of, 204
  expiration or extension of, 203
  U.S. opponents of, 182

Lacey Act, 133, 163
lakes, draining of, 47, 219
land, carbon dioxide added to
    atmosphere from clearing of,
    157–58
land reclamation, 47
land use, and climate change, 156–59
Laos, 99
Laozi, 219
Latasi, Perpetua, 185
Leopold, Aldo, 103

Lewis and Clark expedition, 107
Li Fang, 196
life, miracle of, 228
lifestyle enrichment
    China, 117–18, 160–62, 164,
        199–201, 216
    environmental costs of, 18, 20,
        61–63, 71–74, 199–201
Limits to Growth, The (Club of
        Rome), 15
Li Peng, 50
Li Rui, 56–57
Li Shizhen, 93
Little, Archibald, 26
Little Yu, 55–56
Li Xiao (pseudonym), 91–92
log depot in China. *See* Zhangjiagang
        log depot
logging
    illegal, 162–64
    modern technology of, 143–44
    restrictions on and disincentives to,
        147–48
    selective, 126–27
    sustainable, 162
    and tree extinction, 126–27
logging concessions
    destructive to local societies,
        167–68
    in New Guinea, 135, 165–68
    tactics of companies to get
        permission to log, 153–54
Lovejoy, Thomas, 115–18
Lovelock, James, 45
Luo (businessman), 51
Lynas, Mark, 207, 211

MacKinnon, John, 72
Madagascar, 83–84
Madang, Papua New Guinea, 165–68
"made for man" assertion, 169

made-in-China labels, 8
mahogany, 126–27
Mahto, Ram Kumar, 186
Malhotra, Tykee, 75, 104–5
Malthus, Thomas Robert, 14, 46
Manamaging, Papua New Guinea,
        165, 167
manufacturing jobs, U.S., loss of, 8
Mao's War Against Nature (Shapiro), 46
Mao Zedong, 46–48, 50, 129
Marine Biological Laboratory, 155
Marx, Karl, 57
Massachusetts Institute of Technology,
        213
materialism, Chinese, 54
Mattel, 147
Matthiessen, Peter, 83
    The Birds of Heaven, 220
Mauritius, 84
Mayans, 101
McKinsey Global Institute, 201
meat, exports, 161
medical discoveries, biological diversity
        and, 141
medicine, traditional. *See* traditional
        Chinese medicine
Mencius, 43
mercury, 12–13
    in air, 5
    water contamination by, 5, 32
Merkel, Angela, 206
Mexico, economic growth, and
        resource consumption, 224
Miliband, Ed, 207–8
"Millennium Ecosystem Assessment"
        (UN), 16, 86
mining, in Colorado, revitalization of, 4
Ministry of Environmental Protection,
        China, 58
monitoring, 210
monsoons, 185

mountain lions, near extermination of, 107

Mount Bachelor, Oregon, 4–5

Muir, John, 149, 172

Musée d'Histoire Naturelle (Paris), 84–85, 87

mussels (*Mytilus californianus*), 111

Myanmar, 130, 163

Myers, Norman, 124

National Center for the Performing Arts (Beijing), 130

National Forest Protection Program (China), 129

National Oceanic and Atmospheric Administration (NOAA), 5–6

national parks and reserves, protective perimeters around, 109

NATO, 148

natural resources, unsustainable demands on, 16–17, 71, 224

nature, balance of, 169–70

Netherlands Environmental Assessment Agency, 180

New Elk mine, Trinidad, Colorado, 2–4

New Guinea, 121–26, 137–54
  bush life vs. town life in, 166
  deforestation in, 143–49, 165–68
  exploitation of, 226
  highlands of, 170–72
  jungles of, 170
  lifestyle changes in (materialism), 166–68
  log exports, 147, 163
  population growth, 145–46
  remoteness of, 137
  seen from air, 138
  sustainable lifestyle in wilderness, 150–51

tribal communities in, desire for improved lifestyle, 143–44, 145–46
  wilderness forest in, 123–26
  See also Papua New Guinea

New York City, New Guineans' skeptical view of, 171

nitrous oxide, 159

North America
  fisheries, 37–38
  wilderness cleared in, 107–8

Northern River terrapin, 100

Notebooks from New Guinea (Novotny), 140

Novotny, Vojtech, 139–45

Nursing (guide), 106

Obama, Barack, at Copenhagen conference (2009), 203, 206–7

Oceana, 72

oil palms, 159, 161
  cultivation of, 130

On the Origin of Species by Means of Natural Selection (Darwin), 122

Opium War, 178

orangutans, 13, 134

Orwell, George, *Animal Farm*, 104

ozone, 5

Paine, Robert, 111

Palais De Fortune villa complex, Beijing, 161–62

pangolin, 10

Pan Yue, 181–82

paper, Chinese demand for, 130, 131

Papua New Guinea, 123, 134–35, 137–54
  founding of, goals, 166–67
  See also New Guinea

Papua New Guinea Forest Authority, 146–48

particulate matter with diameters
    smaller than 2.5 millionths of a
    meter (PM 2.5), 137
    coal dust, 4–5
pastures, and carbon released to
    atmosphere, 157
Pauly, Daniel, 41
peacocks, 44
peasant society, 57
Pengzhou, Sichuan Province,
    China, 11
permafrost, 188–89
Permian period, 188
personal actions for environmental
    health, 228–29
pet trade, 101
Pew Charitable Trusts, 212
philosophers, Chinese, 44–48
pig, killing a, 175–76
Pitman, Robert, 14, 61
planet Earth
    balance of, 224
    China's impact on, 8–10, 116–18
    humans' shaping of, historically,
        7, 214–15
plants
    carbon stored in, 156
    stripped by herbivores uncontrolled
        by predators, 110
plywood, Chinese demand for, 130
poaching, 13, 68, 71, 78–81
    organized crime involvement in,
        72
population. See human population
Port Moresby, Papua New Guinea,
    146, 154
Potsdam Institute, 213
Poyang Lake, China, 219–23
predators. See top predators
Putin, Vladimir, 104

quagga (Equus quagga quagga), 85
Quammen, David, 84, 105
    Monster of God, 107
Queen Alexandra's birdwing
    (Ornithoptera alexandrae), 139

rain forest, 127
    clearing of, 130
recycling programs, 197
Red List (of IUCN), 29, 72, 86–87,
    100
Red River giant soft-shell turtles, 100
Reducing Emissions from Deforestation
    and Forest Degradation (REDD),
    148
reforestation, carbon capture from, 158
renewable energy, China's lead in, 212
Republican Party (U.S.), 210, 211
Retreat of the Elephants, The (Elvin),
    43, 46
rhinoceros, 10, 44, 71–72, 91
rhino horn, 91–92, 93–94
RISI timber consultancy, 129, 132
Roy, Stapleton, 208–9
rural China, 175–77
    lifestyle and income, 198–99
    "not our future," 177, 201–2
    population of, 177, 195
Russia
    economic growth, and resource
        consumption, 224
    exploitation of, 226
    logging in, 9, 130–31, 163

Sachs, Jeffrey, 65, 229
Saffron, Inga, 38
saiga antelope, 91
sal trees, 105, 109
Sanskara, 75
Sariska Tiger Reserve, 81

Sarkozy, Nicolas, 206
Save the Rhino International, 72
Schaller, George, 83
sea level, rise in, 184
sea otters, 111
sea urchins, 111
Semcars (guide), 170–71
Shanghai, China, 177–78
Shapiro, Judith, 46
shared responsibility of Western nations
    for planetary health, 226–29
shark fins, in soup, 72
sharks, 10, 72
Shearman, Phil, 148–49
Shenyang Forest Wildlife Zoo, 70
Shenzhen, China, 177
shifting baseline syndrome, 41, 86
Siberian cranes, 63, 219–23
Sichuan Province, China, 31, 69, 91
Sierra Club, 3
Silk Road, 79
Singapore, 138
Singh, Honey Prabhujot, 108–9
Sino-Forest, 130
solar cells, 212
Songhua River, 13
Sopoaga, Enele, 185
Southeast Asia, logging in, 9
South Korea, 13
South-North Water Diversion Project,
    56
soybeans
    cultivation of, 130, 160
    exports, 161
sparrows, Mao's war against, 47
special economic zones (China),
    177
species, diversified, in tropical forests,
    141–43
species extinctions, 9–10, 14, 27–31
    in the fossil record, 86, 188

human-caused, in four centuries,
    83–86
lifestyle pressure and, 61–63, 71–74
natural rate of, 86
predicted, 116–17
threatened, 86–87, 225
twentieth century rate of, 86
spirits, belief in, 151–52
starfish (*Pisaster ochraceous*), 111
State Environmental Protection Agency
    (China), 58, 181
State Forestry Administration (China),
    164
Steller's sea cow (*Hydrodamalis gigas*), 85
Stern, Nicholas, 214–17, 229
Stern Report, 214
stewardship concept, 88
sturgeon
    past exploitation of, 37–38, 107
    worldwide threat to, 27–29
suburbanization, in China, 160–62
Sudan, 207
Sullivan, John, 210
Sumatra, 138
Sun Yat-sen, 49, 55–56
superpowers, 207–8
Sustainability Institute, 213
sustainable lifestyle in wilderness,
    150–51
sustainable resource use, 87–88,
    162, 226

talk-yes money, 168
Tans, Pieter, 6–7
Tanzania, 163
temperature, global
    goal of limiting to 2-degree Celsius
        maximum rise, 189–91, 213
    predicted rise in, 188–89, 213
    rise of, in 20th century, 184
Theroux, Paul, 23

"think globally, act locally" environmental mantra, 225–26

Thoreau, Henry David, 149–50

Three Gorges, on Yangtze River, China, 25

Three Gorges Dam, 25–30, 49–61, 221
criticism of, 56–57, 60–61
tour of, 60

Tiananmen Square protests (1989), 57, 99

Tibet, 31, 129

Tibetans, 68, 80

tiger bone, 69–71, 79, 91–92, 93–94

Tiger Bone & Rhino Horn (Ellis), 94

tiger bone wine, 70

tiger farms, 70–71, 73

tiger parts
Chinese demand for, 68
price of, 71
trade in, 79–80
See also tiger bone

tigers, 10, 19
amount of meat needed daily, 110
mating of, 112–13
as perfect killing machines, 113
poaching of, 68, 71, 78–81
reason for saving, 103–4
sight of, in the wild, 74, 112–15
in the wild, 67–71, 74, 112–15
worldwide population decline, 69

tiger skins, 80

timber
imports, legal and illegal, 133, 138, 163
imports by China, 9, 13, 129–35

toolache wallaby (*Macropus greyi*), 84

top predators
extermination of, in most of world, 112
importance of, to healthy ecosystems, 74, 110–12

traditional Chinese medicine, 10, 69–74, 92–95
cost to wildlife, 88, 95
fear of death and resort to, 92, 94–95
scientific tests of efficacy of, 94

Traffic, 69, 73, 89, 99

tragedy of the commons, 15, 213

train travel in China, 193–96

travel, desire to, 154, 199–200

trees
as carbon storehouses, 140–41, 148
extinction from logging, 126–27

tribal communities, desire for improved lifestyle, in New Guinea, 143–46

Trinidad, Colorado, 1–4

tropical logs, trade in, 127, 129–35, 143

Tucker, Richard, 87

Tuojia village, China, 176–77, 192, 201–2, 216

turtles, 96–101
"Asian crisis" of, 100
collection and export to China, 97–101
threat to, 100–101

Turvey, Samuel, 61–63

Tuvalu, global warming's effects in, 184–85

Tyndall Centre for Climate Change Research, 189

UN Environment Program (UNEP), 117, 138, 161, 211, 213

UN Framework Convention on Climate Change (UNFCCC), 179, 189, 204, 227

United Nations
and climate talks, 207–8
environmental millennium goals of, 117
Millennium Ecosystem Assessment of, 16

United States
  carbon emissions, 181
  coal consumption, 2
  commitment to emissions
    reductions, need for, 204–9, 211
  economic demands on environment,
    87
  electrical capacity, 179
  environmental destruction in, 101
  import laws, 133, 163
  refusal to accept a global warming
    treaty, 8, 181
  responsibility for environmental
    action, 229
  See also Americans
University of Papua New Guinea, 145,
  148
UN Office on Drugs and Crime, 71
unsustainable resource use, 16–17, 71,
  224
urban China, 190, 201
U.S.–China Clean Energy Research
  Center, 208
Ussuriyskaya Taiga, 70

Van Damme, Jean-Claude, 150
van Dijk, Peter Paul, 96–102
vehicle fleet of China, 200–201
vehicle fuel-efficiency standards, 200
Venezuela, 111–12, 207
Ventana Systems, 213
Vietnam, 98–99

wallabies, 125
Wallace, Alfred Russel, 122–24,
  137–40, 168–70
  The Malay Archipelago, 122, 140
Wanang, Papua New Guinea, 150–53
Wang Chengyou, 29–36, 50
Wang Song, 73–74, 95, 96
Wang Tao, 189–91

Wasser, Samuel K., 71
water pollution, 5, 12–13, 25, 32, 58
Watts, Jonathan, 45
Waxman-Markey bill, 204, 211
Wei Qiwei, 29
Wei Sicong (pseudonym), 132–35
Wen Jiabao, 203, 205, 206–7
Western nations, shared responsibility
  of, for planetary health,
  226–29
WildAid, 72
wilderness
  clearing of, in Western nations,
    107–8
  last remains of, 123–24
  spiritual value of, 172, 225
  worldwide destruction of, 99–102
wildlife
  China and worldwide destruction of,
    99–102
  consumption of, 90
  illegal trade in, 10, 13, 89–92
  international trade in, 73, 97
  protecting, in India, 77
  protecting, in Western nations, 87
Wildlife Protection Law (China, 1998),
  91
Wildlife Protection Society of India,
  68, 78, 79
Wilson, Edward O., 1, 17, 44, 124, 227
wind turbines, 212
Witness to Extinction: How We Failed to
  Save the Yangtze River Dolphin
  (Turvey), 61
wolves, near extermination of, 107
wood, Chinese preference for, 130, 162
Woods Hole, Massachusetts, 155
Woods Hole Oceanographic
  Institution, 155
Woods Hole Research Center, 155
World Bank, 103, 167

World Commission on Forests and
    Sustainable Development, 155
World Resources Institute, 131
World Wildlife Fund (WWF), 16, 132,
    163, 209
Wright, Belinda, 78–81, 103–4
Wu Bo, 51, 53–55

Xu Jintao, 208, 216

Yangtze River, 9, 23–39, 49–63
    called *Chang Jiang*, 26
    environmental degradation of, 32–33
    flooding episode (1998), 129, 146
    history of, 31–32
    species endemic to, 31

Yangtze River dolphin (*baiji*),
    extinction of, 14, 33, 61–63, 86
Yangtze River Fisheries Research
    Institute, 29–30
Yang Xiaohua, 34
Yawan, Papua New Guinea, 170
Yichang, China, 62

Zhang Chao (David), 176–77, 191–202
Zhang Dejun, 175–76, 198–99
Zhangjiagang log depot ("horizontal
    forest"), near Shanghai, China,
    127–28, 132–35, 168
Zhang Yuge (Edmund), 196
Zhuangzi, 44–45
ziran (natural), 45